BROADWAY BUTTERFLY

Also by ANTHONY M. DESTEFANO

The Deadly Don:
Vito Genovese, Mafia Boss

Gotti's Boys:
The Mafia Crew That Killed for John Gotti

Top Hoodlum:
Frank Costello, Prime Minister of the Mafia

The Big Heist:
The Real Story of the Lufthansa Heist, the Mafia, and Murder

Mob Killer:
The Bloody Rampage of Charles Carneglia, Mafia Hit Man

King of the Godfathers:
Joseph Massino and the Fall of the Bonanno Crime Family

BROADWAY BUTTERFLY

VIVIAN GORDON,
THE LADY GANGSTER
OF JAZZ AGE NEW YORK

ANTHONY M. DESTEFANO

CITADEL PRESS
Kensington Publishing Corp.
www.kensingtonbooks.com

CITADEL PRESS BOOKS are published by

Kensington Publishing Corp.
900 Third Avenue
New York, NY 10022

All Kensington titles, imprints, and distributed lines are available at special quantity discounts for bulk purchases for sales promotions, premiums, fund-raising, educational, or institutional use. Special book excerpts or customized printings can also be created to fit specific needs. For details, write or phone the office of the Kensington sales manager: Kensington Publishing Corp., 900 Third Avenue, New York, NY 10022, attn Sales Department; phone 1-800-221-2647.

10 9 8 7 6 5 4 3 2 1

First Citadel hardcover printing: July 2024

Printed in the United States of America

ISBN: 978-0-8065-4314-7

ISBN: 978-0-8065-4316-1 (e-book)

Library of Congress Control Number: 2024932363

In memory of my parents,
Louise Jean and Michael William DeStefano

CONTENTS

BROADWAY BUTTERFLY

THE WOMAN
IN THE PARK

FEBRUARY MORNINGS IN NEW YORK City, even with the approaching spring, can be a mix of chilly winds and freezing temperatures. So it was when Harry Francis, early on the morning of February 26, 1931, began his journey through the bracing cold, dressed in a heavy jacket and warm Yukon trapper hat, from his home in the Bronx on Story Avenue westward to the shore of the Hudson River. A truck driver by trade, Francis's destination that day was to the terminal of the Tide Water Oil Company on the riverbank in Yonkers, just over the city limits. Once in his tanker truck, Francis would spend the day making heating oil deliveries. Even with the waning winter days people still needed heat to ward of the persistent chill.

It isn't clear if Francis, a rugged man used to brisk physical activity, walked all the way from his home—which would have been a few miles' distance—or got a lift to the edge of Van Cortlandt Park in the very northern section of the Bronx. One of New York City's largest public areas and together with adjacent historic Woodlawn Cemetery, which is perpetual home to hundreds of thousands of deceased, the park serves as a green space buffer between the city and the suburban north.

It was just before 7:00 A.M. and no matter how Francis got so quickly to the park, he walked past the cemetery's gates to where Mosholu

Avenue intersected with Jerome Avenue. Turning left in a westerly direction, Francis was on the final leg of his ambulatory commute to the oil terminal, a distance of just about a mile. In more temperate weather, the park greenery, the undulating hills, and the odor of city-run stables made his final leg of the walk seem like a jaunt through the countryside. But in February the trees and shrubs along the avenue were barren, stripped of leaves, and there was really nothing much to see apart from the stubby greens of a municipal golf course and clubhouse that wouldn't have golfers for a few months. With little distraction, Francis could stride briskly, lost in his early morning thoughts.

But Francis was barely a few hundred yards along the macadam road into Van Cortlandt Park when he was jolted back to reality. Lying off the avenue and down a slope amid some large rocks was the unmistakable body of a red-haired woman. With a length of clothesline tied in a slipknot so taut against her skin that it dug into the flesh, the woman was clearly dead. Her eyes were open in a death stare and her legs spread, as if she had been sexually assaulted before she was killed. Her head was tilted to the left, obviously pulled in that direction by the rope used to kill her.

Francis knew there was a park stable not far from where the body lay and found Emanuel Kamma, a stable hand who was also an early riser. After he told Kamma of the body in the park, the police were alerted and an officer from the local Kingsbridge precinct was the first to respond.

As later official reports would describe the scene, cops determined from some drag marks that the victim, a somewhat plump woman of about 35, had been pulled along the frozen ground for some distance before being dumped so cruelly among the brambles and boulders. Her clothing indicated she wasn't some vagrant and obviously was a woman of means. The victim was clothed in a black velvet dress trimmed in cream lace. Her shoes were of black suede and adorned with rhinestone buckles. The shoe from her right foot was found nearby, as were two white gloves. She also wore no coat, which seemed odd in winter.

As police scoured the area, they found two crumpled newspaper articles featuring stories about the local political scandal of the day: an investigation into police corruption involving charges that the NYPD vice division was in cahoots with court officials and others to falsely accuse women of prostitution. One story mentioned how Governor Franklin D. Roosevelt was prepared to pardon all the falsely accused women. The newsprint containing the stories was fresh and not weathered, a sign that they weren't just random park litter but maybe discarded around the time the dead woman was tossed away like garbage. Perhaps the victim had the articles with her when she died. Or maybe some passerby had discarded them. For the moment the significance of the articles was of little importance, and cops scooped up the body and put it in a metal morgue container.

Who was the mystery dead woman? Aside from her attire which indicated she had been well off, police were stumped. Patrolman Daniel Sullivan was the first officer to arrive at the scene and he found no identification papers or jewelry with the body. Clothing tags wouldn't indicate anything. A doctor from nearby Fordham Hospital estimated the corpse had been dead about five or six hours, which would have put the time of death at shortly after midnight on February 26. Still, she was an unidentified corpse.

Today, cops would be able to take a crime scene victim's fingerprints with their smartphones, electronically upload them to the massive New York State fingerprint databases and quickly come up with a match if the victim had been known to the criminal justice system. But in 1931, the responding detectives went to the Fordham morgue and had to ink the dead woman's prints—a combination of unique whorls, peaks, and loops on each of her cold digits—and physically get them to NYPD headquarters in Lower Manhattan. Housed in a grand Baroque-style building on Centre Street, police headquarters was the repository for thousands of fingerprint cards. Using an arcane manual filing system of pinpointing fingerprints, skilled analysts in the Bureau of Identification working in a windowless office had a way of zeroing in on the type of prints before them and through a process of elimination come up with a match. It was an art form in its own way. Still, the process took time and several hours passed before detectives learned that the body in the park was that of a woman named Vivian Gordon. The fact that Gordon's prints were on file

showed she was a person who had a history of involvement with police—quite a history as it would turn out.

Born Benita Franklin and educated in a convent, Gordon was a onetime struggling, pretty chorus girl, vaudeville performer, and occasional
film actress who was part of an army of women—some talented, some
not so much—who had become entranced with New York City during
the Prohibition Era. Like the other women whose aspirations took
them to Broadway, Gordon had visions of fame and fortune. The image
of the Jazz Age popularized by *The Great Gatsby*, the good times, the
parties, the speakeasies and easy money ready to be picked up with little effort created the vision of an elusive Nirvana that Gordon and so
many others sought. It might have been the Depression but plenty of
businessmen and gangsters had money to burn.

The fingerprint check showed that Gordon had a minor police record
containing one arrest for a prostitution charge in 1923. Her killing would
be one of 343 in New York City for the year, the majority of which were
by shooting, not strangulation. What really set off alarm bells ringing
within the police department were records found at Gordon's apartment
on 37th Street. A particular set of voluminous diaries covering seven
books showed that Gordon wasn't just some unfortunate, down-on-
her-luck lady of the night. Instead, she was the consummate sexual extortionist, a blackmailer, a lady racketeer whose modus operandi was to
bait rich men with pretty women and get them into compromising situations—often sexual—so that they were ripe for shakedowns. It paid off
well, reaping police estimates of millions of dollars, a number that might
have been overblown but still provided Gordon with a comfortable lifestyle. Gordon also had business deals involving a group of questionable
characters.

Trolling as she did in New York's demimonde of Prohibition, police
discovered that Gordon was associated with several major gangland
figures. Jack "Legs" Diamond worked the extortion rackets with her;
Arnold Rothstein was another associate whose familiarity with Gordon was embedded in his role as the city's preeminent Broadway man
about town, gambler, and political fixer; Charles "Vannie" Higgins, the
ruthless Irish bootlegger who escaped conviction in at least five gangland murders, rubbed shoulders with Gordon and knew her well. Then

there was Judge Crater, the bon vivant jurist who, before he disappeared forever in 1930, partied with Gordon and some of her women at her apartment, up until the very night he stepped into a Manhattan taxi and was never seen again.

Polly Adler was the city's preeminent madam of the day. Her racket was fairly straightforward: provide celebrities, racketeers, politicians, sports figures and businessmen with top-shelf ladies in her select Manhattan brothels and the cash would roll in. No need for extortion and trickery. It made Adler a celebrity in her own right, even if she had to put up with the occasion arrest. Adler admitted knowing Gordon and once said she was "an attractive brunette" in the sex trade out to make a quick buck. As biographer Debby Applegate noted in *Madam: The Biography of Polly Adler, Icon of the Jazz Age*, the celebrity madam at first admitted that "Viv" was a good friend but then, unconvincingly, tried to minimize her contact with the dead woman.

"But the Broadway rumor mill said otherwise," noted Applegate. "It quickly became clear from Gordon's personal diaries and other underworld sources that the dead woman had once been one of Polly's top-dollar call girls, before striking out on her own and parlaying her little black book in a lucrative blackmail enterprise."

After leaving Adler, Gordon's particular scheme was a Jazz Age version of the old *badger game*, a racket known as far back as the early days of the republic which once implicated, of all people, U.S. Treasury Secretary Alexander Hamilton in a tawdry scandal with 23-year-old Maria Reynolds, a married woman ten years his junior. The trickery was fairly simple. Women enticed men into what they thought were sexual encounters, only to suddenly have male accomplices—often posing as a husband—burst into the room of the assignation and express fake outrage. The duped male victim, picked because he had lots of money or a prominent position, would then quickly panic and agree to fork over money to keep his indiscretion a secret. Sometimes the threat was more subtle, and just the mere possibility that the woman shakedown artist would make a disclosure was enough for the male victim to fork over lavish payments, jewelry, property or even business tips.

Police discovered there was another wrinkle to Gordon's death, and it would set off a furor that rocked the police department and city government. It turned out she *did have* a connection to the investigation described in the discarded newspaper articles found near her body. For months the probe by former judge Samuel Seabury had disclosed shocking details of a different kind of shakedown racket run in the New York City magistrates' court system. The targets were usually women who had been arrested on trumped up and bogus prostitution cases. It was kind of a reverse badger game. Court officials and cops would then force hundreds of women, under threat of blackmail and social ruin, to make payoffs to have their cases dropped or forgotten.

Gordon always believed that her 1923 prostitution arrest, for which she spent three years in a women's prison, was a scam, and when she saw that Seabury was probing things in the corrupt magistrates' court, she sent him a letter telling him she had evidence that would be useful to him. Gordon had talked briefly to Seabury's staff earlier that February and was supposed to return with more evidence but never did. When police discovered Gordon's tie to the investigation, it took everything into another direction. Gordon was killed because she had evidence of police corruption, the newspapers speculated. The city was a lawless rotten apple and her death proved it, sounded a drumbeat of social critics, clergy and pundits.

With the sexual extortion and corruption angles the juicy fare for journalists and tabloid editors, New York City, national and international newspapers exploded for months with stories about Gordon's murder and soon dubbed her the "Broadway Butterfly" for her fast company, gangster friends and nightlife. The Great White Way was the flame which attracted the women in droves. The New York dailies including the *New York Times* covered the story feverishly. Gordon's murder even made the front page in the papers in Anchorage, Alaska, squeezing out the more mundane local stories of shipping news and bush pilot schedules.

The murder of Gordon was the most sensational crime in the city during a time when the glamor of the Jazz Age was giving way to a dark undercurrent in the decade of Prohibition. Rothstein, the biggest gambler and political fixer in town, had been murdered in 1928 in a shooting during a card game, a crime that would never be solved. In

August 1930, Judge Crater vanished after dining with his mistress. Over the decade, the city was also rocked by the killings of a number of other young, hard-partying women, all attracted to Broadway nightlife. Cops were in perpetual alliance with bootleggers and emerging Mafia figures like Charles "Lucky" Luciano and Frank Costello, helping them smuggle mountains of booze to stock the estimated 32,000 speakeasies. Manhattan's district attorney, the man who was supposed to be the city's main law enforcement official, was shown to be incompetent and inept.

Many thought that Prohibition would cut down on crime and vice which seemed to plague New York City. But the opposite turned out to be true in the Big Apple and was beginning to distress a growing number of reformers and other do-gooders. The nascent Italian mobs were run by old-timers like Joe Masseria, who would soon be deposed in a bloody coup. His successors, like Luciano, would organize the rackets in a way that made an army of two-bit gangsters into something more powerful and rich.

The man who became the object of the emerging criticism was Mayor James "Gentleman Jimmy" Walker, the City Hall occupant who first won election in 1925 (he won reelection in 1929) and promptly showed that work running the municipality was a distraction he had to put up with in the daytime, something that got in the way of his bon vivant existence as he careened around town, burnishing his reputation as a good-time Charlie—or in his case Jimmy. Walker, a natty dresser who showed up at speakeasies as often as he did his desk at City Hall, had a carefree and scandalous private lifestyle, demonstrated by the way he would ultimately dump his wife Janet for showgirl Betty Compton.

"Mayor 'Gentleman Jimmy' Walker was the ideal politician for the times: he voiced the opinion that the greatest of all sins was going to bed the same day you got up," said historian Thomas Aylesworth. "New Yorkers agreed and kept their pin-striped, top-hatted mayor in office as long as they could."

To be fair, Walker did work hard in the early days of his tenure. He was said to have kept up a pace of sixteen-hour days in the office, at least for the first two months after he was elected. But the pace contributed to a physical and mental breakdown of sorts and led to Walker paring down his effort. He took a brief vacation to Atlantic City and hung up his nightclub suits—but only for a little while.

As reported by Donald L. Miller in *Supreme City,* "Walker returned to the banquet circuit and cut back on the part of the job he detested—the grind of morning office work." With a busy nightlife, Walker stopped getting to work at City Hall in time to put in a full day.

If truth be told, politics was not Walker's first choice for a career. He was said to have been an aspiring songwriter. His first lyrics were for the 1906 song "Will You Love Me in December as You Did in May." But eventually, he conceded to the aspirations of his family and entered politics, serving in the New York State Assembly for four years and getting elected to the State Senate for a combined total of nine years covering two districts. With the support of political mentor Al Smith, Walker defeated the sitting mayor John Hylan in the run-up to the 1926 mayoral election and became the city's 97th mayor.

For reporters, Walker was good copy, the "Dude" who was always quick with a quote or witty repartee. Walker didn't work very hard as mayor. While his critics were deeply troubled by the way Walker comported himself, the public loved his persona, since it legitimized the lawless, booze-filled and licentious times the average citizen admired and, secretly or not, tried to emulate. Gordon was part of the times and she was, as top police officials acknowledged, a lady racketeer who ran investment schemes and also swindled men through extortion rackets, usually involving sex.

Walker seemed genuinely troubled by Gordon's death, although there was no indication he had ever met her in his rounds of speakeasies or nightclubs like the Central Park Casino where he drank black velvets and kept a private office. The casino had been transformed with the help of Walker's intervention in 1926 into a playground for high society and was said to have been financed by Arnold Rothstein. Still, the implication that her murder had *something* to do with police corruption forced Walker to pay attention to what Police Commissioner Edward Mulrooney was up against. Until the case was solved, there would be a stain on every cop in the city, Mulrooney said.

Gordon's murder—be it tied to police corruption or something linked to her numerous connections to racketeers—showed that all was not right in the underbelly of the nation's largest metropolis. Revelations of the Seabury investigation and the brutality of Gordon's killing began to turn the usually adoring public against Walker. Reformists had long held the hard-partying mayor in their sights and the sensational murder gave them, and influential editorial writers, ammunition to demand that he do something about the corrupt times. They were particularly angered by the stunning fact that Gordon's 16-year-old daughter, Benita, was pushed to suicide just days after her mother's death and the calamity that followed.

"You can't laugh off the rope around the neck of a dead woman," the *New York World-Telegram* told Walker in an editorial. "A grave situation confronts New York.... [I]t calls for action, resolution, leadership. Jimmy Walker should supply all three. If he is unable to do so, he should step aside and let someone take the job who can and will."

Those were words of tough criticism and rooted in the growing exasperation with the mayor. Walker encouraged Mulrooney and his task force of scores of detectives to spare no effort in breaking the case, and for a time detectives ran the investigation out of the dead woman's apartment. Within two months, cops had arrested three men who knew Gordon well—one was even her part-time bodyguard—and charged them with abducting her, killing her, robbing her of her jewelry and expensive fur coat and then tossing her out of a taxicab in Van Cortlandt Park. The motive was believed to be robbery, something that seemed too pat, too easy an explanation given the extensive criminal associations Gordon had developed over the years in New York.

With the arrests, Walker and the police hierarchy breathed a sigh of relief that Gordon's death didn't seem to be connected to the police corruption and thus wouldn't taint City Hall. But the political winds in New York City would blow unpredictably, in ways that Walker couldn't have anticipated from Gordon's murder. The stars were aligning the wrong way for Walker, who up until the Seabury investigation and Gordon's killing had led a charmed existence as a creature of the powerful Democratic organization Tammany Hall. But the Seabury probers had uncovered indications that not only the magistrates' court was corrupt but also that Walker himself had been cavalier and dishonest about his affairs, amassing large amounts of monetary assets, access to wealth and bank accounts which indicated that he was, quite bluntly, on the take.

When Walker actually took office with his first electoral win in 1926, the economy was percolating along at a grand pace, fed by stock market speculation and a sense that there was an endless supply of money and jobs. But with the stock market collapse in 1929, the city economy began to erode and Walker and his inability to deal with financial problems was seen as a greater liability. He won reelection against Fiorello LaGuardia but would not have an easy second term.

History would show that Walker was a practitioner of what the old Tammany Hall stalwart George Washington Plunkitt called "honest graft" in politics. As far as Plunkitt was concerned, politicians were presented with all sorts of opportunities for enrichment because of their position in government. Plunkitt didn't mean blackmail and extortion; rather he was referring to, among other things, profiting from inside information, something that would get a Wall Street investor a prison sentence today but which Plunkitt thought was perfectly fine in the political sphere. In a 1905 interview he boldly gave an example of how he made a bundle of cash from the expansion of the New York City reservoir system.

"Up in the watershed I made some money, too," Plunkitt said. "I bought up several bits of land there some years ago and made a pretty good guess that they would be bought up for water purposes later by the city. Somehow, I always guessed about right, and shouldn't I enjoy the profit of my foresight?"

But by the Depression Era, the notion of politicians profiting from their positions—be it called honest graft or outright corruption—was fast falling out of disfavor with the public and increasingly vocal reformists. Gov. Franklin Roosevelt, himself harboring plans to run for president in 1932, had to find some way to harness the growing public outrage about what had happened to Vivian Gordon and the stench of corruption which had pervaded the city under Walker's watch. Samuel Seabury's sprawling investigations would provide Roosevelt with the perfect vehicle to do something about the partying mayor.

In 1932, under Roosevelt's prodding, Seabury initiated a review of Walker's tenure as mayor, holding a series of public hearings in which Hizzoner was the star witness. By all accounts, Walker did well under sometimes condescending questioning by Seabury, who seemed like a bit of a stuffy patrician. The *Daily News* called the verbal fencing a battle of the ages, covering the hearings like a prize fight in which Walker's reputation and legacy were at stake. Walker used his rapier wit to spar against Seabury's ponderous legal blows. If Walker scored verbal points the public audience cheered, so popular was the mayor still.

But the evidence couldn't be denied. Although he had gotten by for years on the strength of his wits and fine tailoring, Walker was no longer a gentleman above suspicion. Bank records showed that Walker had nearly $250,000 in cash in a safe in his apartment, money that had come from the brokerage account of a friend in the publishing industry. In another deal, a company that won a city contract secured a $10,000 letter of credit in Walker's name. It all sounded corrupt, and Seabury said as much, charging that Walker had been involved in gross impropriety by taking money from those doing business with City Hall.

No doubt believing his press coverage, Walker thought he could weather any storm. The public loved him and the will of the electorate was worth more than anything Seabury could hurl at him. Seabury had no power to remove or penalize Walker. It was up to Roosevelt to decide what to do. For the governor, the timing was delicate.

Vying for the Democratic nomination as president, Roosevelt knew he couldn't alienate Tammany Hall. Although wounded by various allegations of corruption, the Tammany machine still had clout and Roosevelt needed the organization's support if he wanted to make a credible run for the presidential nomination. But Roosevelt also had to show some fairness to Walker, and in the summer of 1932, likely to buy some time, conducted his own hearing into the mayor's activities. The result was not much different from Seabury's findings. Roosevelt then had to decide.

In the end, Walker made it easy for everyone. Sensing that he really had no choice, Walker sent Roosevelt a terse telegram the night of September 1, 1932: "I hereby resign as Mayor of New York, said resignation to take effect immediately." A week later, Walker set sail for Europe where he met up with girlfriend Betty Compton, who was waiting for him in Italy.

Walker's political ouster and ruination capped an extraordinary series of events that was impelled by the killing of Vivian Gordon. Had there not been such a public outcry over her killing as a symbol of the lawlessness wracking the city—both from the entrenched gangster culture and the corrupt officialdom—Walker might not have become such a lightning rod for the storm brought on by reformists and good government types. But at this particular moment the stars were aligned against him. It would be the first time in the modern history of New York City that a sitting mayor of the nation's biggest metropolis would be chased from office by scandal.

When she died, Vivian Gordon would be buried in an unmarked grave in Westchester County with only a few pallbearers, a nurse and her grieving brother to watch as she was put into her final resting place. But while virtually no one mourned Vivian Gordon, her story has become a vital part of the social and political histories of New York and is the basis for *Broadway Butterfly: Vivian Gordon, the Lady Gangster of Jazz Age New York*.

The term "Broadway Butterfly" is one that applies not just to Vivian Gordon but also to the parade of women who were attracted by Broadway's glitz, glamor and promise of fame and fortune. Some had talent and would make it. Many, even with a modicum of talent, just couldn't get the breaks and had to confront the reality that they either had to go back home to the quiet towns they came from or make a living somehow. The tabloids sometimes called them "singed moths," consumed by the lights of Broadway, or third-class gold diggers. Vivian chose prostitution and then her own style of dicey business deals, questionable associates and racketeering to make a living. Others, like attractive singer and model Dot King of the Bronx and Louise Lawson, an accomplished church piano player from Texas, would befriend wealthy men, often those who were married, and become kept women. It might have been hard times for some, but there was no lack of well-heeled men looking for mistresses.

Rich men in New York City eagerly sought out younger women. These were sexual and economic arrangements and the women profited well with nice apartments, fine things like jewelry and lifestyles they couldn't afford on their own. The men always had the upper hand and control in such relationships through their money. At times the relationships would run their course and the men would go on to other conquests and their women would find other sugar daddies. However, before Vivian Gordon's demise some of the other Butterflies met untimely murderous fates. Dot King, who had as her benefactor J. Kearsley Mitchell, the son-in-law of one of America's richest men, Edward T. Stotesbury, was found dead in her apartment off Central Park on March 15, 1923. King was in a fetal position on her bed and appeared to have been strangled. Police found a bottle of chloroform on the floor, apparently used to subdue her. Her substantial jewelry collection was also missing.

About a year after Dot King was killed, Louise Lawson, 26, who had some minor success landing a supporting role in one film with Lillian Gish, was found dead in her West 77th Street apartment. Lawson had been in various relationships with rich men, the last being businessman Gerhard M. Dahl. The night she died, Lawson let in a couple of men who ostensibly were going to restock her bootlegged liquor supply. When cops discovered Lawson's body, they determined she had been suffocated and that $15,000 of her jewelry had been taken. The King and Lawson killings, which were never solved, were the most notorious of cases dubbed by the tabloids as the "Butterfly Murders."

As the old song said, "There is a broken heart for every light on Broadway." And if aspiring women who failed to make it weren't killed, the sting of failure on the Great White Way was too much for them to handle. For as another stanza in that song said, "The lights above you, think nothing of you"; this was something many found to be the harsh truth. One chorus girl, after failing to find work, stuffed her powder puff in the door keyhole, turned on the gas in her apartment and suffocated to death by her own hand. Another gal who came to New York with dreams of making it on Broadway was so weak from not being able to earn money to eat that she was found by police unconscious after fainting on the Upper West Side. After recovering, the poor woman had to go to court, where a sympathetic judge and court bailiffs passed the hat and collected $10, not enough money to send her back to her native Ohio but sufficient to get her to the home of friends in New Jersey who could take care of her.

Not all of the so-called Broadway Butterflies who tried to make careers on the stage would be defeated or wind up dead. A notable exception was Peggy Hopkins Joyce. Born Marguerite Upton in Virginia in 1893, Joyce did carve out a modest career on Broadway and made a couple of film appearances. But what she became remembered for most was her series of six marriages to millionaires and men of celebrity, all of which resulted in her getting millions of dollars in jewels, homes and other assets, as well as healthy alimony settlements. Sometimes it was the men who pursued her who met untimely ends. Such was the case of Chilean diplomat Guillermo Errazuriz, who wound up taking his own life after Joyce said she spurned his advances. Nine days after Errazuriz's death, another Chilean diplomat committed suicide by a drug overdose after he reportedly became despondent when Joyce spurned him as well. She had quite an impact on Chilean men it seems.

If she didn't have a breakout career singing and dancing like Joyce's, Vivian Gordon certainly got by with her schemes and crimes. In the end she ended up on a morgue slab as well, her murder being one of the most celebrated of the Butterfly killings. Yet like the slayings of Dot King, Louise Lawson and socialite party girl Starr Faithfull—found dead on a Long Island beach a month after Gordon's death—no one was ever held legally responsible for the homicides. Modern forensic science might have made these cases slam dunks for police. But in 1931 there was no DNA analysis, no surveillance cameras, and in trying to figure out what kind of rope was tied around Vivian's neck, cops used a relatively primitive comparison with samples of clotheslines. When Vivian's suspected killers finally went to trial, the defense attorneys aggressively showed that the star witness had his own criminal history, casting doubt on his veracity. The result was a verdict of acquittal.

Still, the search to discover who killed Vivian Gordon captivated the public for years on end and is detailed from start to finish in *Broad-*

way Butterfly. The challenge today in telling the story is that everyone who had any connection to the case is long gone. In piecing together Vivian's life, I had to sort through her various identities. She was born Benita Franklin and after marrying John Bischoff took his surname. Where necessary, I used Vivian's earlier names to search records and for story clarity. But in *Broadway Butterfly* for the most part I decided to stay with Vivian Gordon throughout the text, often using the short form "Vivian."

An author today has the benefit of archives and databases, particularly Ancestry.com and census records, which serve as trails allowing a person, no matter how obscure and how dead, to be tracked through time much as I did with Vivian Gordon. Unlike some of the gangsters I have written biographies about—Frank Costello, Vito Genovese, John A. Gotti—Vivian had a relatively small paper trail of criminal and civil cases. But thanks to digitization, newspapers would help expand the story with coverage that was colorful, sensational and, if not, sometimes a bit suspect in terms of veracity. Archivists in the United States and Canada proved to be helpful as well by digging out facts and documents which had long remained hidden.

However, as much as *Broadway Butterfly* is about one murder victim, it is also a story with a broader historical context. Vivian Gordon is a symbol of the excesses, police corruption and wide-open criminality of the day. Her story also reflects the status of women in the Jazz Age in a realistic way. *The Great Gatsby* was emblematic of life in a certain elevated cut of society in post–World War One America and spread the mythology that life was one constant good time, with parties on Long Island's North Shore and endless amounts of libations. Iconic newspaperman Damon Runyon pushed his own version of Broadway myths with fictional gangsters loosely modeled on real-life characters like Costello and stories about the dazzle of Manhattan. What both Gatsby and Runyon did was to create worlds only partly rooted in reality. However, for the average folk those stories told of a fairy-tale existence about things that were unattainable and not part of New Yorkers' everyday struggle to survive.

"Damon Runyon invented the Broadway of *Guys and Dolls* and Roaring Twenties, neither of which existed . . . but whose names and

phrases became part of theater history and the American language,"
said Jimmy Breslin in his biography *Damon Runyon: A Life*.

As Breslin explained, just blocks from Broadway, a longshoreman
like Gus Barrett scratched around for two hours' work and then was
told to go home, after making a pittance. He was part of an army of
marginal workers who were afraid to complain out of fear of being
sent home with nothing at all. The Jazz Age to them was an illusion,
something that existed in the newspapers and in stories told by Runyon and Fitzgerald. The average income for a New York State resident
in 1929 was just under $1,200 a year, under $1,000 for neighboring
New Jersey.

"Prohibition, then, was a time when hundreds danced wildly while
tens of thousands stared at the floor and tried to find a slice of bread,"
Breslin said.

Vivian Gordon bought into the myths of the era and in her way
tried out her own particular hustle to make it in New York, far away
from the life she had growing up in the Midwest and in a Canadian
convent. Gordon wasn't a political creature and, in her world, couldn't
have cared less about Jimmy Walker and Franklin Delano Roosevelt.
She was a mother who at the core of her existence—as *Broadway Butterfly* will show—had one overriding obsession centered on the care of
her daughter. But she was also a hooker, hustler and vindictive conniver who made poor choices. Yet her death was cruel: strangled and
dumped like an animal in the park. Her demise, which nobody could
have foreseen at the time, served as a catalyst for change in one of the
most important political battles of the age among two of the most
dominant men of the times. Roosevelt got his presidency and led the
country until his death from a massive stroke in the waning days of
World War Two. Walker was ruined but didn't fade away entirely. He
stayed in Europe until 1935 and, when he came back to the U.S., eventually took a corporate position as head of a record company, which
was probably the better career choice.

Roosevelt's funeral was a state affair leading to a burial in Hyde
Park, New York, home of his presidential museum, where his final resting place is a tourist attraction. The nation mourned him. Walker died
in November 1946 at the age of 65 from a blood clot on the brain and

was buried under a maroon marble tombstone in Gate of Heaven Cemetery, in Valhalla, N.Y., in the company of many notables like Babe Ruth and gangster Dutch Schultz, another character from his days as mayor. He rated a funeral at St. Patrick's Cathedral in Manhattan.

Given all that happened in her life and the impact of her death, Vivian Gordon turned out to be a New York historical figure as well. But over the decades she lay in an unmarked grave, largely forgotten, with not even a piece of a stone or metal marker to show she lived on this earth.

PART ONE

CHAPTER ONE

CATHOLIC HILL

THE WELL-KNOWN STORY IN Canada about the founding of the settlement of Guelph in southwestern Ontario province was that businessman John Galt showed up one day around 1850 with his axe and went to the tallest hill in the area. After cutting down a tree, Galt told God that he hoped his friend Bishop Alexander McDonell would use the particular spot for betterment of Roman Catholicism. In fact, Galt did more than hope and pray; he actually deeded the land on the hill to the church. Bishop McDonell didn't disappoint and soon Guelph became the place where the church started building edifices in earnest.

A big stone church in Gothic style was crafted from limestone. An order of nuns known as the Loretto sisters soon followed, and a convent was also built, serving as a sparsely furnished living area where the ladies could live out their vows of chastity, obedience and poverty. But the good sisters of Loretto weren't recluses. They had a God-given mission to teach, and over the years in the grounds around the church and convent oversaw the construction of places where young girls—and later young boys—could get a good Catholic education. The venue seemed idyllic, described by one historian as having tall maple trees and well-kept green lawns. The entire religious complex, standing as it did on the highest spot in Guelph, became known to the locals as "Catholic Hill," something it is still referred to as today.

True, the curriculum was aimed at making good Catholics. But the nuns knew the value and attraction of a well-rounded education and classes at the Loretto Academy were taught in music, art, and domestic skills. Night classes were added for the locals and some young women earned certifications for teaching. One of the nuns, Sister Antoinette McQuillan, was among some very talented musicians and the academy became a mecca of sorts for promising girls who wanted to advance their musical education. At times, when needy children either had lost their parents or required help, the sisters would take them in for an education.

All in all, Loretto Academy was a progressive place for the times and its reputation spread easily, becoming known to parents in the American city of Detroit, some 100 miles away across the border formed by Lake St. Clair. John Franklin was the father of five, including three girls—Lillian, Arnolda and Benita—who he knew were musically gifted and could benefit from the Loretto Academy experience. Franklin and his wife, Margaret, had raised their family initially in Michigan City, a small city in Indiana on the shores of Lake Michigan. The only distinguishing attractions of Michigan City was that it had a lighthouse and peculiar shifting sands along the lake shore. Not the most inspiring place for a child with musical talent.

Old newspaper reports claim that John Franklin worked as an assistant warden in Joliet Prison, a notorious penal institution in Illinois, although it is unclear what his specific duties at the jail were. With its crenellated walls and towers, Joliet had a foreboding Gothic look and over the years after its founding in 1858 became filled beyond capacity. Unsanitary conditions and other problems eventually brought calls to close the prison, although it would take until the 21st century for that to finally happen.

By the early 20th century, specifically around 1906 when reports grew about problems at Joliet, John Franklin changed whatever job he might have had at the prison and took on a position as a salesman for what was then known as the Acme White Lead and Color Works, an up-and-coming industrial concern in Detroit that fabricated metal products. It is likely that Franklin took the job as a way of earning enough to pay for the Catholic education of his three daughters who had to board at the Loretto Academy in Canada.

School records show that Lillian, Arnolda and Benita first enrolled at the academy in 1904 and that their residence was listed as being in Chicago, which would make sense as Franklin was working for the Illinois prison. Lillian and Arnolda remained enrolled in the academy through the 1908 school year, when their parents had moved to Detroit to accommodate their father's new job with Acme. During the school's golden jubilee concert in 1906, Arnolda and Lillian were listed as performing. Arnolda was noted as playing the harp and as a soloist while Lillian played the piano and violin.

Born in 1891, Benita was the youngest of the three sisters, and while her family said she had great musical ability, she wasn't listed in the concert program. However, an official of the Archdiocese of Toronto recently said that Benita studied music as part of her coursework, although she didn't participate in the jubilee concert. Family members said she was accomplished at the violin, piano and clarinet.

As talented as Benita—the girl who would become later known as Vivian Gordon—was musically, she had what can only be called serious behavioral problems. After enrolling in the academy around the age of 14, Benita began showing signs of being incorrigible and psychologically troubled. Benita's issues ran so deep that according to a doctor who later in life came to know her well, she attempted suicide several times while at the academy. The attempts to take her own life involved slashings with knives and other sharp instruments. Benita was "wild and stubborn," the doctor reported, and "helpless from protecting herself," an apparent reference to the suicide attempts.

A convent education clearly wasn't working for Benita, and she decided around 1909 at the age of 18 to leave, the school records indicated. It is likely that in the short term Benita returned to Detroit where her father had his job with the metal fabricating firm. Relatives would later say that John Franklin and his wife, Margaret, had split up while their daughters were teenagers, and that Benita and sister Lillian went to live with another Detroit family known as the Thurstons.

Benita finally left Detroit and her artistic ability and temperament led her to travel around the eastern part of the United States working vaudeville shows, mostly in choruses. Vaudeville, essentially a variety show, was a popular form of entertainment in the late 19th century and well into the 20th. Vaudeville—a French term—incorporated all kinds of performances: comedy, dance, musicians, trained animals, strongmen and even female impersonators. Some well-known American actors and musicians got their start as vaudevillians and Benita saw this as a way of striking out on her own with what her family and friends said were her accomplished musical abilities.

It was during her early vaudevillian period that Benita Franklin adopted the stage name of Vivian Gordon. It isn't known how she settled on that particular moniker, although it was sometimes a character name in high school and community theater plays. Between the time she left Detroit and 1914, there was no trace in newspaper stories of a performer named Vivian Gordon showing up in the cast of any local or regional vaudeville shows in the United States. The same held true for the name Benita Franklin. So it is likely that the young aspiring musician from Detroit got only small, insignificant chorus roles in small towns where the shows weren't worth any mention in the local press.

But in 1914, things started to change personally and professionally for Benita. It was during one of her vaudeville trips to South Carolina that she met John E. C. Bischoff, a native of Charleston, with whom she would begin a common-law marriage which would later become official. Then, in the same year, Benita—now regularly using the stage name Vivian Gordon—landed a role with the New York–based Shubert variety production known as *The Passing Show*.

In a competitive market where stage performers and chorus girls had to struggle to beat out thousands of others, Vivian Gordon finally had her foot in the door. Later stories about her life reported that she was an actress and singer who was well known on Broadway but gave no real details about where she appeared. In fact, a check of newspaper archives found no mention of "Vivian Gordon" in the theater listings or stories anywhere. But thanks to the Shubert Archive and its extensive collection of memorabilia and artifacts, we are now able to show that Vivian didn't remain as some backwoods theatrical drifter but like a few other Broadway Butterflies was able to do something of note, if only for a brief period.

On Broadway in 1914 the established variety stage show was the *Ziegfeld Follies*. Formed in 1907, the *Follies* ran for decades and became known for what were lavish productions, impressive scenery and beautiful women—the Ziegfeld Girls—who paraded all over the sets. Some top names of the day—W. C. Fields, Sophie Tucker, Ray Bolger, Bob Hope, Eddie Cantor and Josephine Baker—took part in the productions.

It was in an effort to compete with the *Follies* that two well-known producers from a major Broadway family, Jacob J. Shubert and Lee Shubert, began a series of reviews in 1912 known collectively as *The Passing Show*. The Shubert family was no marginal player on the Great White Way. Far from it. The family is credited through its real estate holdings with establishing the Broadway theater district of today, with early flagship venues like the Winter Garden, Sam S. Shubert and Imperial theaters. Theatrical historians said that during the Depression the Shubert family poured its resources into keeping theater alive in New York.

The *Follies* had been running for a few years when the Shubert family decided to launch its competitive revue. Critics would later say the Shuberts merely latched on to the tried-and-true Ziegfeld formula of pretty women, snappy songs and impressive staging. *The Passing Show* even sparked the threat of legal action by Florenz Ziegfeld when he believed one production number disparaged his wife, actress Billie Burke, who later went on to play the Good Witch in the film *The Wizard of Oz*.

But as Broadway historian Jonas Westover said in his book *The Shuberts and Their Passing Shows: The Untold Tale of Ziegfeld's Rivals*, the Shubert family had been innovating for years and recognized that the time for vaudeville and the revue had come. *The Passing Show* got some good reviews and notices, although not all the critics were thrilled, a usual state of affairs on Broadway.

The bench of talented composers, singers, actors, dancers, performers and pretty women—all necessary elements for Ziegfeld and

Shubert productions—was very deep in New York. To fill chorus lines, the Shubert Organization was able to pick from a horde of aspiring young women like Vivian Gordon who were eager, desperate even, to get a job. As it turned out, Vivian, a pretty redhead with engaging eyes and what was at the time a good figure, landed two positions with *The Passing Show of 1914*, according to the Shubert Archive. She was cast as the character "Miss Heather" in the November 23, 1914 show at the Shubert Theatre in Boston. The character name for Miss Heather derived from one of the show's skits which was set in Scotland, and according to Broadway historian Westover featured five women, including Vivian, with character names that reflected Scottish motifs and settings—Miss Leeds, Miss Glasgow, Miss Edinburgh and Miss Heather, for example.

For shows in June and August of that year at the Winter Garden, Vivian was in the chorus, including one large production set in what was described as "The Beautiful Persian Garden Scene," where she and dozens of other ambitious and pretty chorines were arrayed around a man who was supposed to be a sheik but was dressed in what looked like an outfit of tights and a hat that made him look like Robin Hood. "An Uproarious Upheaval of Lingerie and Laughter—A Mastodon of Musical Extravaganza" was how the playbill described the show, using a noun that didn't seem to be the best choice of words.

A role with a Shubert production wasn't anything to look down upon. But for Vivian it doesn't seem like the jobs she wrangled with *The Passing Show* were a springboard to any continued success. By the end of 1914 or early 1915, Vivian was pregnant and would have a daughter whom she also named Benita Fredericka. Theater work would have to take a back seat for a while to childcare, and at some point Vivian and the child's father, John Bischoff, finally decided to get married (he would later tell police it was in 1922) and live in Pennsylvania, although temporarily.

For a woman like Vivian who thrived on Broadway excitement and had a taste of it with *The Passing Show* spectacle, the choice of Bischoff as a spouse seemed a bit of a mismatch. Born in South Carolina in 1888, Bischoff had a job that was far removed from the world Vivian was familiar with on Broadway. Bischoff had a position in an offshoot of the federal prison system, spending much of his workweek in Virginia and commuting back home to Vivian and his daughter in Pennsylvania.

Bischoff's job has been described as that of a revenue officer at the Lorton Reformatory of the District of Columbia. Some reports said he was a federal marshal, although today the U.S. Marshals Service doesn't have any record of Bischoff working for the agency. The jail facility wasn't in the district but some miles away in Lorton, Virginia. Under the prison system in place at the time, Lorton served inmates who offended in the District of Columbia. The facility was established under the policy of President Theodore Roosevelt to be a model "prison without walls," where inmates were supposed to be rehabilitated before being sent back to society. The inmates were housed in large dormitory settings, not cells, and Lorton became known for its brickworks where the inmates worked. The reformatory gained notoriety when in 1917 some suffragettes were taken there after being summarily arrested for picketing outside the White House. The mistreatment the women received became a scandal. Eventually, the United States Bureau of Prisons would take over Lorton, which finally closed and was sold off in 2002 to Fairfax County in Virginia.

A thin-faced man with a stern countenance, Bischoff was essentially an accountant for the reformatory. Between commuting back and forth to his job, Bischoff likely didn't have much of a full family life, and it wasn't long before Vivian decided she had had enough of what for her must have been a boring existence. Around 1922 she left him, taking young Benita Fredericka with her. The destination for mother and child was New York City, the dreamland for Vivian and so many other women. The small taste of success Vivian had of Broadway stayed with her and she thought she could try it all over again.

It would seem that Vivian, while brought up by conservative parents, turned out to be an abusive spouse. Her husband would later tell the police that Vivian would pummel him, claw at him and throw dishes at him during arguments. The countless episodes of domestic fighting were the basis for Bischoff's later winning a divorce from Vivian on the grounds of cruelty.

In 1920 the titian-haired Vivian was almost 30 years old and not really old by Broadway standards. But she also had a young daughter to think about and to care for. There is no record of a returning Vivian finding work on the stage, although it is possible she found a few jobs that never made it to print. It was clear that in postwar New York City in the early days of Prohibition there were other more immediate ways a pretty woman in need of cash could get what she needed through the sex industry.

Polly Adler will always be remembered as the *Grande* Madam of New York City, the so-called "Queen of Tarts" of the era. Adler, a Jewish emigrant from Russia in the early 20th century, lived in New York and New England before finally settling down permanently in a Manhattan apartment on the Upper West Side. But instead of the manual jobs she'd taken after first immigrating, Adler found herself introduced to a notorious bootlegger and pimp named Nicolas Montana, who set her up in her own apartment and got Adler launched in her own business of procuring prostitutes, which earned her about $100 a week. The year was 1920, the very time Vivian Gordon had made her way back to Manhattan.

Occasional arrests were an occupational hazard for procuring and prostitution and Adler experienced her share. But she also learned to grease the palms of police when she met them, a petty kind of bribery that helped protect her from too much harassment from the law. A shrewd operator, Adler steadily expanded her operation and was her own best publicity, showing up in nightclubs with some of her best-looking girls. Her clientele was a mix of rich and famous—as well as the rich and infamous. Tony clients like *New Yorker* editor Harold Ross and playwright George S. Kaufman were regular visitors to Adler's 75th Street brothel and later at West 50th Street, as were mob beer baron Dutch Schultz and gangster Charles Luciano, who had a voracious appetite for what he would later call "straight" girls.

"I didn't go in for none of that leather and whip crap," Luciano would recall. "I liked good-looking girls who could screw good and that is what Polly always sent me."

For Luciano, an afternoon with one of Polly's girls was how he would start his day. He would relax a bit and then get dressed for what would be a long evening with his cronies out of his suite in the Waldorf Astoria. But while he made a bundle from bootlegging rackets along the East Coast, Luciano had a reputation for being a terrible tipper to the girls, maybe forking over an extra five dollars into their bras above the $20 tab that was Adler's standard fare.

If Luciano was a cheapskate, a lot of Adler's other clientele were not. She made a bundle and the women who worked for her—minus the parsimonious guys who tipped like Charley Lucky—could do very well. Adler's bordellos were so well furnished that they were once dubbed the "Versailles of vice," antique-filled flesh spots where the well-heeled felt comfortable and money-hungry girls like Vivian Gordon knew they could make good scores.

It is clear from the available evidence that Vivian and Polly Adler had a working relationship. The question remains as to when it started. As will be shown later in this story, when Vivian got arrested on a loitering for prostitution charge and spent three years in a women's reformatory, she would always maintain that she was a victim of a setup by police and wasn't trolling the city streets for a customer as alleged. But with no indication that Vivian was working in the theater at that time she had to be earning cash somehow, although she was said to be getting $50 a week from her estranged spouse. Any of the thousands of young women struggling to make it on Broadway knew that among the jobs available as they waited for their big break on the stage, prostitution was a choice.

Adler admitted knowing Vivian as a pretty woman out to make a quick buck. When scandal would later erupt about Vivian, Adler seemed quick to downplay their relationship. As would later be reported, Vivian was among the 600 or so women on Adler's "call list" and with her looks may have been a big draw for clients.

Vivian, said Adler's biographer Debby Applegate, "had once been one of Polly's top-dollar call girls, before striking out on her own and parlaying her little black book into a lucrative blackmail enterprise."

The parting of Vivian and Adler may not have been amicable. According to a story in 1931 by *Daily News* crime reporter Grace Robinson, Vivian and Adler quarreled at the older woman's apartment on 88th Street. The dispute was over the spoils to be earned from a middle-aged "heavy spender" whom Vivian had brought to the apartment for a "rendezvous," said Robinson.

Vivian's shift from a struggling chorine to a crafty blackmailer likely took place sometime after her 1923 arrest, an event which finished off her already dying marriage and shattered her relationship with her daughter, Benita Fredericka. After leaving her husband back in Philadelphia in 1920, Vivian and her daughter made the precipitous move to New York with the meager financial resources of a $200 a month allowance from Bischoff. While she may have loved the child, Vivian wasn't providing much of a secure and stable home life for the girl in the city. Vivian took up with a fellow named Al Marks, a handsome, dark-haired ex-con and financial sponger whose first name was actually Abraham and who shared their small hotel apartment.

Marks had spent about 20 months in Sing Sing prison following his arrest in 1920 on a grand larceny charge. He would later recall meeting Vivian on the street in 1922 and eventually started living with her at the Hotel Langwell in Manhattan. As Marks remembered it, Vivian had stage aspirations for her daughter and was teaching her to dance but lacked the money to send the child for formal lessons. Vivian's life at that point was simple and lacking in the expensive clothes and fine jewelry that would become necessary parts of her lifestyle later. Still, she had class.

"She was far above the ordinary run of woman," Marks remembered later about Vivian.

While Vivian might have been classy, Bischoff was not happy that his estranged wife had abandoned him and taken up with a convicted felon who shared living space with his young daughter. He also did not like the idea that Vivian was trying to mold their daughter into a stage child at such an early age, even if she did have talent. But at the time, Bischoff had little recourse.

"Her husband kicked about the child growing up with me around," Marks would recall. "He tried to take the kid away. But she [Vivian] was crazy about me. She told Bischoff she was in love with me."

But the romantic and seemingly idyllic existence of the financially strapped couple came to an abrupt end on March 9, 1923. As would later come out, Marks had already gone to live in a different hotel and on that particular day Vivian had what was described as a flirty conversation on the street near her lodging hotel with one Andrew J.

McLaughlin. After meeting McLaughlin, Vivian contacted Marks and urgently said she had to see him at his place—possibly because her daughter was at her own apartment. Marks would later say that he had to go and left the door to his dwelling open so that Vivian could gain entry. Well, an attractive 32-year-old Vivian, whatever her motives for picking up McLaughlin, was setting herself up for some big trouble. McLaughlin was in reality an undercover plainclothes vice cop with the NYPD and used the circumstance—the flirting by Vivian and her invitation to come back to the apartment—as evidence that she was a prostitute trying to offer her sexual services.

Marks returned to the apartment to find a number of detectives in the room, and he was promptly arrested on charges of promoting prostitution. Already a felon on parole, Marks pleaded with the officers not to charge him as it would mean that he would be a parole violator and have to go back to Sing Sing. The cops weren't swayed by Marks's pleading, and he was taken to the Tombs, the notorious detention house in Lower Manhattan, where he stayed until he was shipped back upstate.

Vivian protested her innocence, crying out that Marks had set her up, but it did no good. She was taken downtown to the women's court at Jefferson Market in Greenwich Village where she would be arraigned. A parade of pickpockets, drunkards, petty thieves, brawlers and those who loitered for immoral purposes paraded daily through the dilapidated brick building where justice—if it could be called that— was dished out by hack judges whose main qualification for the job was that they had ties to the Tammany Hall organization. Despite earlier complaints and investigations over the years about the way justice was dispensed there, the women's court remained infamous and viewed with suspicion as a place rife with corruption.

It was hardly a place where a woman like Vivian Gordon, with a reputation for fine breeding, educated by nuns and with dreams of being a musical star, expected to find herself.

CHAPTER TWO

"FROM INNOCENCE
TO VICE"

OR DECADES, THE CRIMINAL COURT system in New York City was a hodgepodge of different places run by political appointees where all sorts of criminals could find themselves. For a while, as far back as 1795, a bureaucracy known as police court was presided over by so-called "police justices" who in many ways ran things as if they were courthouse cash registers: if you could pay a bribe into the till, the case would go away. It was like a collection agency. Just as good were polit-ical favors for Tammany Hall that would miraculously spare an accused from trial and conviction.

After the five boroughs consolidated into the City of New York in 1898, the police courts became magistrates' courts with special divi-sions for children under the age of 16 who committed crimes and women whose crimes could range from homicide to petty thievery but for the most part dealt with street prostitution. But Tammany Hall loved thievery, and if any reformers thought the changes to a special-ized magistrates' court for women would change anything they were very much mistaken.

By 1908 the city awakened and realized it had a problem with the magistrates' courts, particularly the one for women at Jefferson Market, and was forced to convene a special investigative committee known as the Page Commission. Whenever it couldn't be ignored that the city had a corruption problem in some area, a commission was appointed. One probation officer testified that even if a prostitute was released after conviction, a so-called "cadet," who in actuality was a pimp who worked in the court, would pursue the woman and force her to go back to her old line of work, using her criminal past as leverage.

The cadet scheme was a nice racket and there were others. Court clerks would deposit fines in their personal accounts and maybe they would remember to send the cash over to the city coffers, if they ever took the time to make a note of it. The courthouse building itself was a shambles. There was no filing system of any worth for records, which would wind up lost and never showing up for a trial. Fingerprints used to be taken of defendants but that stopped for some unexplained reason. Indeed, the Jefferson Market building was a filthy pigsty, and if anyone dared visit the place to look for court papers they would want to leave as fast as they could to get away from the vermin and dust.

Political party operatives sat as magistrates. Faced with the terrible state of the building, they sometimes worked only half the time they were supposed to and pushed through cases with little deliberation or concern for what the law required. It was all enough for the *New York Times* to conclude in one headline that ANARCHY IS BRED IN POLICE COURTS. Magistrates' courts like the one at Jefferson Market were calculated by Tammany to be chaotic because they worked best that way for the powers that be.

The Page Commission was forced to recommend that the lowly magistrates' courts be reorganized and that seemed to appease reformers. The passage of the Inferior Criminal Court Act made things a bit better for a time. But there was one big problem still: the administration of courts like Jefferson Market was still part of the political spoils system overseen by Tammany Hall. Magistrates—they were still known by that title—got their jobs because they had been Democratic Party faithful. The same was true for court clerks and other personnel who knew how to properly genuflect and give the right consideration to the right politically connected people.

So the atmosphere for corruption continued no matter what the Page Commission tried to recommend. Among the worst of it was a new version of the rackets that targeted women arrested in their apartments, likely framed by vice cops on prostitution charges. The cops were quite obvious about their motives to shake down one of these women, questioning her in detail about her finances before even taking her to the police station. There at the station house, a bail bondsman would relieve the woman of her jewelry and take it to be appraised. The bondsman would then tell the confused and frightened lady that there was no way she could beat the cops at their game. But she might be able to help herself.

"We fix these cases all the time," said one bondsman. "No matter how innocent you are, you are going to get yourself in a jam and they might jail you because they all work hand in hand."

Since the magistrates would always believe the cops, the only way the innocent woman could beat the case was to pay the bondsman a nice fee, say $300. She was also told not to call an attorney. When the distraught defendant was brought to court, a man posing as her attorney appeared and asked the cop some planted questions after which she was finally told she could go home. The money the woman paid would be divvied up among the bondsmen, the attorney and the cops.

So when Vivian Gordon was taken to Jefferson Market, she faced a deeply corrupted system that was infested at all levels. It was a stacked deck. If Vivian didn't have the cash to spread around and buy her way out of the prostitution jam, she would find herself with no other option but to take the fall. Despite her protestation of innocence and that her old lover boy Al Marks had set her up for the arrest, Vivian pleaded guilty to the charge of prostitution and was sentenced by Magistrate Stanley Renaud to a three-year term in the Bedford Reformatory for Women in Bedford, New York.

With his estranged wife now an inmate and unable to care for their daughter, John Bischoff took young Benita Fredericka back home with him. The eight-year-old child was kept in the dark about her mother's true status and in a letter indicated she thought Vivian had suddenly taken ill and was confined to an institution.

"Dear Mamma: I am very sorry you are sick. I hope you will be better very soon. Daddy will bring me to see you as soon as you are better," Benita Fredericka wrote.

Vivian would insist till the day she died that her conviction was a fraud, a setup by the cops and the courts. Based on what was known about the magistrates' court and in particular Magistrate Renaud, her protest might have had merit. Renaud was a judicial hack and was later found to be a particularly pliant magistrate when it came to the police. In one case involving two women grabbed in a prostitution arrest whose testimony conflicted with the arresting officer's, Renaud said that "defendants are always presumed to exculpate themselves" and sided with the cop. When asked later what would happen if a cop lied, Renaud said it was none of his concern. More than one woman had to spend time in jail because Renaud decided to believe a cop despite overwhelming evidence to the contrary.

The long-standing scheme in the court was that the payment of a bribe to cops, court clerks and attorneys would guarantee that a criminal case would be dismissed. One way to easily assure dismissal was for an arresting officer not to appear in court, at which point the case would be thrown out. Renaud was one of those magistrates who earned the reputation for quickly tossing cases, and cops knew when he was on the bench that a dismissal was easy to get, so they tried steering cases to his courtroom.

Vivian's time in Bedford was hard for her, considering the separation from her daughter and the belief that she had become a victim of the corrupt criminal justice system. Records of her incarceration are no longer available from the New York State Department of Correction. But later accounts of matrons at Bedford during Vivian's time in the reformatory indicated she made the best of things, was "dependable" in her work and "well-mannered," far from her uncontrollable behavior as a teenager at the Loretto Academy.

If correction officials thought that the experience at Bedford would somehow benefit Vivian and rehabilitate her, they were quite wrong. The prison environment was full of negative influences. In letters to her sister Arnolda, Vivian said that if she didn't know about the criminal life before she was arrested, Bedford would turn into a crime school.

"You can't imagine what I learned at Bedford. The class of women there was awful," Vivian said. "They showed me and told me how to do everything in the underworld. Dope fiends, blackmailer—oh, Arnolda you wouldn't understand that I got thoroughly educated to vice by being amongst these women.

"I am not slow to learn," Vivian continued. "In my case, the reformatory reformed me from innocence to vice, just contrary to its purpose. Oh, this is a terrible thing!"

The letter to Arnolda was written by Vivian sometime after she got out of Bedford around 1926. Vivian said her fellow inmates couldn't extricate themselves from the spiral of criminality, that she herself couldn't get on the right track and instead the horror of her new lifestyle was the only way she knew how to live.

It had to be after Bedford that Vivian Gordon began to develop a lifestyle of criminality that would gain her the notoriety which plagued her to her death. But a major concern also was the custody of Benita Fredericka, which Bischoff had as a result of the divorce decree granted by the Philadelphia courts around 1924. Vivian would repeatedly demand the return of her daughter, but Bischoff wouldn't relent. By 1926, Bischoff, who was still working at the Lorton Reformatory in Virginia, had married again. Eunice and John Bischoff lived with Benita Fredericka in the quiet New Jersey town of Audubon about 100 miles from Manhattan, just over the Delaware River from Philadelphia.

Vivian wouldn't stop trying to regain custody of her daughter, the loss of which contributed to a continuing feeling of bitterness that she had been unfairly victimized by the cops, the courts, her old lover Al Marks and lastly her ex-spouse. Events would later show that this sense of betrayal contributed to the spiral of fateful decisions—some with unexpected political overtones—Vivian would make before her murder and the worldwide sensation which followed. But in the interim Vivian still had to make her own way and survive in New York City. Suburban life was not for her, and she made decisions about what she did and who she did it with which would come to define her reputation, character and place in history.

CHAPTER THREE

THE REDHEADED LEAGUE

B Y THE TIME VIVIAN GORDON returned to New York City for the second time in 1920, the metropolis was a different place than when she left in 1914. For a start, the population of about 4.8 million just before the start of World War One had already jumped to 5.6 million by 1920, with Manhattan having the most residents at 2.2 million. Peacetime had brought tens of thousands of returning servicemen looking to resume their lives, get jobs, raise families and have some fun. The latter possibility was only slightly inhibited by Prohibition, what President Herbert Hoover called the "noble experiment" to make the country "dry." With the passage of the 18th Amendment, lawmakers expected that the ban on the sale of alcoholic beverages would improve the health of the citizenry, diminish crime and foster a newfound respect for law and order.

It was true that reports of cases of cirrhosis of the liver, a condition tied to excessive consumption of alcoholic beverages, decreased, but some other diseases connected to drinking saw increases in the years after 1920, the *New York Herald* reported. If there was any hope that respect for the law would grow with Prohibition, that idea was soon dashed. Polls in different parts of the country reported that the public believed efforts to enforce the Prohibition laws were largely a failure;

people were drinking more, not less; there was growing disrespect for laws and bootleggers were making lots of money from all of the smuggling of alcohol.

The money being made from bootlegging was high octane for the New York gangsters who, as it turned out, would become an important part of Vivian's life. Throughout World War One, the gangs of New York had been a bunch of loosely organized head breakers and ruffians scratching around to make a buck. There were some famous names like Owney Madden, Paul Kelly and Monk Eastman, who rose to the top and had gangs that lorded over areas of the city like the notorious Five Points in Lower Manhattan. But overnight with Prohibition, the local criminal combinations began to profit from the smuggling and production of alcoholic beverages in ways they had never imagined. For a while it was a free-for-all, with liquor shipments being hijacked and gun fights erupting all over the city and Long Island. Guys who had been mob head breakers were now earning millions of dollars.

Eventually, the mobs from around the country came together in a meeting in Atlantic City, N.J., and agreed that it took a better organizational structure to move the product to a hungry public, fight off outside competition and make cooperative friends among the police and politicians who had no shame about taking some of the money. This was the early precursor of what Luciano and his associates would later put together as the ruling commission of the Mafia.

The public wanted booze and got it. Some of it came all the way from Europe and was of the finest quality, and some was manufactured at home—the term "bathtub gin" was an apt description of where some of the product came from. This was the time of the Roaring Twenties, the Jazz Age, whatever pundits like Damon Runyon wanted to call it. The myth of a never-ending good time on the Great White Way was pervasive. New York, with an estimated 32,000 speakeasies, needed a constant supply of booze and smuggling ships from as far away as the French islands of St. Pierre and Miquelon just off Canada and the Caribbean. Ships also came in from Europe laden with champagne and scotch whiskey and stabled off Long Island in an area known as Rum Row, waiting to play cat-and-mouse games with the Coast Guard vessels that tried to stop them from landing their illicit, but very much prized, cargoes.

Once the liquor came ashore, trucks run by Italian gangsters like Frank and Eddie Costello, Jewish mobsters like Dutch Schultz and Irish mob bosses like Charles "Vannie" Higgins and Legs Diamond moved the booze to New York City and Long Island. The money they made was amazing and when they needed help in unloading their speedboats, New York City cops would sometimes act like stevedores and assist them. If anybody tried to get in the way of the business, homicide was the answer. Higgins was himself earmarked with responsibility for five murders but none of the charges ever stuck. Swimming in cash, gangsters like Costello were able to dangle plenty of dollars and convince Tammany Hall to be a political friend.

The man who became known in this period as "The Brain" of organized crime was a Jew named Arnold Rothstein, born to affluence in Manhattan to an Ashkenazi family. While his father, Abraham, earned a reputation as a devout businessman of substance, Arnold took to gambling and by the age of 31 was throwing around tens of thousands of dollars in wagers, often on baseball games, so much so that in 1914 he is reported to have lost $75,000 in game bets for the season, a sum that would be valued at about $2.3 million in 2023. If there was a card game anywhere in Manhattan, Rothstein could find it, and his name surfaced in 1918 when he was rounded up with other luminaries caught gambling not far from City Hall.

What made Rothstein a power in the world of the Prohibition rackets was the money he was said to have lent Costello, Luciano and others to fund their growing bootlegging operations, which in time grew into major syndicates and spawned what would become known later as the Mafia or La Cosa Nostra. Rothstein also had his own transatlantic shipping operation for high-quality scotch—and quite possibly heroin. In time, Rothstein became one of the biggest players in bootlegging operations and used Luciano, Costello and Meyer Lansky for his business plan, which was to bring in high-quality scotch from Europe. He knew that the market for good booze wasn't going away anytime soon so Rothstein decided that the best sources of scotch were England and Scotland. As David Pietrusza described in *Rothstein*, it was Lansksy's job to get the scotch from Europe to the U.S. any way he could.

Of course, the big legend to follow Rothstein through his life was that he fixed the 1919 World Series so that he could bet against the Chicago White Sox and make a killing. But despite a federal grand jury investigation into the "Black Sox Scandal," no charges were ever brought against Rothstein, who claimed he was an innocent businessman whose name was used by others to pull off the fix.

It is unclear exactly when Rothstein met Vivian Gordon since she didn't return to the city until somewhere between 1920 and 1922, when Rothstein was busy with horse betting and other sports endeavors and becoming a big *macher* on Broadway. But Rothstein liked attractive women. He is said to have used beautiful *Ziegfeld Follies* women like Lillian Lorraine to steer well-heeled gamblers to his establishment. Since Vivian hung out around the theater district scene it was inevitable that they would meet even if she wasn't doing anything on the stage. Eventually, Rothstein provided Vivian with cash for her own prostitution racket, something The Brain knew could be as lucrative as printing money.

Around this time Rothstein was into a great many strange dealings that an aspiring sex entrepreneur like Vivian could take note of, mainly his involvement in a blackmail scheme involving a pretty auburn-haired woman named Nellie Black, the so-called "Pajama Girl" who set about trying to extort cash from a couple of wealthy men. Black, who earned her nickname after chasing burglars in her pajamas, was accused of trying to carry out shakedowns against a wealthy stockbroker who was later accused of fraud, and also Westchester businessman Walter Ward, who liked red-haired women, a category which included Vivian. Court testimony indicated Rothstein acted as an intermediary for Black, trying to get her victims to make payments to settle things without further embarrassment.

According to one newspaper account, Ward was a murder suspect and associate of Rothstein. For a time, Ward owned a defunct Brooklyn baseball club. The stories circulated in the sporting world that Ward fancied red-haired women and became the target of a group of blackmail conspirators who used women with flaming red tresses to lure tempting targets like Ward, who had a particular fetish for auburn-haired young ladies. According to another account, Ward, while married, kept a Manhattan apartment in which a handful of kimono-clad women came and went, including one described as a "Titian-haired girl of striking appearance" known as "Peggy." The latter may very well have been Peggy Hopkins Joyce, the woman known for her serial affairs and marriages. Another Ziegfeld girl who had a penchant for snaring men, Joyce is said to have been used in the 1910s as a steerer of rich men to Rothstein's gambling operations.

It was never made clear why Rothstein played a role in trying to help Black in her shakedown attempts. He was nearing the apex of his power in the underworld and running lucrative major floating gambling operations around New York. His bets were followed as closely in the sports world as baseball scores. When he won, which was often, it was for big money, like he did when he backed boxer Gene Tunney over Jack Dempsey in 1926 and collected a $200,000 payout.

However, Rothstein couldn't help himself. He appeared to relish the role of fixer, a go-to man, bailing out gangster friends and in 1926 helping negotiate a contract between the International Ladies Garment Workers Union and some manufacturers. He even sent around gangster Jacob "Little Augie" Orgen to placate a hat manufacturer whose partner was beat up in a labor dispute. Rothstein only touched situations where he felt it was a sure thing that he could make money. It appeared to be more than coincidental that the big-shot gambler became involved in the conspiracy to use red-haired women in the blackmail scheme, acting as an intermediary, his favorite role, in getting extortion payments.

As her letters to her sister Arnolda indicated, Vivian claimed to have first learned the blackmail ropes through her fellow inmates in the Bedford Reformatory. But it is through her acquaintance with Rothstein and his flaming-haired ladies that Vivian would see the way the blackmail racket—a variation of the old badger game—could work among the rich in New York. But after her prostitution arrest, red-haired Vivian didn't have much time to become bait for somebody like Ward since by March 1923, she was off to serve her three-year sentence.

In some ways, the three-year trip to "college," as the gangsters called time spent in custody, just might have kept Vivian out of the way of some serious harm which befell some other women on the

Broadway hustle. The year 1923 stood out for Vivian because she got
arrested and lost custody of her daughter. But around the time Vivian
was getting locked up, Broadway saw the beginning of what would become high-profile killings, all the victims young, aspiring women who
wanted desperately to make it in show business but who would wind
up dead by the strangler's hand or some other kind of misadventure.

The first of the so-called "Butterfly Murders" involved Dorothy Keenan, a pretty, petite and shapely first-generation Irish immigrant.
Keenan, thanks to her good looks, became a model for high-end fashion stores in Manhattan, and apart from modeling clothes was
expected to go out wining and dining with out-of-town buyers. Not
long after, Dorothy was easily persuaded by a lady friend to join a new
line of business, becoming what the newspapers called a "Broadway
gold digger." Apparently, it took little to convince Dorothy, who had
been making about $100 a month at the stores, to begin some serious
prospecting for men.

"There is no use for a girl who looks like you to be working for $25
a week," Dorothy was told by a girlfriend. "What you need is a 'friend.'
Why not let me introduce you to some rich men." With that, Dorothy
changed her name to Dorothy King—Dot for short—and joined the
ranks of gold diggers.

"Dot King came to know the Broadway of the parasites, the immac-
ulate road agents, the press agents, the lounge lizards who lived on
women . . . the out-of-town businessmen bent on sprees of liquor or
sex, the bored millionaires who seek some new thrill," was how the
Daily News summed up her new lifestyle.

King graduated up the feeding chain, first with men with small
amounts to spend and then gradually hitting it big. It was at a café
that King met millionaire businessman J. Kearsley Mitchell, president
of a rubber company and married to the daughter of Main Line Philadelphia blue blood E. T. Stotesbury. Smitten by King, Mitchell offered
her $1,000 a month, a promise to pay the bills and an apartment in
Manhattan on West 57th Street, just down the block from Rothstein's
building. She took the deal.

But King didn't just stick with Mitchell. She took up with another
millionaire, one from Puerto Rico named Albert Guimares, a stock

trader but also a swindler, whom she plied with money and even joined in a business venture. In return, Guimares would show his gratitude with his fists. He beat King and mocked her desire to get married. There was also Draper Daugherty, described as a habitual drunk and drug user, whose brother was a top federal law enforcement official. But apparently, Mitchell remained in King's life, continuing to give her jewels, furs and clothing and sending her a letter dated two days before March 15, 1923, saying how much he missed her and couldn't wait to see her back in New York when he could "kiss [her] pretty pink toes."

It was March 15, just before 11:00 A.M., that the maid entered King's apartment and found her dead on the bed, with her two rooms showing signs of being ransacked. While police at first thought King might have killed herself, that theory was quickly discounted after cops noticed bruising around her neck and concluded she had been strangled. A bottle of chloroform was found near the bed as well. Some $15,000 in jewelry, gifts from Mitchell, was gone, as were two fur coats of ermine and squirrel. The soppy love letter Mitchell had sent the dead woman a few days earlier, where he mentioned kissing her pink toes, was also missing.

The tabloids went wild with the story of King's murder, a prelude to what would eventually become the media feeding frenzy a few years later over Vivian's killing. Despite efforts to keep himself in the background, Mitchell's name surfaced in connection with King, including the fact that he had spent a few hours with her—in the presence of his attorney—at the 57th Street apartment in the hours before she was killed.

The police determined that Mitchell had left the apartment and didn't try to conceal the fact that he been there. It seemed there was no proof he killed King. But the disclosures in the newspapers effectively ruined his standing on the Social Register and the Philadelphia social circuit, at least for a while. While police would initially fixate on robbery as a motive for King's slaying, the *Daily News* conducted its own investigation and determined that Mitchell was the object of a blackmail attempt, in which an extortionist tried to squeeze him for $100,000 in the badger game that Vivian Gordon would later exploit so well. The plotters, the *News* reported, tried to recruit King in the scheme but she reportedly refused. The extortionist was banking on the notion that shame would get Mitchell to pay to keep his indiscretions secret and protect his social standing.

Affairs by rich men in Mitchell's social and economic strata were not uncommon. "On the contrary," said the News in its take on the mores of the elite, "a large percentage of the millionaire crowd engage in these butterfly chases and consider them a necessary diversion from the correct routine into which a society man's life is likely to fall."

Neither Mitchell nor Guimares, who curiously was noticed a couple of days after King's death with bite marks and scars on his hand, were charged in the killing. To this date, the case remains unsolved.

Louise Lawson had a brief career trajectory on Broadway similar to Dot King's, although she had true musical talent and was not just a pretty face. While Lawson didn't come from a poor family like King's, her hometown of Walnut Spring, Texas, had little in terms of cultural stimulation and outlets for her music, apart from the church choir. What she saw of New Yorkers and other big-city folks she liked, and after completing studies at Baylor University headed to New York, staked to a few months' living money by her father.

But Broadway was filled with aspiring actors, singers, dancers and performers of all types, each trying to get the big break. Lawson studied her music and although she got a couple of small stage roles, it was all temporary and short-lived. Lawson appeared in a publicity still for the Ziegfeld Girls, an indication she made it to the chorus for one of the Ziegfeld projects at a rate reported to be $75 a week. Films offered only a bit more opportunity. Lawson was cast as an extra in the Lillian Gish feature Way Down East.

But for Lawson the only steady way to keep up appearances for the folks back home was to get a rich male friend, one of whom was Gerhard M. Dahl, a married businessman with what was called a "traction business" who helped her financially. As in the case of Dot King, Dahl provided Lawson with an apartment on West 77th Street and tens of thousands of dollars' worth of jewels. Dahl would later say he used to visit Lawson at her apartment and play mah-jongg and listen to her play the piano. Near her bed Lawson had a photo of her well-heeled benefactor.

Louise Lawson was said to be a teetotaler but for some reason had plenty of liquor in her apartment since friends would regularly send her shipments. The night of February 8, 1924, both the elevator operator in the building and a neighbor recounted how two men came carrying a bundle and wanted to deliver it to Lawson's apartment. The men rode up the elevator and knocked on the door; the neighbor remembered hearing Lawson answer the doorbell ring by telling the deliverymen that she wasn't dressed and that they should leave.

"I can't wait," one of the deliverymen answered, and then the neighbor heard Lawson open her door. The neighbor found it strange that she didn't hear another sound until the Lawson maid screamed, "Murder!"

Lawson's bruised body was found in the apartment. Her dog was found tied to a chair in the parlor and no one heard him bark. The medical examiner would determine the cause of death to be strangulation, clearly a homicide. As in the case of Dot King, some $15,000 in jewelry—diamond, sapphire and emerald rings and expensive watches—were all missing.

Dahl had connections high up in the NYPD and cops at first agreed to keep news of his friendship with Lawson quiet. But word got out and the label of "Butterfly Murder" was stuck on the case by detectives and the newspapers. Lawson's friends were irked by the way she was painted as a Broadway party girl. Her ambition was to be a movie star, although despite studying at the Carnegie School of Acting her career was going nowhere.

Meanwhile Dahl's attorney painted the businessman as a worthy and caring friend of Lawson, whose motives for friendship were strictly platonic. No toe sucking in this relationship.

"Miss Lawson was a talented pianist and Mr. Dahl was quite interested in her musical achievements," Dahl's attorney Frederick Landeck told reporters. "His shoulders are broad—he hasn't the least desire to shrink from anything. That's why he called up the police and I know he made a clean slate of everything."

The killers of Lawson were never caught and despite the effort by police to watch pawnshops and known fences in stolen jewels, nothing turned up.

VIVIAN WAS EFFECTIVELY off the streets and out of any of the danger that befell the other good-looking party girls until 1926, when the doors of the Bedford Reformatory sprang open and she could head back to New York City. Her first important stop it seems was to Polly Adler and her house of pleasure. As Debby Applegate wrote in *Madam*, citing the reportage of *Daily News* writer Grace Robinson, Vivian and Adler were "well-seasoned comrades and occasional competitors."

According to Applegate, Robinson wrote that "[w]hen Vivian found herself broke she often worked for Madame Polly herself.... [Vivian] constantly boasted to others of her rich boyfriends, said she didn't have to go to Adler's and just worked to keep her mind occupied."

Polly treated Vivian, Robinson said, as something of an equal and more than an employee. She was sort of a high-ranked, cultured girl in the Adler stable, who even wrote poetry, said Robinson. At some point though, Vivian appeared to have amassed a significant amount of cash and began a series of forays over the years in other business ventures. She was helped along the way by a group of men—some lovers, others businessmen of questionable character and honesty.

A pundit once said that the concrete sidewalks and buildings of Broadway smelled of larceny and the rumble of the subway was like the sound of a safe being blown open. If that were so, it was a place where Vivian's old friend Arnold Rothstein was at home. Rothstein was the King of Broadway. What he made from his gambling and conniving made Rothstein rich and that led him to believe he could trick everyone into assuming he was going straight. He was done with gambling, real estate was the wave of the future, Rothstein said. Thinking he had some inside information about the site for a new airport in Queens, Rothstein around 1927 bought up land in what is known as Juniper Swamp, a soggy area of peat not far from Lutheran Cemetery. But the site wasn't picked for the project and Rothstein, stuck with the parcel, decided to build some 143 homes in two clusters that resembled apartment buildings. But the construction of the housing was cheap, and no streets connected the area to the local neighborhoods, although some sewer lines had been laid. It all eventually would be torn down to make way for a park today known as Juniper Park.

The Juniper Swamp project was a poor attempt by Rothstein to become a real estate baron and he soon reverted to card games, dealing in stolen securities—as well as more nefarious criminality, the kind that brought him the scrutiny of federal narcotics prosecutors and in which Vivian's name would later surface. While overshadowed by the Black Sox Scandal, Rothstein appeared to have been at the epicenter of a drug smuggling operation which one federal official called the largest such ring in the country. The extent of the smuggling would become known after Rothstein's murder in 1928 but included operations overseas in France, Holland and Belgium that directed the movement of heroin. The King of Broadway's files found in his office by police would ultimately lead to the seizure of $3 million worth of drugs in baggage aboard the old Twentieth Century Limited train out of Chicago as it traveled in December 1928 on its way to Buffalo, as well as the arrest of some of Rothstein's associates.

Vivian didn't appear to have any involvement in Rothstein's drug operation and was never arrested as part of the federal seizure. But years after the drug bust and after Vivian had been murdered, a renegade group of federal grand jurors, angered by the appearance of corruption and malfeasance within the federal narcotics investigations in New York, asked government officials to look into a series of questionable situations, including the way a stock swindler who was a friend of Vivian's was granted immunity from prosecution. Rumors circulated that Vivian had provided information about Rothstein's burgeoning drug empire to the U.S. Attorney's Office in Manhattan, which was led by George Z. Medalie, a prosecutor who in private practice had been an attorney for Rothstein. The grand jurors thought Vivian was talking, possibly in return for immunity for herself and the crooked friend, Joseph Radlow.

CHAPTER FOUR

"BEAUTY AND THE BLACKJACK"

GROVER ALOYSIUS WHALEN BECAME NEW York City's fifteenth police commissioner when he was appointed in 1928 to the job by his old friend and Tammany Hall cohort Mayor James Walker. Now, there will be much more about Hizzoner later in this story, but he is mentioned here because he put Whalen in as top cop, even though he had no law enforcement experience to speak of and his previous job was as a top official at Wanamaker's department store. But he had the backing of Walker and was a Tammany favorite so that was really all that mattered.

Whalen's main policing priority was to enforce Prohibition, and his idea of good police work can be summed up by this one statement: "There is plenty of law at the end of a nightstick." That toughness was something that would come back to haunt him later. But this was the era of the speakeasies and it soon became apparent to Whalen that Prohibition couldn't be enforced by swinging a billy club. Lawlessness when it came to Prohibition seemed to be the rule. Cops were seen off-loading bootlegged liquor up and down the East River and Walker himself was a regular habitué of his choice of speakeasies.

The police involvement was more than just off-loading the rum-running boats. An investigation would later reveal that an NYPD inspector in Queens named Thomas W. Mullarkey courted boot-leggers who made liquor in local stills. Mullarkey, as the investigation determined, was getting a cut of bootlegging operations for himself and his son. Mullarkey was so tuned in to bootlegging that he could quote current prices for alcohol and accessories to make stills. If Mayor Walker liked speakeasies and booze, why should cops be worried if they were giving him and the public what it wanted? Mullarkey was allowed to retire and then with his son promptly disappeared. It was found that Mullarkey, who had a yearly salary of $5,900, deposited nearly $28,000 in six months before disappearing, over half of it with his stockbroker.

Whalen was hardly a year on the job when he bemoaned the crime increase he faced in New York, blaming it all on the great failure of Prohibition to make things better. In a speech before the Rotary Club at the Waldorf Astoria on April 4, 1928, Whalen said that the rise of speakeasies and what he called the "hostess problem" had reversed years of progress. He also took a swipe at "sob-sister" judges who Whalen said were unfairly critical of his cops.

"In the old days, you could wipe out a vicious saloon," said Whalen. "Nowadays, all you need is two bottles and a room and you have a speakeasy. We have 32,000 speakeasies in this city."

Whalen could have added that pliant and complicit cops were also part of the problem. It wasn't that cops didn't try to shut down speakeasies. But it seemed that the low-level officers, because of certain regulations, couldn't go after high-class speakeasies, just the small fry that couldn't pay for protection. The big places were only to be raided if there was a complaint and many weren't targeted because they could afford to pay protection—much like Madam Polly Adler could. In the Bronx, old saloon operators formed the "Liberty League" and got a special blue card they hung behind the speakeasy bar to let cops know the place paid off and was protected. A skillful low-level cop could have received only "crumbs from the table," as one said, but that didn't stop them from banking nearly $100,000 during ten years of Prohibition.

Whalen was either willfully blind to what was going on in his department or just plain naïve and stupid about what the reality was on the streets of the city. Speakeasies, he insisted, were the source of all kinds of problems—including the way women worked the business.

"From the speakeasy comes dining and dancing and out of that grows the hostess game," Whalen continued. "This hostess problem verges seriously on a vice that we wiped out many years ago. It is very difficult for the police to get the necessary legal evidence to wipe out these places."

The "hostess problem" was a euphemism for the women who worked the bars and speakeasies, pushing drinks and themselves on customers. It was within this world that Vivian Gordon, once she got back to Manhattan from Bedford, found room to develop her own racket separate and apart from Adler. With backing from mobsters like Rothstein and Legs Diamond, Vivian assembled a stable of young, beautiful women—she had a list of at least 40 in her diary—who played the blackmail game targeting rich and vulnerable men who, despite the Depression, were around in sufficient numbers to make the scheme work.

It was what one writer called a "unique combination of beauty and the blackjack." Vivian set up the women, often at parties or in clubs, to meet the men and put them in sexually compromising situations. The women were told to find out as much as they could about the men, their wealth, occupation and marital status. It was a variation of the old badger game but without the phony aggrieved "husband" or boyfriend discovering the woman bedding the wealthy mark. Instead, Vivian was able to use the likes of Diamond to make sure the marks paid.

In Vivian's racket the coercion of the men could be through a subtle understanding of the embarrassment they could face if their escapades became known. But with Diamond in the picture, the value of *his* bad reputation—he had a lengthy criminal record and had been a close associate of Rothstein's—made it clear the kind of additional trouble the victims could face if they didn't pay.

Jack "Legs" Diamond got his nickname, so the story goes, because he had a reputation for being a good dancer. Although married, the handsome Diamond played the field and became a player on Broadway, claiming that he backed some shows and put some money into a couple of nightspots like the Hotsy Totsy Club, and is said to have backed a couple of boxers. Diamond told one journalist that he was just like any other businessman who wanted to make a return on his buck. But he was also involved in the bootlegging rackets and eventually got into a long-running dispute with Dutch Schultz, who claimed supremacy over the beer distribution in the city, as well as some other upstate gangs. Their feud would go on for years, with a high body count of dead gangsters.

These disputes among the bootleggers sometimes led to violence and Diamond found himself at the receiving end of gunfire so often that he was labeled the "clay pigeon" of gangland. He survived being shot in 1924 and when "Little Augie" Orgen was gunned down on the Lower East Side in 1927, Diamond was standing next to him and got hit three times, luckily surviving. In October 1930, Diamond was shot five times by two men who broke into his room at the Hotel Monticello in Manhattan and again survived, although he had to spend a couple of months in hospital.

"Ain't there nobody that can shoot this guy so he don't bounce back?" rival Dutch Schultz remarked.

It was not only good luck for Diamond that he was able to survive. He also seemed to fare well in the courthouse. Arrested at least 13 times since he was 17 years old, Diamond had a rap sheet filled with cases, including a number of homicide charges, that were either dismissed or led to acquittals. By the time Diamond met Vivian, the Broadway gangster seemed to have a streak of luck that made him a good partner for the criminally ambitious lady.

By mid-1930 Diamond and Vivian were working the sexual extortion racket in a deal apparently sealed at the Club Abbey, one of his nightspots. As part of the arrangement, Vivian would use her stable of party girls to take in gullible men and leave Diamond to do the rest of the strong-arming, if necessary. Diamond made a specialty of shaking down stockbrokers so he knew how to handle them. *Daily News* reporter Martin McEvilly would later report that a girlfriend of Vivian's related that Diamond and the hustling chorine would meet most nights at the Club Abbey, which had garnered a reputation as a gangster dive.

"Vivian was always lucky when it came to meeting rich men," her friend told McEvilly. "I don't know why but she seemed to attract the fellows with important money.

"And nobody had more nerve than Jack Diamond when it comes to muscling in on a proposition," McEvilly was told. "He would just walk in on one of Vivian's chumps and take him for everything he had."

But, at some point, possibly by late 1930 or early 1931, Vivian and Diamond had a big dispute over money. According to reporter McEvilly's informant, whom he did not name in his story, one night at the Club Abbey Diamond tossed a roll of cash containing $2,000 on the table towards Vivian. It was his way of buying her out.

McEvilly's source indicated she saw the whole incident and related that an infuriated Vivian told Diamond the payment was a lousy cut for what turned out to be a lucrative extortion deal and called him a "piker." An angry Diamond called Vivian a "dirty little bum" and told her to take the cash if she knew what was good for her. Vivian took the cash and later walked out of the club.

Diamond was clearly good muscle for a schemer like Vivian to have in her corner. But she was not without other resources to help her in the blackmail racket. It turned out that Vivian had a fairly well-organized operation that included a catalogue of the women in her employ, complete with nude photographs, to entice the men. Her instructions to the women were straightforward: they were in it for the money, as much as they could get, and should use stealth and craftiness to find out the identities of the "chumps" and how much they were worth.

Later investigation found that Vivian didn't have to use mob muscle to get the money. She had the services of a lawyer out of Brooklyn named John A. Radeloff of Court Street. Back in the day, calling someone a "Court Street lawyer" might be grounds for a slander suit, so dicey was the reputation of the legal profession on that particular block of downtown Brooklyn. Radeloff was just what Vivian needed in that he could make all of the right kinds of legal noises to threaten obstinate men who didn't want to pay up. If the money wasn't forthcoming, then Radeloff would file a lawsuit.

She might have been taught by nuns early in her life but Vivian the racketeer and shakedown artist had a bad reputation on Broadway. One woman interviewed by the *Daily News* related how she ran into Vivian at the Club Abbey in the company of Diamond and was quietly approached by another woman who was in the ladies' room and warned about Vivian.

"Listen, I am a good friend of yours and I don't want to see anything happen to you. Stay away from Vivian Gordon, understand," was the warning given in the bathroom. When the friend was pressed for more of an explanation, she replied in no uncertain terms about Vivian's bad reputation.

"She is red hot. She travels with a bad mob. She will get hers someday," was the explanation. "Vivian Gordon is the toughest, most desperate blackmailer, extortionist and shakedown artist in this man's town. She is strictly bad medicine."

On top of being a racketeer, there were reports that Vivian was using drugs and when drunk, which was often, could turn extremely nasty. She also had a vindictive streak when it came to the prostitution racket. Vivian had a couple of "resorts" in Manhattan and Brooklyn, according to the *Daily News*, although there was some competition from a woman named Dora Murray who operated in the same area off Eastern Parkway.

Murray finally left Brooklyn and put down stakes in Rockville Centre, a town on Long Island, taking one of Vivian's partners named Nick the Greek with her. Together Murray, Nick the Greek and another woman opened a business in the Hotel Miramar. After that move, Vivian's remaining business in Brooklyn was raided twice and she suspected that it was Murray, or one of her associates, who tipped off the cops.

In Long Beach, the setup at the Hotel Miramar was a place where Wall Street brokers had a private hideaway described as having "luxe fittings, soft music and an apparently limitless supply of beautiful girls." The hotel even had an office on Wall Street that discreetly told the local business elites of the good times that could be had out east in Long Beach. Of all the many ports of call for smugglers during Prohibition on Long Island, the City of Long Beach had its own special niche. Gambling and bootlegging were rife within the city limits. One widely circulated story was that a special display of lights in the tower of one beachfront hotel signaled to smuggling ships that it was okay to land their loads of liquor. Cops were in on the smuggling and often found themselves arrested. Once inside the Hotel Miramar, patrons, which in some cases included local police, were able to have what the newspapers would call "Super Whoopee."

After getting raided a few times back in Brooklyn, Vivian decided it was time to get even with Murray and her crowd on Long Island. Sometime in 1928 or 1929, Vivian started sending anonymous tips to the constabulary out in Nassau County about the goings-on at the Hotel Miramar—Whoopee and all. The results of those anonymous notes were predictable. In November 1929, about two weeks before Thanksgiving, police armed with sledgehammers hit the Hotel Miramar and crashed through the heavy oak-paneled back doors.

"When the raiders crept up on the place they found a score of expensive automobiles in the parking yard," the *Daily News* said. "A jazz band was blaring forth in the main-floor dining room, women were laughing, men were singing and lights were flashing on the upper floors."

The cops found more than a dozen patrons making Super Whoopee: in the dining room, with most of the men in dinner clothes and the girls clad in what was described as "décolleté evening gowns." What was exactly meant by "Super Whoopee" wasn't defined in print but it was enough to bring charges of keeping a disorderly resort, which over the years was a term that crept into the vernacular to mean a house of prostitution.

The result of the raid was significant in that a number of cops spent time in jail, including Lester Chadwick, the former chief of police of the town of Lynbrook, who pleaded guilty to extorting payments from one of the woman operating the Hotel Miramar. A Nassau County cop was convicted of neglecting his duty by visiting the Miramar but saw the verdict overturned on appeal and was acquitted on a retrial. Dora Murray, whose big idea was to leave Brooklyn and set up the operation at the Hotel Miramar, was reported for a time to have been a fugitive in the case but eventually pleaded guilty to a charge of maintaining a disorderly house. If Vivian was looking for vengeance against Murray, she certainly got it.

VIVIAN'S DEMAND FOR revenge when she thought she had been wronged showed itself a number of times as she plied the sex extortion and nightclub scams, usually with all sorts of legal repercussions. Perhaps the most notorious involved a party at the Palace Hotel on March 1, 1930. According to entries in Vivian's diary, she had gone out to dinner on February 28 with a male friend to have a couple of cocktails, spent some time at a club on West 45th Street in the theater district where she said the place was "Ye Gods! Nothing but gangsters there," then headed over to the hotel where one of her girlfriends had an apartment.

Vivian described in her diary that at the hotel she had a "harrowing experience" that nearly killed her. The diary entry, in a staccato writing style, reported what happened.

"Really attempted rape. Everything taken from purse while I was conscious—went down fire escape to avoid more—police met me on fire escape—took me in lobby—Dr. wanted to give me morphine. I said Nothing Doing. I think it was hotel Dr. Officer Tempora gave me $1 for taxi."

The diary entries, as released by police, had names removed. But later accounts and a litigation related that at the hotel Vivian got into an argument with businessman Theodore Schweinler, owner of the Schweinler Press, a printing firm in Manhattan. The party got so out of hand that when police were called they found Vivian on the fire escape, acting hysterical with bruises on her head and face and complaining about Schweinler. News reports indicated that Vivian had registered at the hotel as "Mr. and Mrs. Lerner of New Orleans," perhaps a cover for the couple's true identities.

Cops who questioned Vivian over the Palace Hotel incident asked her a number of times if she wanted to press charges against Schweinler and she explained that she had hired a lawyer—John Radeloff. About two weeks later Radeloff filed a lawsuit for assault on behalf of Vivian against Schweinler for $50,000, a sum that would be valued at close to $900,000 in 2023 dollar value. Schweinler denied he did anything wrong and in short order the case was dismissed. His lawyer would tell reporters later that Schweinler paid nothing to Vivian, an indication that her attempt at extortion was a hollow one that couldn't stand legal scrutiny.

However, the dismissal of the Schweinler lawsuit didn't end things. Shortly after Vivian's lawsuit over the Palace Hotel beating was dismissed, a car pulled up to the Schweinler mansion in East Orange, New Jersey. Gunmen sprayed the home with gunfire. There was one problem: the house wasn't that of Theodore Schweinler, who had been Vivian's alleged assailant. Instead the home was that of Schweinler's brother and business partner, Carl, the real person sitting in the living room with his wife. No one was hurt. It is a fair bet that Vivian's allies were behind the abortive hit attempt on Schweinler. But in the end police made no arrests.

If Vivian failed to squeeze Schweinler for cash, there were plenty of other opportunities over the years for her to make money from the sex and extortion racket, and the indications were she did pretty well financially. She often didn't have to resort to even the threat of litigation and got large sums of cash through extortion. First, there were her living arrangements, usually in Manhattan hotels which, after a while, made her persona non grata for the ruckus and unsavory activity she was involved in with all the pretty women who were part of her retinue. But Vivian was making enough that it wasn't difficult for her to find a place at a nice building at 156 East 37th Street in Manhattan. The rent wasn't high by modern standards but in 1930 at $1,200 it translated to $22,000 in 2023 dollars. The third-floor apartment was nicely appointed, with a piano and plenty of closet space for Vivian to store her numerous shoes and fancy dresses, as well as fur coats and jewelry, things every successful sexual extortionist in this Jazz Age of New York had to have.

One reporter who got a look inside the East 37th Street apartment recalled that it was done in subdued colors and the bedroom exuded "a soft seductiveness." The plush bedding included a bedspread that seemed handmade. One particular touch noticed were several small, clothed dolls arrayed around the dresser and end table, almost like a strange throwback to childhood that Vivian found some comfort in, amid a life that was filled with scheming and betrayal.

With all the money Vivian was hauling in, she used some of it for investing, probably more likely loansharking, as a portion went to various borrowers on Broadway. Borrowers could get as little as $1,000 or as much as $10,000, which in 2023 value would range from $18,000 to $178,000, not counting any interest or good-old vigorish Vivian might have charged.

For her own portfolio, Vivian made an investment in real estate through a company known as Vivigo Corporation, an entity formed by her favorite lawyer, John Radeloff, in 1929. The company took an ownership interest in two adjacent buildings in Jamaica, Queens, at 129-08 and 129-14 Jamaica Avenue. The structures were apartment houses which were rented out. Also on the premises was a local Democratic club which operated its own speakeasy. Police would later find Vivian held a mortgage on a garage on Navy Street in Brooklyn and had extensive stock dealings with a Wall Street brokerage.

While she could sell sex and earn a good living from squeezing the rich men who were clients, Vivian lacked the Midas touch when it came to real estate. As the *Daily News* discovered, she had invested $75,000 at Radeloff's suggestion in sixteen foreclosed pieces of property in Brooklyn, properties that even at a distress sale she found weren't worth the value she paid. Strapped for cash to pay the interest on the Brooklyn property mortgages, Vivian did a swap with a Brooklyn realtor who gave her money in exchange for the two Jamaica properties. But even that exchange failed to earn Vivian the needed cash flow. She proved to be a terrible property manager and according to the building superintendent in Jamaica would show up drunk and cause all kinds of problems for the tenants. In the end Vivian had to turn over the rental income from the Queens buildings back to the Brooklyn realtor to satisfy the mortgage interest.

If real estate wasn't working for Vivian, the rich, lonely men in New York gave her enough alternate sources of income. Take the case of millionaire Henry M. Joralmon who, according to Radeloff, showered Vivian with clothes, jewels and the best perfumes coming out of Paris.

"Joralmon would pass out hundred-dollar bills or a thousand-dollar bill simply for the companionship of Vivian," Radeloff recalled. "Old and lonesome, he found his money piling up and no outlet for it. He admired her flashing wit, her devil-may-care arrogance."

According to Radeloff, Joralmon was Vivian's special sugar daddy, who would give her the money she needed and sit around as she shopped at Nat Lewis's, an expensive shop on Broadway run a well-known clothier and Broadway outfitter. Joralmon's wife Katharine had died in 1923, so he had money and time to spare. With a blank check, so to speak, Vivian would buy up Paris fashions and intimate apparel like negligees while the elderly Joralmon read the newspapers, remembered Radeloff.

But it seems that Radeloff the lawyer was more than a disinterested observer in terms of Joralmon's money and may have taken some for himself in a swindle of Helen Dorf, a model. Dorf was another woman who caught Joralmon's eye and since he was very free with his money— he had plenty and had holdings worth over $10 million—the lonely millionaire gave her a gift of $25,000. Vivian then jumped in and suggested that Dorf give the cash to Radeloff, who would find a good investment that would reap the young model some nice dividends. The unsophisticated Dorf turned over the cash to Radeloff, who invested the $25,000 in a laundry business in Brooklyn. But as was later revealed, Dorf only got stock in the company worth about $3,300 and the rest of her cash was simply unaccounted for on the laundry firm's books.

The big returns Dorf was promised on her investment never materialized, although she got some pieces of her original investment back. An angry Dorf then sued Radeloff to force him to account for the money. The entire transaction also soured Dorf on Vivian and their friendship ended. It seems that Radeloff was having his own relationship with Vivian and the two worked hand in hand to take advantage of the naïve Dorf.

Another woman linked to Joralmon who saw the way Vivian could be duplicitous was Annette Franco. Pretty with a full head of dark hair, Franco met the millionaire while she was working at the souvenir counter in the Hotel Biltmore. By all accounts, Joralmon was smitten with Franco after he first met Vivian. Franco also benefited from Joralmon's stuffed money belt, from which he would pluck $1,000 bills (legal tender at the time) and stuff them into her hands. As Franco would later recall, the aging widower talked to her of his love and even quoted from the Bible.

"He asked me to marry him and I accepted his proposal," Franco said. "He said we were going to Arabia as a honeymoon and that he was going to buy me a castle overlooking the Mediterranean. The closest I ever got to those places was by looking at them in my high school geography book."

Joralmon went as far as to buy Franco an engagement ring but never actually gave it to her. He did want to slip a wedding band on her ring finger but Franco said she didn't want to do that until they were married. For reasons known only to Joralmon, he never married Franco and she responded by filing a $250,000 breach of promise lawsuit. When news of the litigation hit the newspapers, Vivian saw an opportunity for a little conniving and, according to Franco, contacted her old sugar daddy Joralmon. Vivian's plan was to double-cross Franco after she approached her to find out the details of why she was suing. Then Vivian secretly met with Joralmon at the Marguery Restaurant on Park Avenue, a fashionable place inside the sumptuous Marguery Apartments, said at the time to be the biggest apartment complex in the world. Over champagne, Vivian told Joralmon about Franco's lawsuit and at some point, instead of going to Franco, the diamond ring was given to Vivian, according to Radeloff.

Vivian would also lash out at good friends. Jean Stoneham, a pretty mob moll who shared an apartment with Vivian, said that even she was falsely accused by Vivian of stealing some clothes, an allegation that led to a bogus charge of larceny which a judge later saw through and dismissed. When Vivian demanded a payment of $1,000 for the clothing, Stoneham said a lawyer told her not to pay Vivian anything and she was never bothered again.

Stoneham herself was no babe in the woods when it came to the Broadway and bootlegging crime scene. She had been a former girlfriend of Irish mob boss Charles Higgins, whose bootlegging operations stretched from Long Island to New York City and who was suspected of nearly a half dozen homicides but was never convicted. Both she and Vivian would visit Higgins and Diamond at the Hotel Monticello, said Stoneham.

Another woman who was suspicious of Vivian and her constant duplicity was Florence Sharp Willard, a former actress who was locked in a paternity lawsuit with millionaire candy manufacturer F. Joseph Haan. In her diaries, detectives were able to piece together that Vivian was prepared to tell Haan—for $50,000—that she had information about the real father of his alleged son with Willard, thus scuttling the lawsuit brought by her friend Willard. Haan rejected the idea.

In an interview with the newspapers after Vivian was killed, Willard said her lawsuit wasn't about money. It was just to establish the paternity of her son, also named Joseph Willard. She also had some catty comments about Vivian.

"Vivian's so-called beauty never impressed," said Willard. "She talked of nothing but her beauty and how great an attraction she held for men of wealth. When she kept talking along those lines I kept thinking that her eyes were too slanting and hard, and that she had a brutal jaw. She couldn't have been too clever or she wouldn't have been talking about herself all the time."

Willard remembered that she and Vivian would sometimes go to church together. But she was angry and shocked that Vivian, while professing friendship, was actually trying to ruin her chance at getting satisfaction from the lawsuit against Haan. It appears that the paternity case failed.

Vivian's blackmail hustle led her to try some activity in Europe, although exactly what she was trying to do remains to this day unclear. Police would later determine that Vivian put up $1,500 for what was initially said to be a 1930 effort to buy a bank in Oslo, Norway, a rather small amount of capital for such an important purchase. No details ever emerged about the bank, but it later was alleged that a trip to Norway, which involved Harry Stein and Morris Levine, was actually a scheme to unload $70,000 worth of stolen securities, a more likely explanation, given Vivian's connections. Stolen securities were a big racket on Wall Street and some of Vivian's connections like Diamond and a shady broker named Joseph Radlow were involved in peddling such hot commodities.

Radlow was one of Wall Street's strange characters during the Prohibition years. A pudgy, bespectacled, balding man, Radlow was essentially a stock thief and was said to be a lover of Vivian since 1927, something that is a bit hard to fathom given his rotund physiognomy but would explain her access to stolen securities. A probation report filed about Radlow described him as a "plausibly ingratiating individual who frankly admits that moral principles have no place in a man's business career."

True to his avowed business philosophy, Radlow spent a good part of the 1920s selling stocks in financially distressed companies and making a profit of reportedly as much as $200,000 a year in what today would be known as a "bucket shop" operation used by the Mafia. It was in 1929 that Radlow was arrested for dealing in some stolen securities and passing them to a cohort named Samuel Cohen, a big ex-con, known by the moniker "Chowderhead," who also turned out to be a friend of Vivian's. Radlow's defense was that he was working as an undercover agent for the New York State attorney general, something about which there was no evidence. He finally pleaded guilty in the middle of his trial.

During his swindling days, Radlow and Vivian were living together in various Manhattan hotels, and she was working as a call girl and perfecting her business technique of sexual extortion. Vivian made money, enough so she loaned Radlow $1,000. But when she asked for repayment, Radlow, who already had a wife and an ill child to deal with, pleaded poverty and wanted more time. Vivian apparently relented but when she pressed him again, Radlow took a page from her playbook and set her up for her very own extortion charge. Vivian had been shaking down people for years and her lover boy had obviously learned a lesson. In league with local detectives, Radlow agreed to meet Vivian and carried a small amount of cash as a partial payment in marked bills. On August 7, 1930, after the cash changed hands, Vivian was promptly charged with shaking down Radlow.

But the evidence of extortion must have been very thin, as on September 9, 1930, the grand jury dismissed the case against Vivian. Needless to say, that finished Vivian's affair with the Wall Street swindler. But it was hardly the end of Vivian's troubles with the men in her life. Joseph Radlow, John Radeloff and Sam Cohen would all emerge as central players in the final acts of Vivian's star-crossed life.

CHAPTER FIVE

THE GATHERING STORM

IN THE ANNALS OF BROADWAY, Oscar Hammerstein has his own special place. The German-born impresario, composer and business-man cut a path through the theater business in New York and London in the years before and just after World War One. He carried out grand plans which included a number of productions and financed the construction of numerous theaters, including the old Olympia Theater at Longacre Square, the major road junction in Manhattan that later became Times Square.

But the problem for Hammerstein was that he was a terrible businessman, stretching himself and his companies way too thin and getting into financial troubles that drained his resources. He got involved in convoluted stock deals with his companies that in the end, after his death in 1919, triggered litigation between his daughters and his third wife, Emma. Ultimately, Emma Hammerstein lost in her bid to gain control of her husband's old Manhattan Opera House.

Considered by some to be "the most beautiful woman on Broadway," Emma was nevertheless financially strapped after her husband's death and in the early 1920s was said to be living homeless in Central Park. Then, in May 1930, Emma was arrested by four cops at the Hotel Winthrop where she lived and charged with what was described as "immoral conduct," the old euphemism for prostitution. She allegedly offered to perform a sex act for $30 and for that was hauled off to the infamous Jefferson Market Women's Court.

The court for women in Greenwich Village had been a problem for decades. The Page Commission found corruption issues and while some changes were made and city officials wrung their hands over the terrible situation women were put through, the old system which enriched some at the expense of many women continued well beyond what Vivian Gordon found in 1923 when she was taken downtown on her particular sex charge. The difference in the case of Emma Hammerstein was that by the time she was arrested a small but vocal body of politically active women were making noise about the Jefferson Market Court and the way cops and court personnel seemed to be engaged in the old shakedown racket. Vivian didn't have that kind of public outcry.

From the beginning, Emma complained that she was set up for the prostitution arrest. As she would later testify in court, Emma said she didn't need money because she had just sold her story for $1,200 to a news agency and that as a result she was "more in the money than at any time within the last few years." Instead, she believed a particular lawyer she had complained about to court officials was behind the frame-up. There was some evidence to support Emma's charge. An insurance agent said that a cop he had met in a courthouse approached him and offered him some cash if he would loiter in the lobby of the Hotel Winthrop, arrange to meet Hammerstein's widow at her apartment and notify police so they could barge in at the right moment. As related by the agent, the procedure was similar to what scores of other women claimed had been used to set them up for false arrest.

"Be sure to have your coat off and leave the money in plain sight. I'll give you $150 if she is arrested and $150 more if she is convicted," the insurance agent quoted the detective as saying about Emma. The agent said he told Hammerstein about the conversation after he saw news of her arrest but apparently didn't carry out the cop's planned setup.

Unlike in the case of Vivian Gordon and other entrapped women, Emma Hammerstein's predicament caught the eye of the newspapers and Catherine Parer Clivette, head of the Greenwich Village Historical Society, who a year earlier had run for a spot on the Board of Aldermen as a candidate of the Square Deal party. After Hammerstein was con-victed, Clivette and others were full-throated in their denunciation, charging that Emma's case was an example of the corrupt practices being carried out against women in the magistrates' court.

Clivette and her political allies formed the Society for the Preven-tion of Unjust Convictions and got publicity by demonstrating on Broadway at the Tivoli Theater. Clivette said a "public-spirited and aroused citizenry cannot afford to sit idly by and permit innocent women and mothers to be falsely and unjustly accused and arrested with the possibility of an unjust conviction, involving disgrace and shame."

With the headlines and the protest, as mild-mannered as they may have been, the matter of the dirty doings in the magistrates' court were again in the limelight. But there were other reasons that a critical mass of interest—none of it good—was brewing over that particular court. The culprits were two magistrates who were getting into deeper trou-ble and raising the specter that the Mob on Broadway and dirty money were again ruling the courthouse.

It was December 1929 that Magistrate Albert H. Vitale, a staunch political ally of Mayor Jimmy Walker's, returned home from an ex-tended trip to Virginia. Vitale's friends threw him a welcome-home dinner at the Roman Gardens restaurant in the Bronx. Things were going great until seven men—only one wearing a mask—invaded the restaurant and, as the news reports described, leisurely went through the banquet hall forcing the guests to give up cash and jewelry. One detective in attendance thought about making a move for his revolver but one of the thieves stuck his own gun into his stomach.

"So you are a cop, eh? Sit right down, Mr. Cop, and don't make a move or you will be a dead cop," one of the holdup men said as he took the detective's gun from him.

A quick-thinking Vitale stayed calm and later told police that he slipped a 4.5-carat diamond pinky ring into his waistband where it stayed hidden. A few other guests hid their jewelry or tossed cash under the table, which the thieves overlooked. The armed men cleaned up about $2,000 in cash and when they were finished got into two wait-ing cars and sped away. No one was hurt.

"I told the guests to obey the orders of the men," Vitale recalled. "'Let them take what we have,' I said. I felt that any resistance might end in murder."

While the holdup should have gained sympathy for Vitale, everything backfired. It turned out that among his guests at the Roman Gardens were seven men with police records. Why would he be associating with them, NYPD commissioner Whalen wanted to know. Whalen was also angered by the fact that one of his detectives had been stripped of his gun during the heist.

Whalen's allegations about Vitale's questionable guests snowballed. The Bar Association, which at that time played a role in disciplining judges and lawyers alike, dug more deeply into Vitale and found things out about him that troubled the white-shoe lawyers. It turned out that Vitale had taken a $19,940 loan from none other than Arnold Rothstein, the King of Broadway and crooked benefactor to Vivian Gordon. The revelation about the loan came about a year after the King of the Jews had been shot and mortally wounded during a high-stakes card game on November 4, 1928, at the Park Central Hotel on West 56th Street. Rothstein lingered in the hospital before passing away on November 6, which turned out to be Election Day.

The loan from Rothstein caused enough trouble for Vitale. But as it turned out the entire dinner became a series of embarrassments for the judge. Since a detective was at the banquet, police commissioner Whalen started an investigation which dredged up a number of allegations, all of which raised questions about the company Vitale had been keeping as a politician and a judge. The hapless detective who lost his gun to the crooks admitted to Commissioner Whalen that it seemed like 25 percent, maybe even 30 percent, of those at the Vitale dinner were known gangsters. A few mobsters from the Bronx, notably the notorious Ciro Terranova, dubbed the "Artichoke King" because he had a corner on the market for that product, even took out advertisements in the banquet program: "Compliments of Ciro Terranova and Rock Delarma."

Apart from an appearance that Vitale was the Mob's man, cops came up with a story that the holdup was staged as part of grand conspiracy by Terranova to avoid paying for a contract of two murders.

The story, which even the newspapers called a "startling explanation" and "weird," was revealed during a hearing Whalen called to find out why the detective at the dinner didn't shoot it out with the robbers and instead surrendered his firearm to them. But in an unexpected twist, Whalen asked Inspector Joseph J. Donovan to take the stand. Donovan was head of the NYPD's Bureau of Criminal Identification and ran a stable of undercover cops posing as bootleggers and thieves, as well as informants who sniffed around the underworld to glean intelligence.

The story Donovan related was a claim about a convoluted murder conspiracy behind the Roman Gardens robbery. In 1928, fabled New York gangster Frankie Yale was pursued in a car chase and shot dead on a Brooklyn street, crashing into a residence as he died behind the wheel. About a year later, Frank Marlow, a friend of Rothstein's and a nightclub owner, was found shot dead on Queens Street after being tossed from a car. Both murders remained unsolved. But according to Inspector Donovan, it was Terranova who put out a contract on both men and drafted a Chicago gangster to kill Yale and Marlow for a combined price of $20,000.

Usually, mob murder contracts are done with a handshake or a nod of the head. But in Terranova's case he actually drafted a written contract which was given to the Chicago assassin, according to Donovan's testimony. If true it was a strange element to the case. But written contract or not, Terranova only paid the hired hitman $5,000 of the agreed upon $20,000 price, New York cops learned. The assassin was angry at being stiffed on his fee and threatened to turn the written contract over to the police and incriminate Terranova, stated Donovan.

Facing a problem, Terranova came up with a Machiavellian-like scheme to get the contract back so it couldn't be used as evidence against him for the murders. The plan, Donovan testified, was for Terranova to invite the Chicago gangster to the Vitale dinner as his guest. Then the seven holdup men who were hired by Terranova would come in and pull off the robbery. The holdup was a ruse since the real goal was to take the written contract from the killer.

It sounded crazy: a gangster walking around with a written murder contract. But Donovan said the police learned that Terranova's plan was ingenious; the hired killer showed up at the Vitale banquet, unaware that something was afoot when the holdup men arrived.

"They were to go through the motions of robbing all the guests," said Donovan. "That was considered necessary to prevent the Chicagoan from becoming suspicious of a frame-up. But their special instructions were to search the Chicago killer and take that contract from him."

The trickery worked. According to Donovan, cops learned that Terranova got the physical contract back and the Chicago hitman returned home, none the wiser. A key suspicion of the cops was that the stolen property would all be returned by the fake robbers. The detective, Arthur C. Johnson, was given his gun back by Vitale personally, who declined to say how he got possession of it. When asked, Vitale also claimed he couldn't say if the other stolen property was returned.

The police hearings were devastating for Vitale. He appeared to be under the thumb of gangsters and oblivious to the way such associations looked to the public. Even his political ally Mayor Walker said that Vitale's usefulness to the public and to the Tammany Hall organization was coming to an end. But there was little Walker or the police could do about Vitale. His career as a judge rested with the New York City Bar Association and ultimately the Appellate Division First Department, the arm of the state judiciary that had jurisdiction over New York City courts.

By February 1930, Vitale saw that it was best to step aside and not hear any more cases in the Bronx. He didn't quit but he knew that charges were looming from the court system, so he didn't need to serve with that kind of distraction. Things then happened quickly. On March 13, 1930, a five-judge panel of the appellate division stripped Vitale of his judgeship, citing the loan from Rothstein as a major factor. However, they didn't disbar him.

"Judge Vitale's retention of Arnold Rothstein's check, when he had the choice of accepting or repudiating it is proven," the appellate panel found. "He did it though no necessity has been shown. On the contrary he had ample resources to obtain any desired loan. Concededly he knew Rothstein's character."

The judges said the loan had the power to put Vitale under the thumb of Rothstein and that it brought the magistrates' court into public suspicion. The appeals judges also were troubled by the way the scandal had put the courts in the crosshairs of a political campaign. The latter reference was to the way the upstart mayoral candidate Fiorello LaGuardia had used the Rothstein loan as a way of slamming Tammany Hall. LaGuardia, known for his feistiness, had served as a Republican in the U.S. House of Representatives in the 1920s, representing East Harlem in Manhattan. While in Congress, LaGuardia ran against Walker in the 1929 mayoral race and made issues of the deceased Rothstein's dealings, including the questionable land deal in Juniper Park and the loan to Vitale to beat up on Tammany Hall.

LaGuardia lost to Walker in 1929 but the issues he raised about mobster corruption made Tammany Hall and Broadway gangsters nervous, particularly Frank Costello, who had an up-and-coming slot machine operation in the city.

The trouble in the courts only continued to gather more political attention. As soon as Vitale was stripped of his judgeship, socialist leader Norman Thomas, who had run a hopeless campaign for mayor in 1929 as well, outlined his own attack, charging that Tammany Hall was dictating what went on in the courts. Thomas said 11 magistrates should be investigated but his demands were given little serious attention. In fact, Manhattan District Attorney Thomas C. T. Crain, a Tammany favorite who would face his own problems shortly, laughed at some of Thomas's accusations.

After the Vitale case, the bar association offered to vet all candidates for the magistrates' courts. But Walker, knowing full well the history of Tammany Hall involvement in the whole judicial process as a plum bit of patronage, declined the offer. He would handle the appointments himself. But as the months passed, the issue of the courts kept on cropping up in bad ways. The most significant matter involved Magistrate George F. Ewald, the scourge of bad drivers in traffic court, that is unless the motorist had political connections. Files uncovered showed that Ewald kept a record of cases he dismissed as favors for friends and political contacts. One of the most telling was a notation in Ewald's file which read "Friend of J. Walker—dismissed," an apparent reference to a friend of the mayor's.

Of course, to those who didn't have the right connections Ewald was known as the "jailing judge." Appointed to the bench by Walker in 1927, in a single week he had sent 160 drivers to jail for speeding, drunk driving and other violations. Ewald was conducting his own campaign and once said drunken drivers were more deadly than machine guns—something the late Frankie Yale wouldn't have agreed with.

But the real problem for Ewald wasn't so much the favors he dispensed in traffic court at Jefferson Market but reports that he actually paid $12,000 for his judicial appointment to a Tammany Hall leader. More serious still was the allegation that Ewald, his brother and others had been involved in stock fraud in securities for the Cotter Butte Mines in Montana. Federal prosecutors charged that Ewald had boosted the value of the mine property, falsely claimed the stock would pay dividends and that company officials worked for no salary. In another disturbing claim by investigators, Ewald was said to have squeezed a traffic offender for a $1,000 purchase of the mining stock in return for dismissing the traffic case. And just for added insult, Ewald's estranged wife said he was a bum who hurt her by forcing her to sign a very one-sided divorce settlement.

"He married me, deserted me," cried Betty Ewald, who also accused the judge of bigamy.

If Vitale looked like he was mobbed up, Ewald seemed to be the pinnacle of New York political corruption and fraud. Numerous investigations, federal and city, tried to get to the bottom of things. Walker himself appeared for questioning by Manhattan District Attorney Crain and denied that Ewald's appointment as a magistrate involved a cash payment, an allegation Walker called "a lamentable thing."

"Mr. Ewald was appointed because of the support and advocacy of the Steuben Society of America," a group of Americans of German ancestry who Walker said had lobbied him on Ewald's behalf. Ewald was a good ethnic German, so to speak.

The growing scent of corruption in the magistrates' courts and as well as a few other city officials put wind in the sails of those clamoring for Walker to do something and change the criminal culture that seemed to envelop more and more levels of city government. Norman Thomas wasn't just one voice in the wilderness. Finally, the *New York*

Times had to weigh in. On July 6, 1930, as the Ewald case mushroomed, the paper ran an editorial titled "The City Scandal." The column was a call for Walker to get off the stick and lambasted him for not even seeming to be aware that anything was wrong.

"Till now, nothing has come from City Hall to indicate that Mr. Walker is aware of the discredit brought by his associates and subordinates upon his own record, or serve as a sharp warning to all the members of his official family," intoned the *Times*. "The hour has come for the mayor to summon the demolition and reconstruction crews. The only call which will put them actively to work must come from him."

If Walker didn't act soon, said the *Times*, then the city government was at risk of collapsing. The newspaper noted that Walker himself wasn't connected to any of the scandals and said he had to speak out soon. About two weeks later, Walker called all city agency heads together at City Hall and told them in a speech that was broadcast to the public over radio that corruption and dishonesty wouldn't be tolerated. At the same time, Walker couldn't avoid politicizing the issue and defended his administration by saying some of the criticism of City Hall was an attempt by the Republican Party—which controlled the statehouse in Albany—to find an issue for the next election.

Goaded by the rising voices condemning the corruption in the city, Walker in mid-July of 1930 announced what was called a "house cleaning" of his administration. He appointed one of his commissioners, James Higgins, to begin looking at the way garage permits were issued and piers leased on the waterfront. It was a small step, but critics saw it as an almost desperate attempt by Walker to stave off the calls for wider investigations of the way he and City Hall had failed to act in the face of corruption. Walker also knew that in Albany, Governor Franklin Roosevelt had his eye on the scandals in New York City and could at any time fold to pressure from Republicans who controlled the state legislature and call for a formal hearing.

Given the way the corruption issue was now on everyone's front burner, Walker had to give what was tepid reassurance that things would be different with the appointment of Higgins to sniff out long-standing problems.

"You can rest assured that if Commissioner Higgins gets his teeth in he won't let go until he draws blood," a boastful Walker said.

No matter what Walker did, he couldn't divert attention from the problems in the magistrates' court. Ewald was indicted on state charges that he purchased his judgeship, along with Martin Healy, the Tammany boss whom he was alleged to have paid. Ewald's second wife, Bertha, was also charged in the case with acting as an intermediary. At trial, Healy testified that he simply borrowed the money to buy a house. In the end, the state jury couldn't agree on a verdict and Ewald was given a mistrial. The court ultimately dropped the charges. However, the scandal ruined Ewald, whose legal career never recovered, and eventually forced him to file for bankruptcy. His wife also saw her motion picture booking business fall into ruin.

The mine stock fraud case in federal court took place in late 1931 and Ewald again saw a mistrial after the jurors couldn't agree on a unanimous verdict. Two other defendants were convicted on a conspiracy charge. By the time the federal case was over, Ewald had already been removed from his job as a magistrate. The entire affair left him a bitter man.

"I had a fine career before me," Ewald said years later. "I was a respected man until I got mixed up with that pack of thieves that hangs out in Tammany Hall. They ruined me."

Given what happened in his two mistrials, Ewald was collateral damage from the storm that had begun to swirl in New York over political corruption.

CHAPTER SIX

A COLDHEARTED DAME

IF 1930 HAD SHAPED UP terribly for Mayor Walker, it was not a great time as well for Vivian Gordon. For a start, Arnold Rothstein, one of her longtime allies, moneymen and protectors, had been dead for two years in a murder case that would remain open after a bungled prosecution of the prime suspect. Whatever monies he had were tied up in probate proceedings. The estimated $25 million in Rothstein's possession when he died would be fought over by his girlfriend Inez Norton, his wife and his family. Ultimately the true value was about $2.5 million, with debts, taxes and various claims reducing the amount to $1.1 million—none of it for Vivian.

Legs Diamond was still in league with Vivian as they ran their sex extortion and stock scams from the Club Abbey. But Diamond was distracted by various attempts on his life and the hunt by police and federal investigators who were on his trail for bootlegging and various murders they believed he had been involved in. By late 1930 their scheme was about to end in a dispute over the money Vivian was owed.

Vivian's life path was taking the exact opposite trajectory of another woman whose background was strikingly similar but who was having luck and fortune that was very, very different. Marion Davies was educated in a convent school but decided to break away and seek a career as a chorus girl, a life path many, many women had been seeking in 1917. It was then that Davies landed a film role and then, unlike struggling Vivian, landed a featured role in the Ziegfeld Follies. The rest was part of a history that few women could match. Davies caught the obsessive eye of publishing giant William Randolph Hearst, who began featuring her in films for his Cosmopolitan Pictures.

Hearst soon began a sexual relationship with Davies that endured for decades. He promoted her films at great expense and her career exploded. Davies did have comedic talent and with Hearst's backing became a star. One 1932 film, Blondie of the Follies, about a working-class girl who gets on stage, paralleled the tale of so many Broadway Butterflies. Eventually, the married Hearst moved Davies into his Hearst Castle in San Simeon, California, and his wife was sent packing back to New York. Davies and Hearst's relationship was filled with jealousy and infidelity but they remained together even as he suffered financial reversals and died in 1951. Davies became wealthy and benefited under Hearst's will. But she had her own demons and drank heavily, developed cancer and died in 1961.

From a career and financial point of view, Davies had it made in a way few Broadway woman were able to. But in contrast, Vivian didn't get the same kind of breaks, had crooked friends, took a different path and as time went on was showing more signs of anxiety, paranoia and other psychological issues. To help her sleep, Vivian took drugs, namely veronal, a barbiturate developed in Europe and sold in little stoppered bottles. Usually, she took the drugs after a night of heavy drinking. A friend reported that on one Christmas Eve in Manhattan she attempted suicide and had to be brought to Bellevue. Even while she made money in the sex racket Vivian became more avaricious, manipulative and cruel, particularly with the women she worked with. Apparently, she wasn't above tipping off cops about some of the women who angered her. Jean Stoneham, the old friend of Legs Diamond's who shared an apartment with Vivian, said the sex swindler once bragged about snitching on six of her women and getting them sent to the Bedford Reformatory.

"She boasted about it when she was drunk," recalled Stoneham. "They were girls who crossed her in money matters, who held out money they got from men to whom she introduced them."

Things got so out of control with Vivian, remembered Stoneham, that during one argument Vivian tried to push her out of the apartment window on 37th Street. Not long after that the women ended their friendship.

But the real issue burning deeply within Vivian's psyche was the loss of custody of her daughter, Benita Fredericka. Since Vivian's divorce and confinement in the Bedford Reformatory, the child lived with her father and stepmother in New Jersey. It was a situation Vivian believed until the end of her life was the result of her unjust conviction on trumped-up prostitution charges in 1923. The separation from the young girl, now a teenager in high school, was something that was unacceptable for Vivian, and she tried a number of times to get the child back. Vivian's wealthy benefactor Henry Joralmon was even approached to finance a trip to New Jersey to bring her child to New York. Vivian did make some trips to New Jersey, and she did barrage the Bischoffs with letters demanding custody of her daughter. John Bischoff would later tell police that Vivian at one point tried to kidnap Benita. The demands became so frequent that the Bischoffs said they were forced at one point to move to a new home. But despite yelling and screaming at her ex-husband and his wife, Vivian had no success in getting her daughter back.

The drugs, the drinking, the late nights, the stress of running the sex racket with gangsters and other criminals were taking a toll on Vivian Gordon. Once a slender, pretty woman with bright eyes and that striking titian hair, Vivian had become worn. Although some thought she looked 20 years old, Vivian's face was puffy for a 39-year-old and her weight no longer allowed her to strike pretty poses for publicity photos that might land her a theatrical job. Those days were long gone.

Instead, Vivian was firmly entrenched as a denizen of Broadway's underworld. Sure, she had big connections with the likes of Rothstein, Diamond and bootlegger Higgins. But Rothstein was gone, and the others really played in a different league, where violence ruled the day and women were expensive playthings. The criminals Vivian found herself increasingly relying upon were lower-level guys, stock swindlers, crooked attorneys and street thugs.

Of course, there were still the women, and Vivian knew some of the best in the sex business, those who knew how inveigle the right men and squeeze them for cash. Judge Joseph Force Crater was one of those players who liked the nightlife, the women and the world Vivian was part of. A product of Tammany Hall, Crater became a state supreme court justice in 1930 and handled routine foreclosure and property liability cases, among others. Although married to Stella Wheeler, Crater liked nightlife—and the company of women. Vivian, according to the recollections of one of her associates, had Crater as a visitor to her apartment.

One of Crater's haunts was Club Abbey, where Legs Diamond and Vivian often met and did their business. It was at the club that Vivian met Crater—who was known by the name Joe Crane—and allegedly tried to lure him into a compromising position for sexual blackmail. The club was ostensibly part owned by gangster Charles "Chink" Sherman, a close associate of Rothstein's, with the rest of it under the control of Owney Madden, bootlegger and Irish gang leader. The club would be the scene of a shooting in early 1931 in which Sherman and Dutch Schultz were wounded, an act that assured the place's notoriety in mob history.

It is not clear if Vivian ever got Crater in a compromising sexual situation that led to blackmail, although reports in the newspapers surfaced that a young blond woman had consulted with an attorney about filing a breach of promise suit against the judge—litigation threats were a central part of Vivian's sexual extortion shakedowns. In any case, Crater did like some of the women at the club and was said to have had a particular friendly relationship with showgirl Elaine Dawn, who said the jurist shared "orangeade" with the other women— no doubt spiked with some good Prohibition whiskey or gin.

Crater's meetings with Vivian and the other club women would not have been a big deal had he not suddenly disappeared on the night of August 6, 1930. Crater was last seen outside a Manhattan restaurant on 46th Street after dining with a couple of friends. He had planned to see a Broadway show but apparently passed it up to have dinner. Club Abbey entertainer Elaine Dawn would later recall that Crater had visited the club later that night, possibly into early the next morning.

Crater's disappearance became one of the most notorious and widely publicized missing persons cases of all time. There were reported sightings of him as far away as Cuba and California. His decades as a missing person became the butt of jokes and even made it into popular culture in sitcoms and documentaries. One report had Crater buried under the Coney Island boardwalk at the spot where the aquarium is today. Confounding the case was the claim by a convicted forger named Joseph Lesser and published in the tabloids that Crater actually visited him in Sing Sing prison as part of a plan involving Vivian's associates Stein and attorney Radeloff—to take care of his sentence. Radeloff would later deny such a deal was made despite Lesser's claims to the contrary. Prison officials said there was no indication in any prison logs that someone resembling Crater ever visited Lesser in that time period. A grand jury investigation called over 90 witnesses but in the end was unable to determine what happened to Crater and whether he was alive or dead. In June 1939, Crater was declared legally dead.

The disappearance of Crater and the scandals involving the magistrates' courts came together at a time when New York City's infatuation with the Jazz Age and its image of constant fun was waning. People still frequented speakeasies, bootleggers still did a steady business and the tabloids were filled with stories about movie stars and their divorces and other juicy scandals. The escapism was there. But the political powers knew that the inherent rot in the system, which for decades had been accepted, and engineered miscarriages of justice, particularly victimizing women, and political control for the profit of Tammany Hall had to be immediately addressed. Although he was physically removed from the growing furor, Governor Roosevelt wasn't blind to the public sentiment.

But Mayor Walker, despite his tepid public pronouncements and handwringing over corruption, seemed to go about his own merry way in what passed as the good times. In fact, the night Crater disappeared, Walker was partying out in Suffolk County at a gambling parlor at the Montauk Island Club with his British-born actress-girlfriend Betty Compton. (His wife stayed at home.) Walker had been living something of a charmed life throughout all of the court and corruption scandals and was getting a free pass in the newspapers—at least in the tabloids—for the way he lived his personal life, parading around with Compton and hanging out in speakeasies. In his book *The Tiger: The*

Rise and Fall of Tammany Hall, historian Oliver E. Allen noted that while Walker wasn't gambling at the Long Island club, Compton was playing for high stakes. When the cops arrived, Walker hightailed it and tried to disguise himself.

"Walker ducked into the kitchen and, donning an apron, tried to look like a waiter," noted Allen. "But Betty was taken to a police station and released. New York's tabloids loved it."

As much as the press loved Walker's devil-may-care nightlife and escapades, Roosevelt could sense the best way to tack into the political winds, and now the winds were pushing away from the distraction of the Jazz Age and into the uncharted waters of what an investigation might uncover. On August 21, 1930, Roosevelt urged the presiding judge of the Appellate Division First Department, the body with jurisdiction over all city courts in Manhattan and the Bronx, to investigate the magistrates' courts so that the public could learn the facts swirling over the administration of justice in the city. Roosevelt himself had no authority over the courts and couldn't remove any judges, so he used the persuasive power of his position to get something done.

Curiously, the same investigation, at least for the moment, wasn't going to take place in the magistrates' courts in Brooklyn, Queens and Staten Island. The presiding judge in the Appellate Division Second Department told Roosevelt in a brief meeting during an awards ceremony at a Boy Scout camp near the town of Monticello that there had been no complaints about the activity in the magistrates' courts in those other boroughs. Roosevelt seemed to accept that claim and said there would be no investigation in the courts in those outer boroughs but added, "I am not making any promises for the future."

SAMUEL SEABURY AND Vivian Gordon had lives that were as different as they could be. While Vivian was a bright, musically talented but uncontrollable child who didn't take to education, Seabury was born to privilege and a tradition of faith, learning and service. His namesake and great-great-grandfather was the first Episcopal bishop in the U.S., while his father was also a member of the clergy. Educated at private schools, Seabury became familiar with the law while he worked for a legal publishing company and clerked for a private lawyer. He then

went on to study law formally at New York Law School, one of New
York City's early independent schools from which he graduated in 1893.

As a practicing attorney, Seabury aligned himself against Tammany Hall although his preferred candidates failed repeatedly against
the big political machine. By 1901, with the backing of a prestigious bar
association, he won election as a city court judge and was sworn in the
next year, putting him on track to be elected to the state supreme
court—the court of lowest general jurisdiction in the state—in 1906 at
the age of 33. By 1915, Seabury was nominated for and later won a spot
on the state's highest court, the court of appeals, where he served for
about two years and wrote opinions that set major precedents. It was
a meteoric rise in the legal world and an indication of Seabury's ability.

Theodore Roosevelt, the cousin of Franklin, encouraged Seabury
to run for governor under the Progressive Party banner in 1916. But
Seabury lost and eventually returned to the private practice of law
which made him a very wealthy man, enabling him to buy a great deal
of property in East Hampton, on Long Island.

Seabury's reputation as a man not afraid to go against the Tammany establishment and to take aggressive positions on public policy
was something that Governor Roosevelt had in mind when he pushed
for the investigation of the magistrates' courts. When Roosevelt issued
his plea to the courts to start an investigation, Seabury was in London
and took about a week to get back to New York on the liner *Aquitania*.
By then, Seabury had already been told by the appellate division that
he had been selected to lead the probe and had a great deal to do to
get things underway. It also was a time for political payback for the
way Tammany had been lukewarm in backing Seabury's gubernato-
rial run in 1916.

"Seabury blamed his defeat on Tammany's lack of enthusiasm for
his candidacy and nursed a desire for revenge. Roosevelt's call gave
him the chance," said historian Allen.

Based on his past experience as a judge, Seabury was well aware of
the corrupt reality of the courts and the police. He once prodded officials to indict some cops for corruption. He also presided at the retrial
of NYPD lieutenant Charles Becker, who had been accused of engineering the murder of gambler Herman Rosenthal in July 1912 at the

Metropole Hotel in Manhattan, an incident mentioned in *The Great Gatsby*. Rosenthal had made accusations of corruption against Becker in a series of newspaper articles. The lieutenant's first conviction was overturned and led to the retrial before Seabury. Becker was convicted again, and Seabury sentenced the officer to death. Becker was executed on July 30, 1915, at Sing Sing prison, the only NYPD officer in history to ever face capital punishment.

Seabury had a free hand for his investigation. The appellate division let him decide where and how far he wanted to go in his probe, including a look at attorneys, magistrates, bail bondsmen and court clerks. Seabury was also going to look at a major area of political abuse: the way magistrates were appointed. To help him, Seabury had as his chief counsel Isidor Kresel, an experienced criminal investigator who knew how to follow the money trail and build cases. One of the first things Kresel did was subpoena the bank records of all the magistrates in Manhattan and the Bronx as part of his overall plan to not rely on anonymous complaints but also to look for hard evidence of corruption.

The first indication that Seabury would be focusing on prostitution cases came when a civic group known as the Committee of Fourteen turned over a study of 12,000 vice cases tried in the magistrates' courts since 1926 in the Bronx and Manhattan. The committee, led by George E. Worthington, said vice had gotten worse during Prohibition but didn't give any hard information about who was exploiting the women.

The new police commissioner, Edward Mulrooney, must have suspected that some of his cops were going to be targeted by Seabury. He couldn't have risen through the ranks and not known what was going on in the streets. In strong terms, Mulrooney denied that his cops used "stool pigeons" or paid informants to make vice cases. It was a remark Mulrooney would soon live to regret.

PART TWO

CHAPTER SEVEN

"THAT IS HOW WE MAKE DEMOCRATS"

S EABURY AND HIS STAFF WAITED until after the 1930 elections on November 3 to start having public hearings. At first, he and his counsel Kresel were disappointed that much of the evidence they had received was in the form of anonymous complaints from people afraid to give public evidence. Kresel even offered to meet potential informants away from the courthouse if that made them feel more comfortable in coming forward. Anonymous calls and letters were not evidence, Kresel stressed.

The investigation started by hearing evidence in secret in a grand jury before a series of public hearings were to begin in late November. But as the public phase approached, Tammany and others involved in the vice racket were showing signs of nervousness. A number of witnesses who were going to testify against two cops accused of perjury reported getting threatening telephone calls from people claiming to be gangsters or at police headquarters, telling the witnesses to "lay off."

While Mayor Walker said he was going to back Seabury in any way he could, it became apparent to investigators that what they called the "opposition of the dominant political machine" (i.e., Tammany Hall) was going to try and wreak havoc. City Hall decided it didn't want to pay the salary of Kresel, who was a vital part of the investigation. When Seabury complained, Walker again promised that the bill would be paid.

But this time the city's top lawyer refused to pay Kresel. Walker then never returned follow-up letters from Seabury demanding payment.

Essentially, the angry Democrats were trying to choke off Seabury's inquiry. Kresel was an important part of the investigation and while he was civic minded, he wasn't going to work all those months for free. Seabury then filed a legal action to compel payment and this time Walker showed his true stripes, saying, when he was pushed up against the wall, that the whole investigation was unconstitutional. The courts ruled that Walker's position was nonsense and ordered payment.

The secret grand jury testimony involved hundreds of witnesses and filled up over 15,000 pages. But it was all behind closed doors and somebody like Vivian Gordon, who felt she had been a victim of the system, wouldn't know what was being uncovered until the secrecy was broken. Even then, unless she was paying attention to what the newspapers were reporting, she wouldn't have a clue about how deeply Seabury was digging into things.

But the public had to be oblivious to what the newspapers would reveal. It was in December 1930 that Seabury started his public hearings, which became a massive spectacle, with all the tabloids and even the New York Times providing nonstop coverage about the scandal the magistrates' courts had become. The main attention focused on the plight of women, estimated to be in the hundreds, who were the victims of shakedowns and coercion by cops, lawyers, court clerks and even judges, much the way they had been victimized years earlier. The courthouses were Christmas trees, piggy banks for the greedy denizens of the halls of justice who scooped up as much money as they could.

The main attraction of Seabury's choreographed hearing was the appearance of a police informant named Chile Mapocha Acuna, a dapper, slender man who as it turned out was an immigrant from Chile. Married with a small boy, Acuna was a gutter-trolling man of the wild side of the city who was, as even the Times called him, "a little stool pigeon." He proved to be an important cog in the police racket aimed at fabricating prostitution cases. Acuna was part of a strange fraternity of stool pigeons that included characters like "the Dove," Pinto, "Harry the Greek," "Chico" and Meyer Slutsky.

Acuna was in New York for a few years when he met two detectives in Manhattan who, because of his knowledge of Spanish, used him to learn about crimes in the Hispanic community. He was paid by the detectives and in 1929 joined up with the vice squad, which had more money to spend on informants than the other detective units. Acuna's usefulness was soon realized by a Lieutenant Peter Pfeiffer, who molded the small-statured Chilean into a special kind of operative in the East Harlem area of Manhattan.

Acuna's brief, as given to him by Pfeiffer, was that during a prostitution arrest he was to always give a false name or address and to expect a slight beating by cops at the time of the bust, to make things authentic. Acuna was also told never to show up in court—that could help in getting the fake case dismissed—and claim that he didn't know the arresting cops.

When Acuna took the stand during Seabury's public hearing, the results were astonishing. He described a system of corrupt cops who preyed on innocent women through a ring of perjury. The *Daily News* called Acuna's testimony something the city had not seen in terms of police corruption since the first 1912 trial of Lt. Charles Becker for the Rosenthal murder. It was "wholesale dishonor," as the *News* called the revelations by Acuna.

Perhaps the most shocking moments in Acuna's testimony occurred when he was asked by counselor Kresel if any of the cops involved in fabricating cases were in the courtroom where the hearing was being held. By command of the NYPD, a number of cops were ordered into the courtroom for the particular session.

At Kresel's prompting, Acuna got up from the witness chair, walked over to the spectator gallery and asked if he saw any of the cops. He answered he did not.

Then Kresel had the courtroom doors opened and 50 officers, who had been ordered to court by Commissioner Mulrooney, came in and lined up along the wall in three lines.

"Now do you see any of the men here?" Kresel asked.

"Yes," answered Acuna.

"Pick him out," ordered Kresel.

Acuna walked down the lines of cops, some in uniform and others in civilian clothes, pointing to them, tapping them on the shoulder and naming them. He got only one name wrong, which he readily acknowledged. Altogether, Acuna identified some 28 officers as being part of the perjury ring. He made an exception to the list of dirty cops by saying that officer Thomas Tunney, brother of boxer Gene Tunney, wasn't part of the vice ring but just worked robbery investigations.

Commissioner Mulrooney was in the courtroom as Acuna implicated the two dozen cops and seemed aghast at what he had learned. Months earlier, Mulrooney had scoffed at the notion that stool pigeons were used by the NYPD and now he was shown to simply have spun a falsehood and proven to be unaware of the level of corruption among the vice officers. It was probably one of the most embarrassing moments Mulrooney would ever face in his career. Later that night he would repair to his offices at police headquarters on Centre Street and figure out what he was going to do with all of the tainted officers.

As a witness, Acuna was the linchpin holding Seabury's hearing together. Acuna said that he decided to testify against the cops after he was himself framed and had to spend time in jail on Welfare Island in the middle of the East River. It was shoddy treatment for the once valuable informant. He served his sentence under a fake name as it turned out.

Another key part of Seabury's case was the wrenching testimony of several women, mostly white but one Black, who told firsthand of their own experiences in the vice shakedown and physical abuse at the hands of the arresting officers. Each case generally followed the same basic outline: Acuna and another stool pigeon would get into an apartment with a woman and had marked money. In each case the sexual advances of Acuna were rejected. But then things quickly got out of control for the unsuspecting woman.

One of the victims who testified was Winifred Grayson, who recalled going across 79th Street from where she lived with informant "Nick the Greek" so that she could recover a wristwatch she was having repaired by Nick's roommate, who happened to be a jeweler. She was accompanied by her cousin, a woman named Marjorie Wharton. Earlier in his testimony Acuna said when he saw Grayson enter the apartment, he put a chalk mark on the door and ran downstairs to notify the cops.

"The jeweler came out of another room when we entered and said hello," Grayson said. "Just then there was a knock on the door, and Nick opened it. He talked to someone outside and then there was a rush of six officers. They came in and two or three of them showed their badges."

One of the cops, identified as Officer Lamb, hollered at Grayson and then smacked both her and her female friend in the face.

"What is this all about?" a startled Grayson said. "I came up here after my watch."

Lamb smacked Grayson again and said, "Don't lie, you are up here for business," Grayson recalled.

Grayson had $20 cash to pay an electric bill, along with some other money, and Lamb took it from her, along with an address book and some jewelry she had received from her dead sister. As the cops took the woman out of the apartment, one of them pushed Wharton down a flight of stairs, she told Kresel. Grayson said that during the ride with the officers, she and her cousin Marjorie sat on the laps of cops in the car and were driven to Central Park, where the officers made what she said were "improper advances," which the women rebuffed.

Grayson and her cousin were taken to a nearby police station where they were locked in a cell. At the Jefferson Market Court, the women were found guilty of prostitution charges by the court's only woman magistrate, Jean Norris. Grayson was then sent to the Bedford Reformatory, the usual dumping ground for women convicted in such bogus cases.

Even when Acuna told the cops that he didn't think a particular woman was a prostitute, they still went ahead and made a case on perjured testimony. Such was the case of Betty Smith, described as a diminutive woman, who showed up at court for the Seabury hearing seeming frightened. Acuna described how he and another informant named Louis "the Dove" Taube set up Smith by telephoning her from a drugstore and tried to make an appointment for a "friend" who was actually Acuna. Smith replied that she was tired and didn't want to see anyone.

But Acuna said that despite Smith's brush-off, he went over to her rooming house and found her asleep. He then gave some marked money to a police officer, who placed it under the woman's pillow. Smith was then promptly arrested after cops entered her room and found the marked money.

Cops were also prone to outright outlandish fabrications. In the case of Catherine Nolan, when she refused to open her door, a patrolman refused to take no for an answer and broke the lock, causing Nolan to fall back and injure herself. In court, the officer said he found a man in the room with her. The officer gave an address for the man that would in reality have been in the middle of the East River.

One indication of the money cops were making on the frame-up cases came from the testimony of Lt. Pfeiffer. Seabury and his staff had done a pretty thorough financial forensic investigation of the cop and found repeated deposits of several hundred dollars into his bank accounts. Pfeiffer's salary as a cop was only $285 a month—barely $3,000 a year—and rental income from some property amounted to only $60 a month. None of that accounted for the huge deposits which on one occasion totaled $3,500.

Pfeiffer was at a loss to credibly explain where all of that money came from. But it seemed clear that he had been profiting from the prostitution shakedowns in a big way. As the Seabury testimony went on, it was also clear that others were profiting from the scheme. The most astonishing evidence involved actual assistant district attorneys working in the magistrates' courts. Their jobs weren't considered seriously—irksome, really—according to Seabury. Some of the prosecuting attorneys seemed barely qualified for their jobs, having reaped the plums of political patronage. The case of one prosecutor, John C. Weston, seemed typical.

Weston had been a jewelry salesman and eventually got a job with the district attorney's office as a lowly process server, the kind of job that was below the status of an office clerk. Incredibly, Weston found himself in magistrates' court and actually began handling cases, with virtually no supervision. Left to his own devices, Weston became a kind of garbage man. For fees received from crooked attorneys who congregated in an area known "Lawyers Row" opposite the Jefferson

Market Court, Weston made sure cases were dismissed. Over an eight-year period Weston tossed out over 600 criminal cases and collected a fortune in bribes. He admitted getting $25 as the usual rate for dismissal, sometimes $50.

Weston wasn't the exception, either. Seabury found that so-called assistant district attorneys did virtually no work in the magistrates' courts and might as well have not shown up at all. Others were raking in tons of money from the shakedowns. Bail bondsmen would bail out a woman for a very exorbitant fee, recommend a lawyer who would grab more of her savings and then, as Seabury found, pay off the arresting officer and the district attorney's representative like Weston.

Although she wasn't a prostitute, Stephanie St. Claire, queen of the Harlem numbers racket, found it necessary to pay off magistrates, using an assistant district attorney as an intermediary. The payments were made to protect St. Claire's lucrative numbers operation. When Seabury started his investigation, St. Claire provided information that showed how the corruption had spread to protect other kinds of rackets.

As it turned out, the Harlem policy protection racket was similar to the prostitution shakedown system. "Policy" itself was a simple form of illegal gambling in which the "banker" who ran the game each day would pick some numbers that would be the winning ones for the day. Players would write what they thought were the winning numbers on a slip of paper and pay a bet of a penny or a dollar. It was similar to what would become the legal New York Lottery decades later. With so many policy banks in Harlem the money to be made was huge, as was the corruption involved. To prevent arrests, cops were paid off, as were magistrates and other court personnel. People who worked for the bankers also had special-colored buttons they carried to show cops they were part of a bank that was paying the police, thus protecting them from arrest.

The public hearings went on and showed how shockingly corrupt the NYPD's vice division had become, turning Commissioner Mulrooney into a man with egg on his face. He had made so many denials of any problems existing with his cops that he had to take action, and quickly. Based on Acuna's testimony, Mulrooney transferred six cops,

effectively demoting them to inconsequential jobs. One of the pun-
ished officers was Lt. William Delaney, who had initially recruited
Acuna for his role as stool pigeon.

As it turned out, Vivian Gordon was watching with dismay as
Acuna was putting the screws to the cops he worked with. She was, according to later remarks by Radeloff, all set to start a brothel in the
70th Street area of Manhattan, complete with the protection of an
NYPD lieutenant, when the Seabury hearing implicated the officer.
Could it have been Lt. Delaney? It was never clear. In any case, Vivian
saw her plans to compete with Polly Adler go up in smoke.

"There goes my place," Vivian moaned, according to Radeloff. "I
had it all fixed. But the fixer couldn't even save himself."

As Seabury took more public testimony, Mulrooney increased the
number of suspended cops to 18. He also filed departmental charges
against a growing number of officers. It soon became apparent that
the police corruption angle was becoming as important as the probe
of the magistrates' courts. The importance of the revelations was not
lost on Governor Roosevelt, the man who originally ordered the probe
by Seabury into the magistrates' courts.

For years after he contracted polio in 1921, Roosevelt had gone to
Warm Springs, Georgia. The attraction of the town was that it contained thermal waters and when Roosevelt learned that it could help
alleviate his paralysis from the waist down, he began making regular
visits beginning in 1924. The therapeutic swimming and bathing
seemed to help Roosevelt and for the first time in years he recovered
movement in his right leg. So impressed with the promise Warms
Springs held for the disabled like himself, in 1926 Roosevelt bought
the resort and its surrounding 1,200 acres for $200,000 and soon after
organized the nonprofit Warm Springs Foundation.

So it was in Warm Springs in December 1930 that Roosevelt learned
of Acuna's revelations in the Seabury hearings. For Roosevelt, the news
was shocking. The fact that so many women had been railroaded with
fake arrests so disturbed Roosevelt that he wrote directly to Seabury, ex-
pressing in measured words his outrage over the disclosures.

"In common with thousands of other citizens of our State, I have
been deeply disturbed and greatly incensed by the unearthing the in-

vestigation being conducted by you showing framing up of women by some members of the so-called police vice squad," said Roosevelt.

For the women who were convicted, Roosevelt believed that something had to be done and that their cases ought to be reopened and investigated and, if necessary, the victims should be given pardons. Seabury wrote back ten days later that six of the women whose cases were brought up in the hearings were framed and not guilty—including Marjorie Wharton and Betty Smith. Executive clemency by the governor was in order, said Seabury. On December 22, 1930, Roosevelt followed Seabury's recommendation and pardoned the six women.

The pardons were the least Roosevelt could do. The bigger problem lay with the way the court system had become so politicized. As more revelations came out, it was clear that the magistrates' court system was a key part of the way Tammany Hall wielded influence and did business in the city. The courts were a favor bank for the Democratic Party, and its district leaders saw interfering or meddling in a case for a friend, even if they didn't know anything about the merit, as something that should be done if needed.

"That," said one district leader, "is how we make Democrats."

IF VIVIAN GORDON didn't know what Seabury would uncover when he initially started his investigation, as the months wore on into late 1930, she and the rest of Broadway couldn't help but be acutely aware of the dirt being uncovered. The headlines about Acuna, the corrupt cops, the gambling payoffs and slot machine rackets were incessant. Then, when Roosevelt granted clemency to the six framed women, Vivian could finally see a glimmer of hope in her never-ending fight to clear her name and get back into the good graces of her daughter, Benita.

Vivian began her own campaign for vindication in early 1931 when she continued her letter writing to her former husband, John Bischoff, and Andrew J. McLaughlin, the vice cop who had arrested her in 1923. In Vivian's mind, Bischoff had been in league with McLaughlin to make the fake prostitution case against her and cause her to lose custody of her daughter. In Vivian's obsessive and paranoid way of thinking the connection seemed obvious. But there was never any proof shown that Bischoff had any connection to McLaughlin, let alone even knew him enough to plot to get his wife arrested.

However, Vivian was not far off the mark about McLaughlin being a criminal and a con artist. While the newspapers didn't carry the information at the time of Seabury's public hearing, there was evidence presented that as an officer McLaughlin was involved in trumping up fake prostitution arrests. In the case of a Mrs. Delbono, identified in Seabury's files as a Hungarian woman, Andrew McLaughlin arrested her twice on prostitution charges, and in one case after she was taken to the police station Delbono was told by the bail bondsman that she had to pay $300, with $100 going to McLaughlin. At trial, the case was dismissed because the officer conveniently provided insufficient evidence.

Vivian's old business associate Polly Adler also reported incidents with McLaughlin, who was known as the "lone wolf" although there were a few times when he worked on the street with other cops to make arrests. As related in *Madam*, by Debby Applegate, Adler and some of her women were pinched by McLaughlin. Knowing as she did the system of payoffs, Adler did what she had to do to assure acquittals, depleting some of her bank account to make the required bribes. There were some other incidents between Adler and McLaughlin, and they all ended with the right accommodation somehow being made to assure Adler's business wasn't terribly impacted.

But Vivian's preoccupation was not over any business. The way McLaughlin's frame-up had destroyed her relationship with daughter Benita Fredericka obsessed her. With the vice corruption now front and center in the public mind, Vivian realized it was time to do something to save her self-esteem and win back her daughter. She saw the Seabury investigation as the best way now to show the world she had been framed. By late January 1931 five NYPD were indicted for perjury in cases Acuna the stool pigeon had said were frame-ups. Seabury also wanted nearly 80 minor girls who had been arrested on morals charges immediately freed from the Bedford Reformatory. The pendulum was swinging in favor of the framed women and by the time the cops were indicted, Vivian was feeling more emboldened and decided to take her own action.

Just around the time the cops were being charged, Vivian wrote a letter to her ex-husband, Bischoff. It wasn't a friendly note, nor one that was grammatically correct.

"Dear Mr. Bischoff, you have probably heard about the vice investigation now going on New York City which is growing day by day that a number of convicted girls framed by the police and others," Vivian said. "You may think you had the last laugh and that my conviction was caused by a frame-up between you and Detective McLaughlin."

Vivian made it clear to her ex-spouse that she wanted to go to the Seabury commission as a way of sticking it to him and McLaughlin and finally letting her daughter know what really happened.

"When I am through it will be just too bad for you. Little Benita is old enough to know that a dirty trick was played on me," Vivian continued. "I intended to go the limit and you know as well as I do that this will mean your finish [sic]."

Vivian though wasn't finished with her letter writing. On February 7, 1931, she penned a note in her 37th Street apartment to Kresel and offered to help the investigation. The missive was short, about eight lines, and written in precise script.

"Dear Mr. Kresel. I have some information in connection with the 'frame-up' by a police officer and others which I believe will be of great interest to your committee in its work. I would appreciate an interview at your earliest convenience. Very truly yours, Vivian Gordon."

Based on all of the press coverage, Kresel seemed to be the right person for Vivian to contact. He had been the main interrogator of many of the witnesses, in both the private and public hearings. But by the time Vivian's letter arrived at the offices of Seabury and his staff at 80 Centre Street in Lower Manhattan, Kresel had his own problems. He was indicted on February 9 by a state grand jury on charges stemming from the collapse of the Bank of United States. The indictment forced Kresel to resign from Seabury's staff, a move that put the rest of those in the office into gloom and depression. But Seabury said the investigation would continue without the need to hire a replacement for Kresel.

Luckily, Vivian's letter was given to one of the junior lawyers on Seabury's staff, Irving Ben Cooper. A 29-year-old attorney who had been born in London, England, Cooper had been in private practice in Manhattan since the 1920s. During one interview he was conducting for Seabury, a convicted bondsman who was brought to the office suddenly got up and tried to take a swing at Cooper. The bondsman had been shackled to a court attendant and didn't hurt the young attorney. After reading Vivian's note, Cooper wrote her back and said that he would be happy to see her for an interview on February 20 in a state office building, just across the street from the State Supreme Court Building, the place where the hearings were held.

While it was initially reported that Vivian didn't show up for her interview, later news stories related that she did talk with Cooper on February 20 about her false arrest by McLaughlin. In an affidavit later given to police, Cooper said that Vivian wanted to help "right a wrong inflicted on her by reason of the charges of immorality" back in March 1923. Vivian maintained that her conviction resulted from a plot between the cops and her husband, who was motivated by a desire to obtain complete custody of their child.

Cooper listened as Vivian recounted the entire episode: how she had gone to a hotel to retrieve some mail (presumably from her old boyfriend Marks) and was accosted by another man who turned out to be McLaughlin. The story, as Vivian told it to Cooper, was more convoluted than the story related by Marks and indicated that her old boyfriend might have been working in league with the police. In any case, Vivian told Cooper she was falsely arrested on prostitution charges.

"I pointed out to Vivian Gordon that the essential thing was to obtain corroboration of her story to me," Cooper said. "She stated that she would go through her personal effects to endeavor to get whatever she could to substantiate her version of the occurrence of which she complained."

Cooper never heard from Vivian again.

CHAPTER EIGHT

"THEY ARE KILLING ME!"

THE INTERSECTION OF ALLERTON AVENUE and Boston Post Road in the Bronx is a busy one, not far from a subway station. The location is a perfect place for cabs to congregate since they are reasonably assured of picking up fares. Early in the morning of February 26, 1931, there were at least three cabs at the road junction cab stand waiting around when a scream of a woman in a yellow Checker cab was heard.

"They are killing me!" the woman was heard yelling.

Not only the cabbies heard the shouts but also a policeman named Edward Nye who was walking along Allerton Avenue to his Bronx home. According to the reports later released by the police, the three cabbies on Allerton jumped in their separate cabs, with Officer Nye jumping on the running board of one vehicle driven by cabbie Martin Katz. All three vehicles went after the Checker cab and the drivers said it was going towards Van Cortlandt Park, about two miles to the west.

Another cabbie, Frank Ryan, claimed he drew abreast of the Checker livery and noticed a motionless woman seated between two men. Ryan said his cab developed engine trouble and he had to abandon his chase as the suspicious vehicle entered the park. Later, there was some doubt about Ryan's version of the chase since it appeared police said that his cab never actually left Allerton Avenue. Still,

Ryan insisted that he saw the last three digits of the Checker's license plate: "810."

It would be about five hours after the cabbie chase that truck driver Harry Francis and Emanuel Kamma would find Vivian Gordon's lifeless body, with a clothesline around her neck and tossed like rubbish off the side of Mosholu Drive. After detectives worked over the crime scene, Vivian's body was taken to the Fordham morgue where coroner Louis Lefkowitz did the autopsy and determined the cause of death: "asphyxia due to strangulation by cord around neck." The manner of death was homicidal, and the time of death was put at about 1:00 A.M. the morning of February 26.

After Vivian's body was identified through fingerprints, the flood of newspaper stories began at a pace that wouldn't cease for months all over the country. Within 24 hours of Vivian's body being found, the press was filled with details of all sorts about her life, a testament to the fever pitch at which reporters worked at that time in the competitive world of the newspapers in New York City, where over a dozen dailies crowded the newsstands. VICE GIRL MURDER screamed the *Daily News* front page, with a pretty portrait of Vivian, and under it another image of her body among the rocks and bushes. Inside, the *News* ran nearly three pages of a story written by reporter Grace Robinson.

"A red-haired woman, found strangled to death in Van Cortlandt park, yesterday became the center of the seething fires of graft, bribery, frame-ups, shakedowns and judicial corruption which have agitated New York since last October," was how Robinson led her story. "The victim was Mrs. Benita Bischoff, 32, who was also known in the gilded haunts of New York's night life as Vivian Gordon. She was strangled with a clothesline and tossed from an automobile."

Vivian's real age would turn out to be thirty-eight, according to the coroner—not thirty-two as reported by Robinson and other journalists. With a birthdate for Vivian of 1891, even the coroner appeared to be off by a year. But with the NYPD being extremely cooperative in giving out information, the press wasn't too far off the mark with details about Vivian, her personal history and her connections to the underworld.

The *New York Times*, which had been closely following the Seabury investigation, also put Vivian's murder on the front page with the headline WOMAN VICE CASE WITNESS FOUND STRANGLED IN PARK and adding the element that attorney John Radeloff had been arrested—not as a suspect but as a material witness. The *Times* and the rest of the newspaper couldn't avoid making the connection between Vivian and her approach to Seabury's investigators and her sudden death. It all seemed too coincidental.

But Commissioner Mulrooney had to deal in the realm of facts before he could make any arrests. The stakes in the case were high for him and there couldn't be any missteps. The NYPD had been tarred with the revelations about the vice squad shakedowns and extortion and if cops were somehow involved in Vivian's murder to keep her quiet, that would take the scandal to another level, and possibly cost Mulrooney his job.

The job of police commissioner is a powerful one in New York City. But in the 1920s and 1930s job security for whoever had the position was tenuous and subject to public whim and outrage. When Grover Whalen had the job, even though he was an old friend of Mayor Walker's, he had to leave when there was public outrage over the way cops beat and mistreated hundreds of demonstrators during an International Unemployment Day rally in March 1930, in the midst of the Depression. Whalen's tendency was to have his cops use nightsticks to give the protestors what veteran officers called "wood shampoos." Grover resigned about two months later, after less than two years on the job, and went back to his retail position. He would later also serve as an official greeter for the city whenever dignitaries or famous people visited.

Before Whalen, Joseph A. Warren was commissioner, and he immediately ran into bad luck in terms of bread-and-butter police work. A number of unsolved homicides happened on Warren's watch, the most notable being that of Arnold Rothstein in 1928. It took weeks for the NYPD to make an arrest and when it did the trial resulted in an acquittal of the prime suspect, George McManus, who had been playing a card game with Rothstein the night he was mortally wounded. A taciturn man who was an old law partner of Walker's, Warren never seemed to master the job and left after 20 months, and died of a stroke soon after in 1929 at the age of 47.

When he took the commissioner job after Whalen in May 1930, Mulrooney was a dyed-in-the-wool cop and investigator at heart with 34 years on the force. He was nothing like his immediate predecessors who had no police background. In his youth, Mulrooney had been a pilot on a Hudson River barge, and after joining the NYPD spent time in the harbor unit, where according to police historian Thomas Reppetto he filled his days chasing river pirates and carrying out water rescues. It was Mulrooney who pulled nearly 30 bodies out of the charred and sunken hull of the *General Slocum* when she burned and sank in the East River with the loss of over 1,000 lives in June 1904.

Mulrooney, whose family had close ties to Tammany Hall, was part of the Irish niche of career cops who had come from a similar Gaelic ancestry, those who for decades would dominate much of the NYPD hierarchy and command structure. Being Irish and close to Tammany Hall were job qualifications that assured ever increasingly important positions in the NYPD. When he was appointed commissioner the day Whalen resigned, the belief was that Walker picked Mulrooney because, as one report said, the mayor didn't want anybody with a personality that was more colorful than his own.

"The mayor had to find a man who was tongue-tied," one reporter observed.

But if Mulrooney didn't have an outsize personality that rivaled Walker's, the killing of Vivian thrust him into the spotlight which he couldn't hide from. The cascade of events—and there were many which followed the murder—wouldn't take attention away from Mulrooney. In fact, for weeks on end, his comments about the case often made him the man of the hour. He would prove *not* to be tongue-tied.

Within days of the killing, Mulrooney painted Vivian as a female racketeer who was playing the old game other women had tried. There was nothing new about Vivian, Mulrooney said. She was following in the line of other women—like Dot King and other Broadway "gay girls" who put aside the drab but respectable life in exchange for jewels, money and the excitement of the underworld.

"There is nothing new about the women racketeers," said Mulrooney. "We will always have them unless human nature changes."

It soon leaked out that police where looking for another lady racketeer, a woman the newspapers called the "Female Al Capone," who
was believed to hold the key to solving Vivian's murder. At first, the
person of interest wasn't identified. But it soon was learned that the
mystery lady gangster cops were looking for was Polly Adler, who had
disappeared to parts unknown, possibly as far as Havana. Actually,
Adler knew all along where she was: Miami Beach, a place where she
could, as one account said, continue "sunbathing, chain smoking and
keeping an eye on the New York papers." Adler had no advance warning about Vivian's murder, it seems, but the tabloids worked her name
over in stories as though she held the key to case. As noted in Adler's
biography, she didn't have much to contribute to the police investigation of Vivian.

The lifestyle of the Broadway Butterflies was something the Irish and
Catholic Mulrooney couldn't fully comprehend. To him, Vivian fit the
stereotype of the thrill-seeking, avaricious women who had descended
on Broadway for years, leading lives that resulted in either death or dis-
appointment, the stuff that cops found themselves having to sort out.
Given that Vivian partnered with gangsters, it was easy to see how Mulrooney would consider Vivian an "adventuress" and racketeer.

Mulrooney's cops, under the direction of Inspector Henry Bruck-
man, descended on Vivian's 37th Street three-room apartment and
began delving into the artifacts of her life, anxious to find something
that would shed light on her killing. Her closet was filled with shoes
and fine clothes. Perfumes and cold creams abounded. The walls appeared covered in expensive paintings and Japanese etchings. There
was also evidence that Vivian had done well in her life to afford such
a lifestyle. Detectives found various financial assets, cash in bank accounts, her interest in the Vivigo Corporation and evidence of stock
dealings on Wall Street.

There were two other things about the apartment that were of note.
Among the three rooms was what was described by the police as a children's room filled with all sorts of toys, curious because no child lived
there. It was likely a sign of Vivian's obsession with getting back her
daughter or that she was stuck in the past about the child, who was
eight years old when custody was lost.

There was also a curious find on Vivian's nightstand. Next to a photo of Vivian was a copy of the book *Bad Girl*, by Vina Delmar. The novel, published in 1928 and considered so controversial that it was banned in Boston, was Delmar's breakthrough book and dealt with premarital sex, pregnancy, abandonment and the toll they took on the female protagonist. It was an edgy book which obviously resonated with Vivian, who in her own life felt victimized by the men around her. Delmar had a long, productive career and would write additional books, including *Kept Woman* and *Loose Ladies*, the latter being a collection of short stories. Delmar caught the attention of Hollywood and even got nominated for an Academy Award. She went on to adapt *Bad Girl* for Hollywood in 1931—a year Vivian never lived through.

But by far the most important discovery in the apartment were diaries Vivian had kept over a two-year period. The seven volumes were a Rosetta stone on Vivian's later life, filled with a combination of mundane musings as well as ominous notes about people she believed posed a threat to her. The contents were related to the press by Bronx District Attorney Charles McLaughlin, who had no relation to the vice cop. One effect of the discovery of the diaries was to eliminate the possibility that Vivian was murdered to prevent her from testifying on the issues of police corruption and, specifically, whether vice cop McLaughlin was somehow involved in her killing. McLaughlin had been mentioned repeatedly as being part of the police frame-up of women in the Seabury hearings and he would go on to have other problems with Mulrooney. But as far as the slaying of Vivian was concerned, McLaughlin seemed to be of no importance. Besides, he had been three days out on a Caribbean cruise when she was killed.

The diaries, which began in February 1929, showed that Vivian feared her old attorney and lover John Radeloff. Vivian wrote that she decided to keep the diary because "it is best to put down things as they happen concerning John A. Radeloff. He is not to be trusted—he would stoop to anything." Part of the bad blood between her and Radeloff was that he refused to pay her medical bills, Vivian recorded.

Although Vivian believed Radeloff could cause her harm, the diary entries included vague phrases like "if anything happens to me, he's to blame, he and his henchmen." In another undated entry, Vivian wrote,

"The threat has been made—Sam Cohen, who is a client of [Radeloff's] in a case, has brought—the thugs—two of them." Cohen was a career criminal, a burglar who had a record of assault as well. "Who would make a confidant of a common loft thief?" Vivian asked rhetorically.

From what the diaries contained, Cohen is supposed to have told Radeloff at one point that in connection with Vivian, "[w]e'll take her out somewhere. No one will know what has happened to her. Every mark of identification will be missing, especially that ring." That passage about Cohen alerted police, who knew from the crime scene where Vivian's body was found that there was no identification with her and that her ring, valued around $2,500, was missing.

It was clear from the diary that Vivian had come to despise Radeloff, to whom she had loaned money. Radeloff "would stoop to anything . . . Radeloff is the only one who is really an enemy of mine—because of certain things I had told his wife in retaliation for all the rotten things he has done to me—he was just using me for a good thing," Vivian said in one angry entry.

Radeloff knew he could borrow money from Vivian, although he seems to have not repaid it. Vivian also mentioned the strange trip to Norway—ostensibly to buy a bank—for which she fronted $1,500 and involved Cohen. Whether or not the diary was absolute proof that Radeloff and Cohen were involved in Vivian's murder, Mulrooney considered them to be potential witnesses and ordered them arrested on material witness warrants, a standard tactic if someone is believed to have information vital to a police investigation.

Right after detectives found the diaries on February 27 they took Radeloff and Cohen to a police station house in Manhattan and questioned them through the night. The next day both men appeared before a Bronx grand jury as "hostile" witnesses, as prosecutors said. The judge who had ordered them held on witness warrants set bail at $50,000. Neither Radeloff nor Cohen could raise that money so they had lawyers go before the court to order that they be released on the grounds that the diary entries weren't enough to hold them in custody.

A Bronx judge was sympathetic to the efforts of police and prosecutors but was unsure that there was enough to tie Radeloff and Cohen to the crime. The assistant district attorney, I. Adlerman, told the judge that both men had "intimate knowledge of the murdered woman." But the judge wondered still.

"Do you intend to hold these men as defendants?" the judge asked.

In a lowered voice, Adlerman replied, "We can't tell at this time."

The court agreed to keep Radeloff and Cohen as material witnesses for another two weeks but clearly the prosecution was having trouble tying them to Vivian's murder, no matter what her diary stated. As fate would have it, Radeloff was indicted on a relatively minor extortion charge unrelated to Vivian's murder when a suspect in a theft case accused him of trying to shake him down for $1,500 to have the case fixed. As a result, on March 24, Radeloff was released as a material witness because he was now bailed out on the extortion case. For Cohen, despite his claim that he willingly testified to the grand jury and hadn't been indicted for Vivian's murder, things wouldn't go so smoothly in the weeks ahead.

THE MORNING OF February 28, 1931, Pierre Morehead Franklin found himself in the Canadian city of Moncton, in the province of New Brunswick. Moncton is fairly high up in latitude and during the winter is generally cold—below freezing for most of February. Franklin worked out of a Canadian axle manufacturing firm and was a car salesman based in Montreal who happened to find himself in the provincial city on business. To warm himself, Franklin was having a cup of coffee and breakfast in a restaurant. He picked up a local newspaper and what he saw stunned him. Splashed across the front page was a picture of his younger sister—the one he had grown up knowing as Benita, not the stage name of Vivian Gordon—with a rope around her neck and dead in a New York City park. The headlines said that she had been murdered as a witness in a sensational New York vice investigation.

Stunned, Franklin was in a daze for two days before the police in New York City contacted him by telegram and he decided to rush there. Franklin couldn't believe what he had been reading about his dead sister. The words "vampire," "woman racketeer" and "blackmailer" were simply at odds with the young, accomplished musician he had grown up with. The lurid descriptions in the newspapers doubled the shock of Vivian's death for her brother.

Once in New York City, Franklin went through the ordeal of visiting the Van Cortlandt Park crime scene where Vivian's corpse had been tossed. He then was taken to the morgue to view her bruised, cold body. Funeral arrangements had to be made. Although he was a big, beefy man over 200 pounds, Franklin was running himself ragged with virtually no sleep. The worst for him was still to come.

CHAPTER NINE

"I AM GOING TO END IT ALL"

A S A 16-YEAR-OLD, Benita Bischoff had gone through some problems in her young life. The divorce and custody battle between her parents had been draining emotionally, pulling her between the two of them and causing her to be uprooted a number of times. First the family lived in Philadelphia, then her mother, Vivian, fled with her to New York City. Finally her father, John Bischoff, who had remarried, got custody of her at the age of eight and brought her to live in New Jersey.

The intervening years for young Benita had not been quiet. Her mother continued to hector Bischoff over custody, even hatched plans to forcibly get Benita back, once unsuccessfully trying to grab her and drag her into a waiting car. Vivian vacillated between showing love and then turning on her daughter, calling her ungrateful. As Benita grew to be a teenager, she developed her own interests and started making new friends in high school. There was even talk that she had a boyfriend.

But any semblance of normality that Benita was feeling was ripped away when she and the rest of the world learned on February 27 that her mother had been killed in Van Cortlandt Park. With newspapers incessantly covering Vivian's murder, the distraught child told her stepmother, Eunice Bischoff, that her mother had screwed up. In her own diary, Benita wrote on February 28, two days after her mother's killing,

"What an awful mess Mother got herself into. She has been found dead in New York and they are saying terrible things."

Benita's stepmother and other neighbors tried to help her in the days immediately after news of Vivian broke. But the flood of negative stories soon began to overwhelm Benita. Vivian was known as the lady racketeer, running a sex extortion racket, scheming with gangsters like Legs Diamond and Arnold Rothstein, with a few other minor disreputable characters thrown in. Even the local New Jersey papers around her hometown of Audubon were filled with stories. It was a sensation that wouldn't fade away. Benita just couldn't escape the horror and vileness of what she discovered about her mother.

Her stepmother, Eunice, tried to get Benita to think about other things, but nothing seemed to work. Benita was said to be increasingly melancholy, eating little, sleeping in fitful starts that ended with her awakening with a cry. By March 1, Benita's tone in her diary changed and she made it clear she was planning to do something drastic.

"I just can't live any longer," Benita wrote. "This has got to be too much for me. I am going to end it all. If any money is coming to me from my mother, I wish that it be divided between my grandmother, Herbert Trout and Billy. I am in my right mind and I am now going to turn on the jets."

No matter what Benita said, she wasn't in her right mind. She had a calculated plan, yes, to take her life. But it was an act of despair that had driven her so far. When police found her on March 3, Benita had sealed the windows and doors of the kitchen shut and there was gas coming from open jets in the stove. She went so far as to roll up a rug to seal the space between the door and the door sill. Scattered on the floor of the kitchen and the table were newspapers with headline accounts of Vivian's murder. Attempts were made to resuscitate her but at a local hospital she was declared dead.

Benita's handwritten last testament about her monies had no legal bearing. She was under 18 and the suicide note wasn't even attested to by any of the required witnesses. As next of kin to Vivian, Benita stood to inherit from her mother, but it was uncertain what assets might be found. But she was thinking of the few people who had meant something to her. Herbert Trout was a 23-year-old local man, a handsome fellow she had met while ice skating at the local rink. Trout told police he and Benita were good friends, but nothing more.

One of the last people to see Benita alive was Estella Cramer, principal of Audubon High School, who recalled seeing the teenager walking across the school grounds with her school books under her arms, morose. She called Benita into the office.

"The poor child's grief was written on her face, and I spoke soothingly to her, urging her to try and forget the cloud that passed across her life," Cramer later recalled. "My efforts seemed to have little effect on her."

Toward the end of the conversation, Benita pushed her school books across the table to Cramer, mumbling that she wouldn't need them because her family was going to be moving. Cramer didn't buy the explanation and told Benita to keep the books until it was clear the family was going away.

Cramer said she made one more effort to buoy Benita, telling her that she still had the love and friendship of everyone at the school. That seemed to lift Benita's spirits, Cramer said. The child smiled and "seemed immensely cheered and lighter of heart," remembered Cramer.

Benita's father prompted her to visit the local skating rink to take her mind off her grief and she went, aware of the attention she was attracting. Trout was there, a local celebrity of sorts who not only had played for the high school ice hockey team but also the local club. He skated by Benita, nodding in her direction and saying hello. Some took his behavior as a slight, although it just as easily could have been uncertainty about what to say to her regarding the loss of her mother.

Benita's suicide was as big a news story as the death of her mother and only compounded the tragedy. The resulting funeral for her brought out a large-scale police presence in New Jersey, mainly for crowd control. The funeral for Benita on March 6 was a brief service at a funeral home in Collingswood, N.J. Admission was by invitation only and cops scrutinized those who entered. After a local pastor recited some Catholic prayers, the casket was closed and eight girls who were friends of Benita's wept as they accompanied the casket outside to a waiting hearse for the trip to the cemetery in Upper Darby, just outside Philadelphia.

At the graveside service there were more prayers and Benita's step-mother tossed a rose into the grave, as did her daughter Eunice from a previous marriage. Then, the eight schoolmates of Benita who acted as pallbearers each tossed their own roses into the grave. If Benita thought she had been abandoned, the devotion of her friends at her grave showed she was very much mistaken. The grave diggers filled in the open plot. There had been talk that Benita's diary would be buried with her, but that did not happen.

Benita's suicide compounded the public horror which began with her mother's murder. Editorial writers bemoaned the double tragedy, something that the best classical writers could have used as a strange inspiration.

"There is a ghastly and tragic aftermath in the suicide of poor little Benita Bischoff," the *Daily News* editorial writers said. "Recording in her piteous diary that fact that she could no longer face the world for shame, Benita turned on the gas. So much for the plot of this drama. It has all the elements of drama—terror, pity, beauty, wealth, the wage of sin, the suffering of an innocent child. It is elemental. Ibsen could have used this material, or Eugene O'Neill; or Aeschylus, Greek trage-dian of 2,400 years ago."

Benita's funeral drew a large crowd. But her mother's rites the very same day some 100 miles away were a ghostly affair. It was early in the afternoon on March 6 that a limousine pulled up to the door of the Fordham morgue in the Bronx and attendants put Vivian's silver cas-ket inside the vehicle. There were only two regular mourners: Vivian's brother Pierre Franklin and a nurse named Mabel McCabe. Aside from news reporters and photographers, the funeral procession con-sisted of only the hearse and a car for Franklin and McCabe. The short procession drove north, passing about two blocks from Van Cortlandt Park where Vivian's body was found, and went some 15 miles to Mount Hope Cemetery in Hastings-on-Hudson.

At the nonsectarian cemetery, the burial took on a strange note. The funeral director Joseph Abbundi was speaking at the graveside on a gently sloping hill when Franklin suddenly broke down, begging to have one more look at the dead Vivian. After the casket was opened, Franklin fell to his knees and kissed his sister's still lips.

"My God, but she is cold!" a distraught Franklin said to Nurse McCabe.

Franklin had to be led aside as the casket lid was closed and the casket lowered into the grave. No headstone was erected to mark the spot.

A great deal had been thrust on Franklin in a few short days. He had to bury Vivian and learned of the suicide of her daughter, his niece. The newspapers ran incessant stories about Vivian's murder and the distressing aspects of her lurid life. With Vivian dead, Franklin had to also begin to wrap up her affairs and talk to police, all under the spotlight of the New York press. It was proving too much for him.

Franklin's graveside behavior was only the beginning of a period of bizarre actions that created as much a stir as the deaths he so mourned. The evening of March 7, police got a call about a man acting erratically on the seventh floor of the Hotel Lincoln. It seemed that he was talking gibberish and walking around nude except for an undershirt. It was Franklin in the midst of a gigantic nervous breakdown, wringing his hands and calling out Vivian's name.

At 200 pounds Franklin was difficult for hotel staff to restrain. A hotel doctor tried to sedate him with an injection but even that failed. Finally the police were called. Wrapped in a blanket and strapped to a stretcher, Franklin was driven to Bellevue Hospital where he was placed in the psychiatric ward. It took two police officers all they could do to keep him from leaving the hospital. While Franklin had registered at the hotel under an assumed name to assure privacy, the next day the newspapers carried screaming headlines, including: VIVIAN'S BROTHER TAKEN RAVING TO INSANE WARD.

It was reporter Grace Robinson, who had been breaking all sorts of stories about Vivian's case, who succinctly summed up the situation about Franklin's breakdown: "His pitiable condition is the culmination of a week of anguish such as might well drive the strongest to madness."

CHAPTER TEN

"THE SHEIK OF THE VICE SQUAD"

W HILE THE DEATHS OF VIVIAN and daughter Benita provided much of the never-ending drama in the early days of the case, the police still were trying to squeeze solid leads in the ever-widening grand jury investigation. Mulrooney, aware of the way failures by one of his predecessors to quickly and finally solve the murder of Arnold Rothstein in 1928 led to his ouster as commissioner, didn't want to suffer the same fate. The reputation of the NYPD was also at stake because the newspapers had pushed the theory that it was Vivian's threat to testify to Seabury that got her killed. There were plenty of leads; some were solid and others proved to be dead ends. Men and women who knew Vivian came forward to tell what they knew, and it became clear that she was as Mulrooney said she was, a lady racketeer. Somewhere in that troubled life of hers lay the answer to who killed Vivian and why.

Two men mentioned in Vivian's diary as having caused her trouble with the prostitution frame-up were her ex-husband, John Bischoff, and vice cop Andrew J. McLaughlin. Mulrooney wanted to talk with both of them but learned that McLaughlin was out of the country when Vivian was killed, on a six-day cruise to Bermuda aboard the S.S. *California*. A handsome, dark-haired man with a wife in Manhattan, McLaughlin's good looks had earned him the moniker of "the Sheik of the Vice Squad," who had over 1,200 arrests to his credit. On the ship, McLaughlin seemed to be the life of party to the other passengers. The liner was due back in New York on March 2.

The day the *California* docked in Manhattan at Pier 14 on the West Side, a detective captain was there and immediately went on board to McLaughlin's stateroom and told him why he needed to be questioned. As he left the dock quarantine area, McLaughlin, whose name had already come up in the Seabury investigation as a crooked cop, told reporters that Vivian and the entire furor "was all Greek to me." Sure, he had heard about the story on the ship radio and got requests for comments from the newspapers, but he didn't really know anything. McLaughlin swore on his family's honor that he had nothing to do with Vivian's murder or any frame-ups.

McLaughlin was whisked by car to the office of Bronx District Attorney Charles McLaughlin, where Bischoff had already been for close to two hours. The questioning of both men was done by the heavyweights in the investigation: Mulrooney, two of his deputy commissioners and some other police officials. Of the two men, Bischoff seemed to have the most credible explanation of his relationship with Vivian and in fact was eager to talk to the cops. He recounted his marriage to Vivian in 1922 and the action he took after her arrest in 1923 to take custody of little Benita. Bischoff's recollections of his tempestuous marital life seemed fluid. While claiming that he married Vivian in 1922 he also filed a divorce action in December of that year, an indication that things were going quickly downhill between him and his wife. He acknowledged having not seen Vivian or having anything to do with her for years. When asked if he had any idea about who committed the murder, Bischoff said he didn't know.

McLaughlin was on thinner ice. He finally produced a letter Vivian had sent him in January and a note strangely written in the third person. The note said Benita Bischoff had been framed by him in 1923 and that she was going to tell the whole story to the "vice commission." It was signed "B. F. B," likely meaning Benita Franklin Bischoff. The existence of the note put the lie to McLaughlin's statement hours earlier to reporters that he didn't know what all the fuss was about. He knew more than he let on since Vivian had already written to him.

Mulrooney and prosecutor McLaughlin seemed satisfied that vice cop McLaughlin had nothing to do with Vivian's murder. He had a solid alibi in that he was out of the country on the cruise ship. But investigators asked for his bank records, and it was clear from the Seabury investigation that McLaughlin was on the radar in the wide probe of shakedowns by the vice squad.

Mulrooney acted quickly. McLaughlin's bank records indicated he made large deposits over two years totaling $35,000. The vice cop refused to tell his superiors how he got that much money on a yearly salary of $3,000. With that refusal, McLaughlin was promptly suspended. He was then hit with departmental charges for not talking and also with charges related to his testimony in a number of vice cases where he made arrests. It was also revealed that McLaughlin had refused to testify before Seabury's committee, claiming the special investigation into the magistrates' courts had no right to examine his personal finances.

On March 21, 1931, after one of the quickest police department internal trials at that time, McLaughlin was found guilty of eight out of eleven departmental charges. The police official presiding at the trial found that McLaughlin's failure to testify about finances was conduct unbecoming of a police officer. He was also found guilty of having insufficient evidence to make certain arrests and had failed to give the magistrates' court all of the evidence in his possession. With that verdict, McLaughlin was dismissed from the NYPD, as were two other vice cops. In a sense, Vivian got posthumous retribution against the cop she so hated for what he had done to her.

The department trial of McLaughlin and the other vice cops were a necessary sideshow to the investigation of Vivian's murder. As police examined Vivian's diary, prosecutor McLaughlin in the Bronx started calling in the other men Vivian had named in the pages. One of them was Joseph Radlow, stock swindler, occasional newspaper writer and former boyfriend of Vivian's. The relationship between Radlow and Vivian had earlier disintegrated after he accused her of extortion in August 1930, a claim that went nowhere in court. Radlow was seen as having a motive to harm Vivian but there didn't seem to be evidence that he tried to hurt her.

Anytime a person becomes the object of public obsession, often because of some failure or misfortune, people who were friends—or once thought to be friends—come out of the woodwork. Sometimes it is for a fleeting few minutes of fame in the newspapers, other times it is to help set the record straight. Then there are those who just want to settle scores and talk trash. In the latter category was Jean Stoneham, the ex–gangster moll who told reporters Vivian was a conniver ready to pin a friend with a fake theft charge and once tried to shake her down for $1,000.

But there were others whose recollections about Vivian painted her in a more sympathetic public light. Dr. Ann Tompkins Gibson was a doctor at the Women's Medical College of Pennsylvania in Philadelphia and a daughter of a prominent member of the local clergy. She knew Vivian and tried to show how her obsession over her daughter was at the root of all the terrible things that happened.

"Vivian was purely the victim of a plan she had nurtured for years in the hopes of vindicating herself in the eyes of her daughter," said Gibson. "Her impelling motive in life was to prove she had been 'framed' on immorality charges and she was not the woman she had been painted as being."

The Seabury investigation, said Gibson, was the one big break Vivian thought she had for reclaiming her reputation. It is quite possible that those who feared what Vivian had to say were involved in her murder, Gibson suspected.

Gibson had known Vivian for a number of years and saw her in the time before she was arrested as a beautiful woman who "everyone" loved and who had a consuming love for her daughter, the likes of which she had never seen. Prison changed all that.

"When she came out she was cold, bitter and calculating," remembered Gibson. "She wanted to be good and told me, she told me, but it became impossible after her sentence at Bedford."

There was one eerie recollection Gibson said she had about Vivian. It was about a month before she died that Vivian called her physician friend and told her of a dream she had about her daughter and implored Gibson to check up on the teenager. "She seemed unusually anxious," recalled Gibson.

Following up, Gibson said she spoke with Benita's father after Vivian's murder and asked if it was okay to stop by and check up on the child. Bischoff said a visit would be fine. But Gibson said she delayed, thinking it best for the furor over Vivian's death to die down before she made the visit. The hesitation on Gibson's part was something she later regretted.

"I am very, very sorry that I didn't go at once," Gibson later said. "She was a very sensitive child, and she might have been comforted, had I gone. In a way I am not surprised [about the suicide], knowing what bond of love held the mother and daughter together."

With 25 detectives assigned to Vivian's murder, Mulrooney and Bronx prosecutor McLaughlin pulled hundreds of witnesses into the grand jury. Some of Vivian's old friends had intriguing tidbits about her activity in the sex extortion racket. Cassie Clayton, a thin woman from Erie, Pennsylvania, who had known Vivian over the years, was found by an investigator for Seabury living in a boardinghouse. Clayton agreed to travel to New York City to tell investigator Cooper what she knew. Clayton had been mentioned in a "Dear Cassie" letter from Vivian so naturally she was of interest. Reportedly, Clayton related that Vivian told her of a $250,000 floating crap game operating in hotels around the Broadway district and that cops were paid off to protect the gambling operation. Given the fact that Rothstein was known to sponsor such games in his day and had been an associate of Vivian's, the information had a ring of truth to it and was another avenue of police corruption.

But in terms of the actual murder and potential suspects, cops had to focus closely on viable suspects. Adding to the work were the contents of Vivian's seven diary books. There were numerous men and women listed in the diaries and the cops and city officials decided to keep most of the identities confidential. This was the era when big money assured that indiscretions of wealthy men—and to some extent women—were largely kept out of the newspapers by police. So intriguing as the diaries were, many names mentioned stayed hidden from the public eye.

But some identities did surface, and the names showed the kind of men Vivian associated with beyond the gangsters of Broadway. One millionaire was John Hoagland, whose Park Avenue apartment was the scene of numerous parties Vivian and other women attended. Hoagland, who made his money in the baking soda business, was known for having afternoon parties which Vivian attended most days. Other diary names sent detectives to Washington, D.C., in what was a futile attempt to find out anything that might shed light on the murder.

The trip by NYPD detectives to Washington seemed to be an exception to the belief that city cops weren't relied upon to develop leads outside of the metropolitan area, a situation that no longer exists in the modern era of policing. It caused a rift between prosecutor McLaughlin and Mulrooney. Within a week of Vivian's murder, McLaughlin admitted that he believed he needed outside help from the Pinkerton Detective Agency. The reliance on Pinkerton seemed to some pundits to be a smack at the NYPD and an indication that McLaughlin had little confidence in the police to handle everything that had to be done in the investigation.

It wasn't that the NYPD couldn't handle local angles, McLaughlin explained; rather, the Pinkerton agency had resources around the country that the local cops didn't have. Pinkerton's corporate resources would also allow investigators to cut out cumbersome bureaucratic delays which were inherent in public police agencies.

"If the New York police wanted out-of-town information, they would have to communicate with the police department of that town and it would take more time then we think necessary," McLaughlin explained to reporters. "We found that the Pinkerton men will go directly to the place or person indicated, do what we want done immediately and report at once."

McLaughlin said if necessary, he would pay for the Pinkerton services out of his own office funds. But that did little to alleviate the perception that perhaps the prosecutor was at a dead end in the investigation and that relations with the police had deteriorated. So, to calm the water, Mayor Walker finally woke up and made his first public comment on the murder, noting that indeed both McLaughlin and the cops had agreed on calling in Pinkerton. In the end the bill for the Pinkerton work came to just over $1,300, not a sum that was going to break the bank.

Still, Mulrooney seemed stung by the fact that an outside private detective agency was meddling in the investigation. He also had to deal with the inconvenient fact, reported in the press, that with over 70 homicides tallied in the city since January 1, about 80 percent were unsolved. So, as a show of force, Mulrooney ordered a surge of police on the streets of New York City for one weekend. It seemed to be something depicted years later in the film *Casablanca*, where the French police commander Renault, learning of the killing of German officer Major Strasser, ordered cops to "round up the usual suspects." Hundreds of motorcycle cops and patrolmen were ordered out from behind soft desk jobs, as the *Daily News* stated, "to pound the pavement in this gigantic search for criminals." The dragnet may have pulled in a host of thieves, pickpockets and other felons, but it didn't do anything for the investigation to find Vivian's killers.

IT WAS NO secret in the city that its mayor, James Walker, was ministering to his job with his left hand. Walker was known widely for his partying, speakeasy appearances and catering to famous visitors. He ran things through aides and deputy mayors but really never saw to take bold initiatives. He liked the glamour that went with the job and the free publicity he got about his haberdashery and canoodling with Broadway babes.

But if all that superficial publicity is what Walker thought would keep him in good standing, the death of Vivian Gordon showed that he was very wrong. Vivian's brutal murder, and the suicide of her daughter, shocked the public. The double tragedy was also seen as symbols of something deeper and troubling going on in the city, evidence of something that was alarming and needed to be swiftly addressed. At one Baptist church in Manhattan, a pastor in a Bible study class got a resolution approved which condemned the crime that appeared to be rampant everywhere. The Baptists approved of what Mulrooney and Seabury were doing to address crime and denounced the corruption which seemed to abound.

The Bible study group resolution got a short notice in the *New York Times*, which in itself showed that it had some newsworthiness. But it was when two big names in New York City religious life—Rabbi

Stephen Wise and Rev. John Haynes Holmes—took a public stance that the deep issue of crime in the city was put on the front burner. Both men, officials of the City Affairs Committee, put out a strong statement in which they mocked the "wise cracking" Walker and called for action against the evil combination of criminals, cops and courts which were being exposed daily. Wise was a well-known name in Reform Judaism and a avowed Zionist who had been outspoken on a number of public issues. Holmes was a well-known pastor of the Community Church who in late 1930 had criticized both Walker and Roosevelt for not doing enough to deal with what he called the "loath-some vermin" of corruption in the city, including a court system that was "the playground of dishonest politicians and racketeers."

"The murder of Vivian Gordon lights up our city's life as with a light-ning flash," their statement said. "In no more sinister and dramatic way could the alliance between the 'forces of law' and the forces of law-lessness have been exposed."

For Wise and Holmes, Vivian's death showed that anyone prepared to expose the evils of crime would be met with "swift and awful pun-ishment." The committee believed that the murder was sparked by Vivian's decision to talk with Seabury, a view shared by many at that point. The question was what government should now do, and for that Wise and Holmes didn't think that either Walker or even Manhattan district attorney Thomas C. T. Crain could be effective.

"The murder of Vivian Gordon cries not for vengeance but for swift and unrelenting scrutiny," they said. Governor Roosevelt had taken the first step in appointing Seabury but now the first thing to do to push things further along was to organize a "vigilance committee of fifty to one hundred men and women" who could support public offi-cials powerful enough to rebuke the corrupt public officials in league with the criminals who were making New York "the meanest and fou-lest of cities."

The Wise and Holmes statement was one of the first to come after Vivian's murder. There would be others. Notably, the Society for the Prevention of Crime made strong charges against the Walker admin-istration and called for Roosevelt to allow Seabury to conduct a wider probe with the view of working to remove Walker. The society didn't accuse Walker of corruption but essentially said he had a lackadaisical, laissez-faire attitude and wouldn't use the laws on the books designed to combat corruption.

The society was almost mocking in the way it highlighted Walker's pettiness by trying to keep funding for Seabury's counsel and by belittling some of the Seabury findings. District Attorney Crain had bragged about solving the Rothstein killing in 15 days but that proved to be empty braggadocio. The fact that Walker's own personal attorney represented a vice cop accused of perjury also seemed improper, the society indicated.

"We would like to have some proof by aggressive action that the mayor really desires a clean city," the society said in its letter to Roosevelt. "We doubt whether the mayor dares give it to us."

It was time to be done with Walker's flippant attitude in a period when the city faced "dastardly conditions," the letter said. The society called for an investigation into the way Walker was leading the city.

Then, the New York City Congregational Church Association, which represented 42 churches, called in a resolution on Governor Roosevelt to do something to eliminate evil in city government. Editorial writers at various newspapers both inside New York City and in other states were critical of Walker and the city's stagnation over crime. Others acknowledged that it was taking something like the murder of Vivian to get attention to the issue of crime and corruption.

"The fate of the red-haired Broadway play girl is providing the most sensational stimulus to New York's analyzing inquiry into vice and crime," one journalist opined breathlessly.

The drumbeat for action continued. James C. Cleary, a noted lawyer in Manhattan, agreed to support a drive by the Citizens Union to form a massive public committee of 1,000 people to support an investigation into public corruption and encourage those who wanted to come forward—much the way Vivian Gordon had—to provide leads without fear of reprisal.

Walker at this point didn't do himself any favors. In the midst of the constant barrage of stories about Vivian, the Seabury investigation and assorted police scandal, Hizzoner took a vacation, going off to the Palm Springs estate of his old friend Samuel Untermeyer, a well-connected Tammany lawyer. Walker said he was going to sunbathe. Ever the showman, Walker, with Untermeyer's engineering for publicity, met with a group of Indians from a reservation. He was offered a thermal mud bath by the Indians, but Walker demurred, saying he was already in one for the past 18 months of his second term.

In one crazy publicity photo, Walker posed with two masked cowboys who pointed revolvers at him. Walker, wearing a suit and a white hat, always ready to play along, raised his hands as if he was in a holdup. The image could have been a metaphor for what was going on in reality back home for years with the gangsters in the city.

Walker held daily press briefings on the porch at the estate, clad in pajamas and appearing quite sunburned. He explained that the trip was the first real vacation he had in the past 15 years. When asked about the Seabury investigation, Walker pointed out that while he appointed magistrates, as mayor he had no ability to remove them from office. So he shouldn't be blamed for what had happened in the magistrates' courts.

SITTING IN THE governor's mansion in Albany, Roosevelt was quite aware of the tempest brewing on his watch in New York City under Walker. Roosevelt had won reelection in 1931 and ostensibly had four more years to lead. But he was seriously assessing his ability to run for president in 1932 and knew that he had to have the support of the Democratic machine, which meant he had to walk a political tightrope with what he did about Walker and the rest of the Tammany Hall favorites in New York City.

On March 3, 1931, as the vice scandal was escalating after Vivian's death, Roosevelt and Seabury met behind closed doors in Albany. It was a chance for Seabury to brief the governor on the progress of the probe into the magistrates' courts and talk frankly about problems he was having with Walker. While both men said they declined to reveal exactly what they discussed, it seemed clear from the way events had unfolded in the four days since Vivian's murder that her case was a topic of their secretive talks.

It did become known that Seabury related how some 41 vice cops had been implicated by stool pigeon Chile Mapocha Acuna in charges

Vivian Gordon, the lady racketeer, in a publicity photo apparently taken while she was seeking stage jobs on Broadway. *Getty Images.*

New York State Judge Joseph Force Crater, who is said to have partied with Vivian Gordon and some of her women at Gordon's apartment. Crater disappeared in August 1930 and despite a massive search was never found. He was last seen in Manhattan after leaving a restaurant. He was declared legally dead in 1939. *AP Images.*

Irish gangster Vincent "Mad Dog" Coll (left) shaking hands with his defense attorney Samuel Leibowitz after Coll was acquitted of kidnapping charges. Leibowitz was regarded as one of the most successful defense attorneys of his time and won an acquittal for Harry Stein in 1931 for the murder of Vivian Gordon. *AP Images.*

Samuel Seabury (left) and Mayor James Walker during a 1932 hearing into allegations that Walker, while mayor of New York City, engaged in questionable financial transactions. The Seabury hearing was a prelude to a similar hearing by Governor Franklin D. Roosevelt, which ended when Walker abruptly resigned as mayor in September 1932. The sentiment against Walker and the way he handled crime and other matters only increased with the murder of Vivian Gordon. *AP Images.*

Detail shot of an older Vivian Gordon, around 1931, used in a special NYPD bulletin distributed to cab drivers in New York City in search of leads about a cab Vivian was believed to have driven away in before she was found dead in Van Cortlandt Park in the Bronx on February 26, 1931.
Special collections section of Lloyd Sealy Library, John Jay College of Criminal Justice.

Frank Costello (left), one of Broadway's top gangsters when Vivian Gordon was active with her schemes, and Noel Scaffa, a famous private investigator who specialized in recovering stolen jewelry. It would later be revealed that Scaffa provided then–Police Commissioner Edward Mulrooney with an informant who gave information which led to the arrest of Harry Stein for Gordon's murder. Costello and Scaffa are pictured here after they were arrested together in a federal criminal case in 1935. *AP Images/John Rooney.*

Jack "Legs" Diamond, a sometime extortion business partner of Vivian Gordon and a major Prohibition gangster, during his trial in upstate New York for kidnapping in December 1931. This was one of the last photographs of Diamond ever taken. Diamond was acquitted of the charges but had little time to celebrate. Less than a day after his acquittal, gunmen caught him in his Albany hotel room and shot him three times in the head. *AP Images.*

Broadway actress Peggy Hopkins Joyce, who was reported to have steered gamblers to Arnold Rothstein's gambling operations. Joyce had a reputation for loving and leaving a number of suitors, some of whom committed suicide. *Library of Congress.*

Samuel Seabury as a young man. Seabury forged a legal career that led to prominence as a New York State judge. After leaving the judiciary, Seabury was eventually tapped by Governor Franklin D. Roosevelt to lead investigations into the magistrates' court system, of which the Jefferson Market Court was a part, as well as a crucial investigation into the financial dealings of Mayor James Walker and his City Hall administration. *Library of Congress.*

Sam "Chowderhead" Cohen, once a bodyguard and friend of Vivian Gordon, appeared before
a congressional committee to give testimony about allegations of strike-breaking.
Cohen, a big beefy man, had a reputation back in New York City for specializing in
"muscular" labor relations. *Library of Congress.*

The above will call your attention to The Candy of Excellence. Are you a patron for this product? A half century of success and approval of our most valued customers warrant your endorsement for the Page & Shaw candies. NEW YORK, BOSTON, PHILADELPHIA, CHICAGO, LYNN, SALEM and all principal cities.

PROGRAM

CAST — Continued

An Aviator.. Joseph P. Galton
Joe Oswald... Wm. Young
William Bulldoon... Wm. Dunham
Mr. Circle... Arthur Whitman
Mr. Bar.. Stanley Vickers
Mr. Pulley... Walter Smith
Conductor.. Jack Bick
Salvation Nell... Elsie Pilcer
Miss Glasgow... Florence Averelle
Miss Leeds... Mae Tormey
Miss Edinburgh... Emily Miles
Miss Heather... Vivian Gordon

The Steinway, Hume, Weber, and Jewett Pianos used at this theatre exclusively are furnished by the M. STEINERT & SONS CO., Steinert Hall, 162 Boylston Street

Shubert Theatre program from 1914, which included Vivian Gordon (bottom right) among the cast for *The Passing Show* revue. An accomplished musician, Gordon had a few credits on Broadway but never had a career that took off. *Shubert Archive.*

Undated modeling shot of Vivian Gordon. She had a brief career as a performer, including in the Shube Organization's *The Passing Show* in the World War One years. *New York City Municipal Archives.*

Mayor James Walker with Governor Franklin D. Roosevelt in more convivial times. It was Roosevelt who held a special hearing in the summer of 1932 into allegations that Walker engaged in questionable financial transactions. Walker abruptly resigned as mayor in September 1932 before Roosevelt had to decide on his fate. *Library of Congress.*

A younger James Walker, around 1920, before he was elected mayor of New York City in 1925. Walker was known for his fastidious fashion sense and his love of night life, as well as women. *Library of Congress.*

The Jefferson Market Court building in Greenwich Village, around the time it was being used as a criminal court, including for cases involving women. Vivian Gordon's 1923 prostitution case was handled in this building. Vivian would contend to the day she died that she was set up by vice cop Andrew McLaughlin on the charge for which she spent about three years in a women's prison. She was giving evidence to Samuel Seabury and his investigators about the long-running practice of shaking down women at the court when she was killed. The old court building still stands as a prominent landmark. *Library of Congress.*

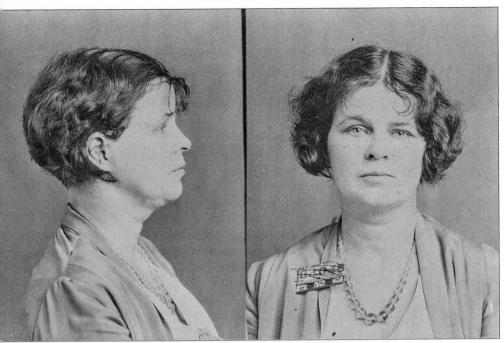

An undated mugshot of Vivian Gordon, likely taken close to the time she was murdered in 1931. She was no longer the svelte dancer and actor she once was.
New York City Municipal Archives.

DETECTIVE DIVISION
CIRCULAR No. 3
MARCH 6, 1931

POLICE DEPARTMENT
CITY OF NEW YORK

POST IN CONSPICUOUS PLACE

CHAUFFEURS' CO-OPERATION

IS REQUESTED BY THE

POLICE DEPARTMENT, CITY OF NEW YORK

Information wanted that may further assist the Police in tracing the movements of

VIVIAN GORDON

An appeal is made to all chauffeur's that might have driven the person whose photographs appear on this circular, at any time. This information will be treated STRICTLY CONFI-DENTIAL and the Chauffeur furnishing same will not be inconvenienced.

THE DESCRIPTION OF VIVIAN GORDON IS AS FOLLOWS:

VIVIAN GORDON also used the name of BENITA BISCHOFF—Age, 38 Years; Height, 5 feet, 2 inches; Weight, 130 pounds; light auburn hair reaching to shoulders, heavy and bushy; gray eyes; fair complexion and full face,

At the time she was last seen she wore black velvet dress, collar and cuffs trimmed with cream colored lace. Cheap ornamental bar-pin 2½ inches long with imitation green jade circle size of 10-cent piece near each end, with a flare of rhinestones protruding from each circle at each end, pinned to dress in center of breast; black pliable straw hat, close fitting, black and white bow on front; gun metal silk stockings, black suede pumps, with square steel buckles.

Brown Mink Fur Coat, 42 inches long, shawl collar, bell sleeves, two-tone brown lining effect, may have label marked "Maison Simone" valued at $1800. White kid gloves wrist length.

Choker of imitation pearls, small size.

Lady's platinum ring, fancy design, one round diamond in center, 2 karats, 9 points; 14 diamonds around large diamond, weight 95 points; 6 diamonds in shank, 3 on each side, weight, 10 points. Scratch No. 26249 on ring, and valued at $2,000.

Lady's rectangular shaped diamond wrist watch, number of diamonds unknown; Meylan movement, Number 41519, Case Number 50865, Scratch No. C-602; Stock No. 8986, made by Black, Starr & Frost, valued at $665.

Post in a conspicuous place where it may be read by your chauffeurs.

PHONE SPRING 6-3100.

PHONE: HACK BUREAU, BARCLAY 7-5720.

EDWARD P. MULROONEY,
POLICE COMMISSIONER

NYPD Commissioner Edward Mulrooney distributed a poster to all chauffeurs after Vivian Gordon was killed in an effort to find out information about a hired cab she is believed to have traveled in just before she was murdered.
Special collections section of Lloyd Sealy Library, John Jay College of Criminal Justice.

Vivian Gordon's body as police found her early on February 26, 1931 in Van Cortlandt Park in the Bronx. Her fur coat and jewelry were missing. *New York City Municipal Archives.*

Vivian Gordon in a Bronx morgue. Notice the rope by her head, which was used to strangle her. *New York City Municipal Archives.*

of conspiracy, bribery and related offenses. Seabury also submitted to Roosevelt a bill to provide some kind of remedy for the various women who had been framed in the prostitution cases.

Two days after meeting with Seabury, Roosevelt disclosed that he had been sent a status report on the investigation of Vivian's murder by Bronx district attorney McLaughlin. Again, Roosevelt was guarded in what he would say but claimed the document didn't contain anything not already known to the public. If that truly was the case, it seemed that McLaughlin's investigation was making little progress. However, one bit of leaked information said that the police had been cleared of any involvement in the murder. So the question remained: Who did kill Vivian Gordon?

CHAPTER ELEVEN

"SHE ONLY MADE ONE CACKLE"

WHEN NEWS OF VIVIAN GORDON'S murder first broke and it became known she was in the Broadway sex racket, estimates of what she had earned ran from $500,000 to $1 million. She showed that she had money from the way she lived. Her closet was filled with expensive clothing from the finer stores—some of it courtesy of sugar daddies like Henry Joralmon. There were her real estate holdings and stock certificates, though some of the latter might have been courtesy of her swindler boyfriend Radlow. When her brother went through her apartment, he found tens of thousands of dollars in assets.

So when it came time to file papers in Manhattan Surrogate's Court a few months after Vivian's death to see what her holdings were, people like funeral director Joseph Abbundi, who had a bill of $1,200 for burying Vivian, expected there to be some money in her estate. Alas, everyone was mistaken. The surrogate's court files revealed that at first Vivian's former husband tried to have the court assign him to administer the estate, primarily since he was already administering the estate in New Jersey of his and Vivian's dead daughter, Benita Fredericka. After Vivian's death, Benita was her sole beneficiary under the law but then her own death complicated the issue.

In the end, the court granted James Egan, who as the public administrator was the official who handled estates of people who died without a will, the ability to find Vivian's assets and figure out what to do with them. Egan didn't have to look very far. Whatever the claims were about Vivian's large financial haul as a racketeer, she died with an estate worth no more than $200. Funeral director Abbundi was left holding the bag for his fee and anybody else looking for a piece of Vivian's stash of cash was disappointed.

Vivian's brother Pierre Franklin doesn't show up in any of the surrogate's court records and there is no record about what he did with the stock certificates and other assets he was reported to have found in her apartment. By March 14, 1931, Franklin was back in Montreal where he gave an interview to the *Montreal Daily Star* which showed that he still couldn't come to terms with what his sister had been doing in her life in New York.

"The things they are saying about my sister, they can't be true," said Franklin in disbelief. "She was a remarkable woman . . . in everything she did there was that touch of distinction. She played the piano, clarinet and violin; she painted rather well and made her own clothes," Franklin noted. "I ask you, could my sister who did all these things, be bad the way they said she is?"

Having not seen his sister in four years, there was little Franklin could have really known about the life Vivian had been living and the pantheon of crooks and gangsters who were in her circle. The lesson was that as well as you might think you know someone, there are always surprises. The reaction to the reality of bad things is usually disbelief. As the Montreal newspaper reporter noted in the story, Franklin preferred to think of Vivian as the demure woman whose portrait he kept in his hotel room.

AS FAR AS Commissioner Mulrooney was concerned, the mention in Vivian's diary of one "Harry Saunders alias Rubin" led him to believe that the names actually related to Harry Stein, a felon with a significant criminal record including an arrest for beating a woman some years earlier. The oblique mention of Stein in the diary was part of an entry that talked about a $1,500 loan Vivian had made to him. But if Mulrooney and the detective had their suspicions about Stein, they had to develop evidence linking him to the murder and that was not an easy task.

Cops had found 32 witnesses to bring into the grand jury, some because they had been mentioned as being gangster associates of Vivian's. After talking with Legs Diamond, Mulrooney ruled him out as a person of interest. After he was arrested for a driving offense in New Jersey, bootlegging boss Charles Higgins talked with New York detectives and admitted knowing Vivian—even talking with her a month earlier—but had no idea about what had happened to her. Then there were the publicity hounds, like George Spanish, who told detectives he knew two men who killed Vivian but recanted and said he made up the story in the hopes of selling it to the newspapers. Some of the focus was on Sam "Chowderhead" Cohen, also known as "Samuel Harris," who was locked up for weeks as a material witness and had a number of friends from a social club he frequented in the Bronx who substantiated his story that he was at the place the night of February 25—when Vivian was last seen alive—playing cards.

One woman who claimed ties to Vivian said she came to grief after it became known that she had been questioned by police. Lenore Halsey, described in the press style of the day as a "colored charwoman," claimed she had given Vivian massages in the past and told police that she had been given a lift home to Mount Vernon in a cab with her and two other men the night of the murder. After Halsey was identified in the newspapers as a possible witness to the fateful taxi ride, she said two men came to her house and told her she didn't have to appear before the grand jury. But before leaving, one of the men threw a caustic substance in Halsey's face, burning her, but not seriously, and missing her eyes. Police expressed some doubt about Halsey's story, but she did get publicity, just not in the way she wanted.

Another old friend of Vivian's was questioned, a pretty dark-haired woman named Vernon Repez. It turned out that Repez had come to Vivian's aid after she sustained injuries in the March 1930 Palace Hotel incident. Repez said she nursed Vivian back to health, saying it "was a thing any woman would do for another." But Vivian got under Repez's skin by constantly trying to entice her to hustle men to get "money in chunks."

Repez eventually stopped seeing Vivian but said she ran into her on the street one day, and she again tried to get her to join a career of hustling. But again Repez refused, noting "I didn't like her way of living."

Since there had been witness reports that Vivian was bundled into a cab and driven away, Mulrooney took the step of producing a special printed police circular. The document contained two photographs of Vivian and a description of what she was wearing when her body was found. Every garage in the city got a copy for posting, as did every cop and taxicab driver who could be located. The circular also listed everything of value Vivian had when she went out for her final ride: a platinum ring with a round, two-carat diamond in the center; 14 diamonds around a large diamond; six diamonds in a shank (part of a ring). There was also a lady's rectangular-shaped diamond wristwatch. Some of the jewelry was estimated to be worth thousands of dollars. The missing long mink coat Vivian wore was estimated to be worth $1,800—about $36,000 adjusted for inflation in 2023.

The missing jewels and fur coat led Mulrooney to believe that robbery might be one motive for the killing. But that was a fallback position. Going through Vivian's records, cops knew she had been doing deals with Legs Diamond and that she was said to have a blackmail list of 200 men who had been caught up as victims in her call girl racket. Just as easily as robbery could have been the motive, Vivian's crazy and dirty financial dealings could have led to her being targeted.

No longer a person of interest in the murder, Vivian's old attorney and lover John Radeloff felt confident enough to spin his theory that it was a cab driver—one who had driven men to rendezvous with Vivian and never got compensated—who may have killed her. Radeloff pushed his theory and had at least one of his own informants flesh it out in a *Daily News* interview, and cops latched onto it. It seemed that one angry cab driver had driven Vivian to a location at 43rd Street and Broadway, and she got out of the vehicle, cursing at the driver. The taxi man got out and continued the argument, striking Vivian and knocking her to the sidewalk, the informant said. Vivian got up, resumed the argument and, instead of asking for help, got in the cab and drove off, according to Radeloff's informant.

The account of the Broadway cab incident had no date and seemed curious in that no one intervened, and that Vivian decided to get back in the cab. But Radeloff stuck with his theory that a cab driver may have killed Vivian over a financial dispute. However, the problem with that idea was that if the cabbie killed Vivian, he would never get whatever money he was owed. Nevertheless, the story sent cops on a search for such a cab driver.

In her own interview Helen Dorf, the woman friend of Vivian's who had received $25,000 from the late Henry Joralmon, showed how Vivian operated and how she used cab drivers in her extortion business.

"When I first met Vivian she tried to interest me in getting money from wealthy men," said Dorf. "This is what Vivian told me of her scheme: 'Helen,' she said, 'there isn't a chance of exposure. And you don't have to give up much. When these men get good and drunk, they forget why they wanted to meet you in the first place and they pay—plenty.'"

The men didn't have to be picked up on the street, Vivian explained, according to Dorf. Taxi drivers were the key cog in getting the scheme to work.

"I have a connection with taxi divers who make a specialty of taking out rich rounders," said Vivian, according to Dorf. "As soon as they are fairly drunk I get a call and meet them. The taxi boy gets a small split—he never knows what I get, and if he does, what's the difference?"

According to Vivian, the scam was safe and profitable and much better than spending time at a party where the "the most you get is drunk on bum liquor," recalled Dorf.

While Dorf demurred when approached by Vivian to be one of her party girls, the unsophisticated model caught the eye of the lonely and free-spending Joralmon, who gave her $25,000. The gift was given by Dorf, at Vivian's suggestion, to Radeloff, who fell through on the promised big returns when he invested the money.

As some cops chased around the city looking for any suspicious taxicabs, Mulrooney and some of his other detectives knew that if Vivian's missing jewels and fur coat turned up, they might prove crucial leads. The market in stolen jewels in New York City was a thriving one. High society women made it easy as they paraded around town in ex-

pensive stones and diamonds, advertising their wealth and letting ad-
venturous thieves know they were lucrative targets. Jewelry heists
targeted so many of the rich that an industry developed to recover the
swag. No one made his own particular niche better than Noel C. Scaffa.

If Damon Runyon ever met Scaffa, it is likely that he saw him as
potential fodder for great copy, worthy of perhaps his own character
in fiction. Dour looking and with a pencil-thin dark moustache that
made him look like some 1930s Broadway matinee character, Scaffa
was one of the better-known private detectives in town. Born in Sicily,
Scaffa took a job in Lower Manhattan's insurance center to support
himself when his father lost his livelihood in the great economic panic
of 1907. From there he moved to the Pinkerton Agency, the detective
firm that would later figure into the Vivian Gordon murder case.

As a gumshoe, Scaffa got his first big break when he was assigned
a jewel heist which victimized the great tenor Enrico Caruso. It seems
that when Caruso and his wife returned from a trip to Cuba to their
home in East Hampton on Long Island, they discovered that thieves
had taken around $450,000 in jewels. Scaffa got the assignment be-
cause the Carusos were Italian speakers, a language Scaffa had known
since his childhood. Try as he might, Scaffa couldn't solve the Caruso
case and told his bosses at Pinkerton that it might have been possible
to make a recovery if the company had connections in the underworld
among the thieves and fences who trafficked in stolen gems.

Scaffa left Pinkerton in 1921 and started his own detective agency,
wedded to the notion that a good sleuth had to have the right connections with thieves. It became apparent to Scaffa that gem thieves
didn't want to keep what they stole but instead wanted to hold them
for ransom and would part with the items if they were paid a portion
of what they were worth. The way the insurance industry worked at
that time, the company would only pay out 60 percent of the value of
the stolen item. For the thieves, if they could get 30 or 40 percent of
the value they would gladly turn over the jewels. That way, the insurance company would get a recovery and would only be out the smaller
finder's fee, so to speak, paid out to the thieves.

Scaffa tried his tactic in a Fifth Avenue caper where $50,000 in
gems were stolen from the Donahue family. How all of the bits and

pieces fell into place was unclear. But after a clandestine meeting in a coffee shop, Scaffa met a character in a Manhattan hotel who passed him a package, and about two weeks after Mrs. Donahue lost her jewels they were returned by Scaffa to the insurance company, and ultimately to the owner.

Such success made Scaffa a Broadway celebrity and his career blossomed, recovering an estimated $10 million in jewelry over the years. He started hanging out in big nightclubs and getting to know Frank Costello and others in the underworld. During this period, Scaffa was building an extensive network of informants and contacts in the stolen gem market. Cops knew this and tried to make cases against Scaffa for compounding a felony, cases which went nowhere and were dismissed.

Mulrooney knew about Scaffa and considered him of some value to the police. Since he had taken personal charge of the investigation into Vivian's murder, Mulrooney started acting like the old pavement-pounding cop he had once been, waiting for the right lead that might solve the murder. In April 1931 Mulrooney and his detectives were focusing on Stein because they had learned he had been trying to sell to a fence a fur coat and jewels very similar to those which Vivian had been wearing the night she was killed.

The complete story of how Mulrooney and the cops got onto Stein wouldn't be revealed until years later. But it was during a conference at police headquarters that Mulrooney left the building to meet a source for information. In later published reports it was stated that a Scaffa stool pigeon disclosed that Stein gave the police enough information to solidify their suspicions about Stein. It is entirely plausible then that it was Mulrooney himself who on that day that he left the office retrieved the information from Scaffa and his people. It seemed that Stein was peddling a fur coat and jewels just hours after Vivian was murdered.

As would later be revealed in court, David Butterman, a well-known fence of stolen property and an associate of Scaffa's, was awakened the morning Vivian was killed by a call from Stein.

"This is Harry," Butterman recalled Stein saying. "I'd like to meet you in the morning. I have something for you." The two met at a coffee shop and haggled over a fur coat. Butterman took out the coat lining and found some numbers which he tried to obliterate with ink but without success. Stein said the coat was from an insurance job—meaning it was stolen. Butterman wasn't keen on buying the coat and asked Stein if he had anything, at which point he said some people "downtown" had a diamond ring and watch. But still, Butterman wasn't buying, even though Stein claimed the ring was at least two carats and others had offered up to $1,000 for it.

From the sequence of events described by Butterman, it seemed like the connection Stein had with the mink and the jewels solidified the police interest in him as a prime suspect in the slaying of Vivian. But it still was circumstantial evidence. There needed to be something more concrete to tie Stein to the crime. Mulrooney and his cops got it in 27-year-old Harry Schlitten.

Detectives already had a focus on Schlitten from the beginning of the murder investigation since he was among several people held early on as material witnesses but later released. But on May 24, 1931, cops figured they had enough on Schlitten and arrested the chauffeur at his home in Newark, N.J. At police headquarters Schlitten was interrogated by several cops, including Mulrooney, as well as Bronx prosecutor McLaughlin. They all gave Schlitten the third degree throughout the night and in police parlance he gave it up, at least as far as he was concerned.

We don't know all these years later what exactly happened during Schlitten's interrogation. The NYPD records of the investigation of Vivian's murder couldn't be found in department files. The NYPD could beat and coerce suspects into saying what they wanted to make a case, a method known as "tuning up," although it is not likely that such methods were used on Schlitten since Bronx district attorney McLaughlin was in the room. On the witness stand, the officer who conducted some of the interrogation vehemently denied that Schlitten had been beaten. But what Schlitten did say put himself, Stein and others in deep trouble.

The next day, it was Mulrooney who told the press what Schlitten had said. Schlitten's role was to rent a Cadillac from a garage on Suffolk Street on the Lower East Side of Manhattan and drive it uptown, picking up Stein and Samuel Greenberg, also known as Greenhauer, along the way. The trio then drove to the Bronx to scout out a place to commit the murder, said Schlitten. Driving back to Manhattan, the group let Stein out so that he could go meet Vivian and drive her back to the Bronx in a cab. Meanwhile, Schlitten and Greenberg drove back in the Cadillac to the Bronx.

The ruse Stein used to get Vivian to go along was a fake story that Greenberg had $250,000 in uncut gems and that she was to "play up" to Greenberg so that she and Stein could get the stones from him. It was while driving in the Cadillac, said Schlitten, that Stein took a piece of rope with a noose and slipped it over Vivian's head. Then Stein and Greenberg forced Vivian to the floor of the Cadillac and Stein pulled the noose harder.

"She only made one cackle," Schlitten would later remember for cops about the moment Vivian died.

Schlitten continued his narrative by saying the Cadillac traveled on the road to Van Cortlandt Park where Stein and Greenberg dragged Vivian's body from the car, Stein holding the feet and Greenberg the head and shoulders. The body was then dumped into the bushes and rocks, making sure that Vivian's fur coat, watch, ring and pocketbook were taken. The trio then left and Schlitten returned the Cadillac to the rental location.

The next day, Mulrooney couldn't hide his exuberance to reporters when he briefed them along with Mayor Walker about the solving of the case. Schlitten as it turned out was given immunity from prosecution for testifying to the grand jury.

"The detective work reflects the highest credit on the department," said Mulrooney. "It is one of the most intelligent, persistent efforts that has been seen in many, many years." But this had nothing to do with the police department, as the tabloid press kept insinuating. The initial suspicion was that Vivian's death stemmed from an attempt to stop her from spilling the beans about vice squad corruption.

Walker also took the chance to harp on the press as he congratulated the police for making an arrest in Vivian's murder.

"Now, I wish we had here the files of some of the newspapers which on the day after Miss Gordon's body was found printed stories and editorials asserting she was murdered by the Police Department of New York," sniped Walker. "How I wish we had those clippings which hinted that police killed her to stifle possible revelations about vice squad patrolmen accused in the Seabury probe."

As to the motive, Mulrooney admitted that the cops weren't certain but held out the idea that since Vivian was stripped of her possessions that robbery would have to work for the moment. But many theories would surface, including that the slaying was revenge for bad business deals, or that Stein wanted to get out from under a loan he had received from Vivian for the Oslo caper, as well as to silence Vivian over what she knew about Broadway's underworld activities.

The case against Stein and Greenberg was largely circumstantial, although Schlitten's confession now provided a more powerful element. Police believed, based in part on the information gleaned from Scaffa's informant, that Stein was in possession of Vivian's fur coat and some of her jewelry. As the top cop said, the case was one of "texture," meaning as the investigators got more evidence they would try and slot it into the prevailing theory of the prosecution.

But for the moment, Schlitten was the prosecution's star witness, and he knew it.

CHAPTER TWELVE

"MORE OR LESS SHOCKED"

THE REVELATION OF THE FRAMING of women on prostitution charges, as well as the crooked way the magistrates' courts had been run in New York City, was not something Mayor Jimmy Walker could ignore. The press simply wouldn't let him. Yet Walker's reaction was that of a typical government bureaucrat, with one eye on the political repercussions as he played things from all sides. Yes, the disclosures about the vice squad were horrible and as he said "more or less shocked" him. But on the other hand, he agreed with the notion that some of the claims were exaggerations. But he still had to strive to keep New York's reputation as the "cleanest, most moral city in the world."

So what did he do? He called a meeting. As Samuel Seabury was getting ready to drop some more bombshells, Walker pulled some sociologists, penologists and criminologists together to talk about things. But talk about what? The experts weren't quite sure of what was expected of them at the meeting: they had arrived with no concrete agenda nor any ideas. After a brief introduction, Walker said he had to leave to attend to other business. So in the end the panel passed the buck, passing a resolution empowering Commissioner Mulrooney to set up a committee to study things in the police department.

If anything of substance was going to happen about the scandals in New York City, the impetus wasn't going to come from City Hall or Walker. The system in the city was too entrenched. On top of that was the fact that the Manhattan district attorney, the chief prosecutor in town, was widely viewed as ineffectual, if not incompetent.

Thomas Crowell Taylor Crain was of Mayflower ancestry and was born in 1860 just blocks away from Tammany Hall. He never strayed far from the Tammany orbit and as a lawyer got some City Hall jobs and eventually was appointed and later elected to the state supreme court. But early in his career questions were raised about Crain's competence. As Commissioner of Tenement House, Crain came under criticism when a fire ravaged a tenement at 105 Allen Street, killing 18 people. Fire officials said the death toll was exacerbated by blocked fire escapes and windows. Crain would later claim his records showed the tenement had been inspected twice a month.

After sitting for about five years on the state supreme court, Crain was elected in 1929 district attorney of Manhattan. Crain's performance in that post was lamentable. He was a genial man but was lost in the world of crime fighting. When Rothstein was shot and killed in 1928, the cops and Crain investigated and brought a suspect to trial, only to have the jury acquit. In 1930, Crain announced a war on rackets but produced few significant cases—this is a city where the early Mafia was beginning to coalesce around Luciano, Costello and Vito Genovese. Crain also tried to prosecute Magistrate George F. Ewald and again failed to secure a conviction. There were other cases that had seasoned cops rolling their eyes over the way Crain didn't want to do anything. Luckily, Vivian Gordon's murder was outside Crain's jurisdiction or else there was no telling what he would have done with it.

It became clear that Crain was in over his head. Civic groups were calling on Roosevelt to remove him. Instead, on March 8, 1931, the governor appointed Seabury to do a full investigation of Crain's office and all of the claims of dereliction of duty. Tammany Hall was angered by Roosevelt's action and thought it was a prelude to the removal of Crain, a distinct possibility but one that would have to wait for the hearings to begin. Seabury got to work quickly and began a hearing within days of his appointment. Among his first witnesses was Raymond Moley, a professor of public law at Barnard College, who presented statistics showing Crain as a prosecutor had garnered the fewest convictions of any prosecutor in the last 25 years.

But to many of Crain's critics the more troubling allegations were his failure to investigate the collapse of the Bank of United States, racketeering in the fish market, garment and hat-making industries and irregularities in the way city docks were leased. More explosive was claims that Crain ignored evidence of bribes involving Tammany office holders. Crain appeared to drop the ball in all those cases. Even a couple of Crain's assistants testified that all sorts of rackets flourished in the city and that even with police and prosecutors working together they couldn't make a dent in crime. It seemed like he couldn't get an alley cat arrested.

Crain also took the witness stand, and his appearance was described as that of a nervous man, biting his lips, and with a face "as white as a sheet of paper in his hands" he admitted to such failings. But he said he would keep on trying for the rest of what was left of his term, a little over two years. Crain also took a shot at Seabury, saying that crime-fighting efforts would be better served if he and the police didn't have to deal with attacks from the rear.

Prosecutor Crain was shown to be lax, inattentive and incompetent. But was that enough to get him fired? Seabury didn't think so. In a final report to Roosevelt released on August 30, 1931, Seabury found that while Crain was unfocused and ineffective in carrying out certain racketeering investigations, his failures didn't warrant Roosevelt terminating him. Just because Crain didn't do a good job in some cases didn't mean that he had to be booted from the office.

Seabury was struck by Crain's long career in public service and the fact that nothing was ever shown that he looked the other way in cases and allowed criminals to get a free pass. There was also no showing that Crain was corrupt.

"There is not a line of proof that any failure to act in any of the cases referred to [in the report] was induced by any improper influence or any untrustworthy motive," Seabury concluded.

Crain wasn't up to the job of district attorney but that was the price the public had to pay for supporting him in his election bid in the first place, observed Seabury.

"The fact that the people of the county do not elect the best man to the position, or one who acts in the most efficient manner, is not ground for his removal," said Seabury. "In such cases, the people must suffer the consequences of their own conduct. They can elect who they please."

Of course, Seabury's unstated notion was that the electorate could choose only the man put up by Tammany for the office.

When Roosevelt got Seabury's report, he effectively rubber-stamped it "case closed" and didn't make any comment about the finding.

Crain, spared the shame of removal, went on to serve the remainder of his term until 1933. No matter what Seabury said about him, Crain was mollified by the fact that even while his record was being raked over the coals, Tammany still loved him. The party even reelected him as a "sachem," a term adopted from the Algonquin Indian word for chief that meant a leader of the Democratic party.

WHEN HE WAS in the final throes of finishing his report on Crain, Seabury would retire to his expansive estate in East Hampton on Long Island to go over the final draft. Over the years Seabury had been buying up property there, and in 1928 topped things off with the purchase of Hardscrabble Farm, a working dairy farm which pushed the sale of milk to make children happy and healthy. Seabury didn't have a hand in running the business, which was under the daily business judgment of the managers.

After mopping up the Crain affair, Seabury would have loved to spend as much time as he could at his estate, isolated as it was from the political drama going on in the great metropolis to the west. He and his spouse loved to entertain. But that was not to be. The Crain case which was given to Seabury was merely a warm-up for what was to come. Crain was just a small target, almost inconsequential except for what Seabury uncovered. The real target of reformers was Mayor James Walker and they wasted no time in letting that be known.

Starting with the deaths of Vivian Gordon and her daughter, as well as the atmosphere of the gangster culture of the city which—justified or not—permeated the homicide investigation, those fed up with the decades of City Hall's laissez-faire attitude sensed this was the time to strike. Vivian was not even buried when religious leaders like Rabbi Stephen Wise condemned the way crime had taken over the city, with nothing pushing back against it. Wise's pungent letters printed in the newspaper and seen by Roosevelt started a cascade of similar calls for action from all over.

In March of 1931, as Seabury was in the early stages of skewering Crain, over 3,000 people crowded in Carnegie Hall to hear speaker after speaker denounce Walker at a meeting called by the City Affairs Committee. Thousands more who couldn't get into the concert venue stood outside. Walker's routine of wisecracking and laughing at early criticism wasn't working anymore, particularly when the city was hit with unemployment as the Depression took hold.

It would be better, one speaker said, if Walker just went away to be "happy on the sunny California coast in the society of actors and actresses in which he is best adapted." Walker, whom one speaker called a "small little man," had just returned from a trip to California and his absence resonated at a time of rising unemployment and fiscal problems for the city.

The committee, which had numerous socialist supporters, had already sent a letter to Roosevelt to ask that the governor take action to yank down the "black flag of Tammany corruption." A couple of weeks earlier Vivian's murder and other crimes were very much on the mind of the Society for the Prevention of Crime when it sent a letter of its own complaints against Walker to individual members of the state legislature in Albany and asked for the appointment of yet another investigation into *citywide* corruption, with the express aim of removing Walker.

"During the last few weeks practically every issue of every metropolitan daily has contained revelations of the vice extortion scandal," the letter stated. "A few days ago a woman who had threatened to give information about her associates was murdered before she would testify. Another woman who was to be called as a witness was burned by acid by those whom she claims represented themselves as officers of the law."

As the reference to Vivian's death and other things made clear, it was not a good time to be a woman in such a corrupt environment and a good Christian society could no longer tolerate the corruption, said the committee. Any politician who stood in the way had signed their own death warrants.

Roosevelt would always maintain that he didn't want to meddle in the investigation of Vivian's killing and was just trying to stay informed when Seabury sent him a summary of the case. But the murder in Van Cortlandt Park was a catalyst, a match if you will, put to a long burning fuse for a bomb Walker sat atop.

It was on March 23, 1931, that both the state assembly and senate in Albany adopted a joint resolution calling for a wide investigation of city corruption. But politics were ever present now and Roosevelt, not wanting to appear like he was ceding responsibility to legislative bodies, said he would wait for a reply to the allegation against Walker, who at this point was posing with Indian chiefs and fake cowboy stickup artists in staged events.

While Tammany Hall was aghast at Roosevelt's action, newspaper editorial writers saw the governor's move as the right step to take. It was up to Walker after returning from playing cowboys and Indians out West to answer the charges. The charges did arrive in Palm Springs in time for Walker to give his daily media briefing, lounging in the desert sun in blue-and-black pajamas and drinking a glass of milk—obviously not from the dairy on Seabury's farm back in East Hampton. Walker had so many curious about the visit that for privacy during his sunbathing he had to go to a nearby hotel.

As he got up to go back indoors, it seemed that Walker forgot about the charging documents and so he went back to pick them up.

"I must put these away before they are changed; one might put something else in them," said Walker.

The next day, Walker was due to go back to New York on the New York Central Railroad's Century train, in the company of theater promoter A. C. Blumenthal and his wife. Both Walker and Blumenthal laughed when reporters asked if it was true the theater promoter had offered $250,000 a year to the mayor for life for a career in Hollywood.

Back in New York, a businessman in the town of Mountain Lakes, N.Y., about 50 miles from Manhattan, made what was termed a gratuitous offer to Walker, to be mayor of that hamlet for $1,000 a year. The one condition was that Walker had to be removed from his current post—so deep was public dissatisfaction running with Walker.

The toll taken on Tammany from all of the investigations and revelations after Vivian's death had been significant. Numerous magistrates—both men and women—were removed from the bench after the revelations about the corrupt vice cop operations and the way the courts were run as criminal enterprises of their own special breed. It was hard to believe some of the myths spread in the media but New York City wasn't living through a Jazz Age of merriment for all. The mob on Broadway had carved up the city with Prohibition, making millions of dollars that would bankroll rackets for decades. City Hall seemed incapable and unwilling to do anything about any of it and Mayor Walker was a man whistling past the graveyard of his own political career.

For readers of the New York City tabloids in the spring of 1931, the big question wasn't what was going to happen to Walker. It was which of the rich and powerful were listed in Vivian's diaries? The good reporters would be digging around for weeks to get the list of names. It was always good copy. There were indications that there were a lot of big names involved in one way or another with Vivian, so it didn't take long for the identities to start coming out.

Just over a month after Vivian died the *Daily News*, relying on tips from law enforcement, revealed that two Broadway producers and a group of millionaires admitted having meetings with her over the years. Some of the encounters were nothing more than casual, friendly meetings in fine hotels and financial offices. Others involved attempts at business ventures. The caliber of men involved showed that Vivian was capable of operating in a different league from the gangsters and hustlers she had colluded with in her sex racket.

William Thornburgh, head of a Chicago-based railroad equipment manufacturer, said he had been introduced to Vivian by a manager at the Hotel Biltmore in New York. That was after he was confronted by a reporter with the fact that his initials, "W. T.," had been found in Vivian's diary. Thornburgh said he chatted with Vivian for about twenty minutes; there was no discussion of money; they never met again.

Samuel C. Herriman was a millionaire patent lawyer in Manhattan and member of the prestigious University Club, who had a quixotic first meeting with Vivian while walking on Fifth Avenue. It was around dinnertime one night when Herriman saw Vivian walking quickly and being followed. Herriman then tried a bit of gallantry to get her out of an uncomfortable situation.

"As she came abreast of me I bowed and she said, 'Oh hello, is that you?'" recalled Herriman. "I asked her if that man was annoying her. She said: 'Yes, he was and I'm glad you spoke to me.'"

If Herriman was looking for a pickup line—which he said he wasn't—he had the right approach. Vivian gave him her phone number and about ten days later Herriman called her for lunch. Vivian's first choice was Ciro's in Manhattan. But after Herriman didn't like the location, Vivian took him to what he remembered being a "high-class speakeasy," a place where she was greeted by many of the customers. It was a glimpse that Herriman had of Vivian's other world.

The next day, Herriman said he sent Vivian a gift and a card which read "from Sam to Vivian." The actual gift was some Chicken Cock Rye, a popular booze once produced in Kentucky but later in Canada from where it was smuggled into the U.S. during Prohibition. The note was found by detectives in Vivian's apartment.

Broadway producer Murray Phillips, who was noted for his revival productions, met Vivian through his wife. It appears Vivian had been eager to back his Broadway production with a loan of $1,500, a deal that later triggered a lawsuit by Vivian to recoup the money. Another Broadway producer, William B. Friedlander, remembered having Vivian in one of his chorus lines in 1915. Friedlander was known as a songwriter and producer who first got his start on Broadway producing some vaudeville shows and went on to a lengthy career in the business. So far as Vivian was concerned, Friedlander wasn't impressed: "Vivian was no flaming beauty."

CHAPTER THIRTEEN

"GOD, I DON'T WANT TO BURN"

AFTER HARRY STEIN AND THE others were arrested and charged with Vivian Gordon's murder, the press put the case on the back burner and the headlines cooled off. In the meantime, until the trial was to begin in June 1931, some of Vivian's old associates in the underworld were seeing things lit up in a very uncomfortable way. Legs Diamond had always been living on the edge as if he had a target on his back and that didn't change.

The town of Cairo in upstate New York's Catskills barely a had fulltime population of 1,800 people in 1930. But being in the mountains, Cairo attracted a good summertime crowd. The hamlet also attracted Diamond, who had a home nearby in the town of Acra, something the state police kept a perpetual watch on seeing that he was known to move bootlegged liquor in the area. Diamond had also been watched in April 1931 because he was suspected of kidnapping and beating a local truckman to near death over a dispute concerning booze.

It was late the night of April 27 when Diamond and another man drove the three miles from Acra to the Aratoga Inn for a meal. For some reason, Diamond rose from a chair and went to the front of the restaurant, which he was supposed to have a business interest in. Suddenly, patrons in the restaurant heard a fusillade of shots, and when they investigated found Diamond on the floor hit by a number of shot-gun pellets in the back. A farmer who passed by outside bundled the wounded gangster in his car and drove pell-mell to a hospital in Al-bany some 30 to 40 miles away.

Diamond appeared to have been prepared for some trouble. Cops found a .25 caliber rifle in Diamond's car and he apparently was wea-ring a bullet-resistant piece of clothing which investigators think may have saved his life. Another tantalizing bit of information was that Diamond had been in a car accident some hours earlier after he started to speed upon seeing something that startled him, a friend re-ported. Diamond had been having a tempestuous affair with Broadway entertainer Kiki Roberts, but after he was shot at the restau-rant he had the presence of mind to tell his dinner companion to make sure that his wife, Alice Kenny Diamond, was looked after. Even a man with a mistress had some marital principles.

"Listen, Gerry," Diamond told his bodyguard John Scaccio. "If I go over the hill, you look out for Alice. They got me Gerry, they got me sure this time."

Well, the shooter did seriously injure Diamond, but it wasn't a sure thing. Diamond made it to the hospital in Albany in time to get treated and have visits from the state police. Diamond was being investigated not only for the torture of a truck driver but also for the suspicion that he had forged an alliance with the Purple Gang of Detroit to move bootlegged whiskey from Canada to New York. His home in Acra had also been raided by order of Governor Roosevelt in what some in gov-ernment believed was an effort to find evidence related to Vivian and her operations. It was a claim that Roosevelt would later deny.

Diamond's recovery and his various legal troubles were easy tab-loid fodder as the trial of Vivian's killers inched closer to starting. New York City never wanted for crime stories and for a while Vivian's case basically took a back seat to other sensational tales. The misfortune of yet another young woman with visions of easy cash and excitement to be found in New York showed how misery and death stalked all kinds of women on Broadway. Take the case of Virginia Brannen, a 23-year-old from Bangor, Maine, who had come to the city to, as one writer said, "live dangerously, as Vivian did."

Brannen had no special skills. She had come to the city and gotten a job as a ten-cents-a-dance girl, a dance hall entertainer who was sought not by the wealthy businessmen whom Vivian targeted but the average working Joes who, if they had spare change, could spend a dime a dance to spin around the floor with a pretty gal for a few minutes and enjoy some human contact. It was the low-end entertainment version of the hostess game being played in Manhattan hotels, posh restaurants and apartments off Fifth Avenue. Some estimated that there were 600 dance halls in the city where the racket was fairly simple. The establishments, some with elaborate displays, had between 50 to 2,000 women—some just girls—who would dance with customers. For $1.25, a customer would purchase a book of tickets which allowed ten dances. If you wanted more, you paid more.

The halls had some dimly lit intimate areas where the women could make arrangements with men to meet later for sex away from the premises. The cops knew of all this but had so many problems that they couldn't keep ahead of the game. In Brannen's case, she worked until about 3:00 A.M. the morning of April 27 at the Primrose Dance Hall at Eighth Avenue and 125th Street in Manhattan. She was then picked up by a group of friends in a car, who then made the rounds of various speakeasies in Manhattan and the Bronx. Brannen was a frequent habitué of those drinking spots and collected their business cards.

After hitting the late-night spots, Brannen and her group took a ride to Ossining, in Westchester County, and had more drinks, broke out some stolen blankets and indulged in what one of the women remembered as "petting." No swank hotels or restaurants for this crowd. Most of those in the car fell asleep as it was being driven by one of the men.

It was then, according to one of the women, that the slumbering folks were awakened by two gunshots. Brannen, with blood covering her dress, blurted out that she had been shot and asked to be taken to a doctor, suddenly slumping into the car's back seat. The car drove farther to an area near the St. Joseph's Catholic Seminary and eventually Brannen was tossed onto the seminary grounds. She was found dead later on the morning of April 27 by Yonkers police. Just hours earlier, Legs Diamond had escaped his shooting with his life.

The ditching of Brannen's body was, as the tabloids pointed out, starkly similar to Vivian's fate. Brannen was clad not in fine-store finery of the kind that clothed Vivian's broken body but what was labeled the "tawdry finery" of a ten-cents-a-dance girl who worked the "Broadway Rhumba rodeos." Vivian had no purse or identification when she was found. Brannen's clutch had some keys, cosmetics and cabaret cards. In terms of the police investigation, unlike in Vivian's case, things moved fast and spun quickly out of hand.

Detectives followed some leads about the revelers and discovered that a couple who had been in the car first wanted to confess to a Catholic priest about what happened the night Brannen was killed and then spoke to investigators. Their testimony implicated Rudolph "Fats" Duringer, the man who was necking with Brannen in the car, as the person who fired the gun. Cops later focused on a crazy sociopath known as Francis "Two Gun" Crowley who, once they cornered him on Long Island, got into a shootout with police, killing one officer named Frederick Hirsch. Crowley was unrepentant.

"Aw, I know I am going to burn, I want to get it over right away," Crowley said after cops arrested him for killing Hirsch.

Duringer was more contrite and during his June 1931 trial said that the shooting of Brannen was an accident and that he didn't want to die in the electric chair.

"God, I don't want to burn," Duringer said within earshot of many in the courtroom. "I'm a guy who likes a good time, Judge, plenty to eat and drink, dames and cabarets. I want to live, I am scared to death to die."

On June 4, 1931, the jury convicted Duringer in the killing of dime-a-dance girl Virginia Brannen and he was sent to the electric chair where he was executed on December 10, 1931. Duringer had a last meal of roast chicken, potatoes and ice cream but only ate a few mouthfuls. He gave the remainder of the meal to his old friend Crowley, who was waiting on death row with some other inmates scheduled for execution.

It took only five minutes for the electricity to kill the 200-pound Duringer. Crowley, who was to meet his fate the following month, liked the idea that his friend gave him his leftover meal.

"I am in a great spot; I got half the dinner," Crowley joked. With only a month more to live, Crowley had decidedly little in the way of expectations about what life would offer.

CHAPTER FOURTEEN

"SHE'S GOT ME BY THE BALLS"

THE TRIAL OF RUDOLPH DURINGER for the murder of Virginia Brannen was over by early June 1931, just in time to serve as a warm-up for the trial of Vivian's killer. In this era, trials could take place fairly quickly. There were no long delays in cases so after being entertained by Duringer's plight, New Yorkers could look forward to the fate of Harry Stein, the man who allegedly garroted Vivian and choked the life out of her.

If there were good lawyers representing an accused that was a plus. The public loved to hear and read stories of good, feisty defense attorneys and that is what they were promised when Stein's trial got underway with jury selection on June 12, 1931. Jury selection is a process that could be as exciting as watching paint dry. But with a seasoned defense attorney like Samuel Liebowitz involved, it was a good bet that the entire trial—from jury selection to verdict—would be worth it.

If Samuel Leibowitz had followed in his father's footsteps after the family immigrated from Romania in the late 19th century, he would have stayed with a pushcart and small shop on the Lower East Side. But Leibowitz's father and mother pushed him to get an education and he graduated from Cornell University and later its law school in 1915.

Leibowitz quickly made a name for himself and in so doing won a great many criminal trials. He became the go-to lawyer in New York in his day. It was estimated that by 1929 he had defended dozens of men and women accused of first-degree murder and not one of his clients was sent to the electric chair. Leibowitz even got to represent Al Capone.

A key to Leibowitz's good track record seemed to be that he didn't take a case where he thought the client was guilty and had no defense. As his son Robert Leibowitz would write in *The Defender*, his biography of his father, the older Leibowitz passed up representing Lucky Luciano, who was convicted in a prostitution case, but took up the successful defense of Albert Anastasia when he was prosecuted for murder.

Jury selection in the trial of Stein and his co-defendant, Samuel Greenhauer, also known as Greenberg, for the first-degree murder of Vivian Gordon finished on June 17, 1931, after a five-day selection process which went through nearly 160 potential jurors. The panel of 12 finally selected were all men and included some who were unemployed or worked in jobs ranging from piano tuner and meter reader to electrical engineer and salesman. The jury foreman selected was Daniel Lister, who listed his occupation as that of transportation agent.

Leibowitz made his mark as an aggressive defense attorney who took any chance he could to knock prosecutors off stride. For Stein, Leibowitz asked that the trial be transferred out of the Bronx because of all the pretrial publicity that had been generated by Vivian's murder. He also asked that Stein be tried separately from co-defendant Greenberg. In each request Leibowitz was shot down by the court.

It was June 11 that the trial of Stein and Greenberg got underway in the Bronx before Judge Albert Cohn, the father of Roy Cohn, who later became a controversial and flamboyant attorney and political figure. True to his style, Leibowitz got the under the skin of Bronx district attorney McLaughlin by telling the prosecutor in open court, "I want you to behave yourself during the trial." With that, McLaughlin seemed to be become apoplectic, reminding Leibowitz that he was in a Bronx courtroom, and not in Brooklyn anymore.

After his earlier flare-up with Leibowitz, chief prosecutor McLaughlin was reported to have become ill and passed the actual trial of the case to his chief assistant, Israel J. P. Adlerman. In his opening remarks,

Adlerman admitted to jurors that the case hinged to a large degree on Schlitten's testimony, particularly a statement that Stein had said "it was necessary to put Vivian out of the way a keep a friend from going to jail."

The problem with the Stein case was that because an accomplice was testifying against him, prosecutors needed to corroborate with additional evidence whatever the accomplice—in this case Schlitten—said. The evidence could be more testimony, eyewitness accounts, scientific or physical evidence, but it still had to be admissible at the trial. The accomplice testimony rule was settled in New York courts and when its standard wasn't met, cases were sometimes dismissed. Such would be the case years later against Vito Genovese when he was accused of murdering Ferdinand Boccia.

Leibowitz's response was that the case was one manufactured by the police and was an attempt to "railroad thee two men at the behest of the lawmen." Schlitten had been given immunity from prosecution and another witness, David Butterman, had problems of his own.

Leibowitz left some tantalizing elements out for the public during his opening statements. First, he claimed that indeed it was Noel Scaffa, the noted jewel theft investigator, who was the liaison between the police and the old fence Butterman. He then suggested that Judge Crater had been at Vivian's apartment at some point, not mentioning the judge by name but just describing him as a man wearing a dress shirt with a high collar and being over six feet three inches tall.

The opening testimony was essentially about the crime scene. Photos were shown of Vivian's body in the bushes. A store manager from I. Miller & Sons shoe store testified about the two lady's shoes found at the scene as being part of a pair and recalled Vivian wearing a fur coat and watch when he saw her the day before she died. Harry Francis, the truckman who found Vivian, and Emanuel Kamma, the stable tenant from Van Cortlandt Park, also testified about finding Vivian's body. The medical examiner, Dr. Louis Lefkowitz, testified that Vivian's time of death was at least six hours before he arrived at the scene and admitted that it was hard for him to fix the exact time. Lefkowitz noted that Vivian had a bruise on her head and said the cause of death was asphyxiation due to strangulation.

These opening rounds of testimony were essentially to get the basics of Vivian's death out of the way and on the record. There weren't any surprises, apart from the fact that the medical examiner conceded that Vivian could have died up to 48 hours before he arrived. The one provocative piece of testimony came when Leibowitz cross-examined Det. Patrick Walsh and through the questions raised the specter that Schlitten had been beaten during his confession. It was as if Leibowitz had seen too many gangster movies.

"Was he beaten in your presence or in the presence of anyone else?" Leibowitz asked the cop.

"Nobody ever laid a hand on him," insisted Walsh.

"Was there a piece of rubber hose there?"

"There is no piece of rubber hose in that office or any other office of the police department."

"If you had given Schlitten a beating or tortured him with the live ends of cigarettes, would you be man enough to come here and admit it?"

Walsh answered by saying that he would be man enough, yes. While Leibowitz never raised the idea of torture through other witnesses, including Schlitten, the mere planting of the idea in the minds of the jurors could be enough to have them at least think about the possibility.

It was June 22 when Harry Schlitten took the witness stand as the main prosecution witness. His appearance was to be the benchmark for the prosecution, the superstructure upon which the story of Vivian's murder was to be built. When he took the witness stand, Schlitten spoke for the most part with his head lowered, as if in shame. His voice sounded very streetwise; one witness described it as guttural sounding. One courtroom observer said Schlitten had a hulking torso, shaggy eyebrows and a button nose that gave him an apelike appearance.

In recounting events, Schlitten seemed to need little prompting from the prosecutors and described how he met Stein a few days before the killing at a Manhattan restaurant and was told that he, Stein, needed a car to take a certain party for a ride or "a good friend of mine will go to jail." Schlitten said he agreed to get the car and drive it for $1,000 and the next day went with his friend Izzy Lewis to get the vehicle.

After reconnoitering Van Cortlandt Park as the scene for dumping the body, Schlitten said that the day of the murder he drove to the Bronx and waited with Greenberg for Stein to arrive with the woman. Schlitten said he and Greenberg saw Stein approach with Vivian at about five or ten minutes before midnight, at which point Greenberg said, "That's the party that is supposed to go."

Once all four were in the car, Schlitten testified, he heard part of the conversation from the back seat. Vivian was asked if she wanted a drink and said to Greenberg, "Where have you been all my life?" As the car drove north, the witness said he heard a scuffle and Greenberg yelled out, "She's got me by the balls."

"Then I heard this awful gasping sound for breath—a screech, like a cackle," recalled Schlitten.

Stein was then heard to say, "She is finished now."

Once inside Van Cortlandt Park, Schlitten said, Stein and Greenberg got out, picked Vivian out of the car and dumped her by the side of the road. Just before driving away, Stein noticed one of Vivian's shoes still in the vehicle and he tossed it out the window. Driving away from the Bronx, Schlitten said that Stein noticed there was $2.16 in Vivian's pocketbook and took the cash and some keys before throwing the pocketbook out.

Once back in Manhattan, Stein stopped by the Upper West Side apartment of a lady friend and went inside the building with Vivian's fur coat. Stein also showed Schlitten a diamond ring. The next few days, according to Schlitten, the activity was aimed at getting the fur coat out of storage, because its description had been reported so often in the news that someone might recognize it. The coat was never found and according to Schlitten might have been disposed of by burning in an apartment building incinerator.

Schlitten said he did get some of the money he was promised, about $329, which he said included a payment of $150 from Radeloff, Vivian's old attorney-boyfriend, who was allegedly the man being protected by Vivian's murder.

Leibowitz's trademark legal tactic was his skilled cross-examination of witnesses and he began working over Schlitten by having him admit to his fringe gangster activities. It turned out that the witness had been something of a labor goon, offering protection to millinery shops from union organizers. Labor racketeering was deeply entrenched in many aspects of the New York garment industry and Schlitten said his name alone evoked just the right amount of fear and respect in some circles. He said that he got $50 a month for offering his protection services.

Schlitten said he ran card games and associated with Chinese opium dens. He also admitted running a small protection racket for a drinking room in Harlem. Schlitten insisted he had no criminal record, despite his questionable activities. The main tactic Leibowitz decided to use to discredit the witness was over his self-interest in testifying with immunity from prosecution for his part in the crime. By showing Schlitten was trying to save his own skin, Leibowitz hoped to defuse the impact of his testimony, which to onlookers seemed substantial, about Vivian's murder.

It was during a point in the testimony about Izzy Lewis that Leibowitz suddenly shifted gears and went directly at Schlitten with a pointed question.

"Would you lie to save your life?" Leibowitz asked.

"I would not," answered Schlitten.

Leibowitz then asked the witness about his immunity deal with the prosecution, and if anyone else aside from the district attorney's office had made him any promises for testifying.

"No sir," said Schlitten.

"Were you ready and willing to tell this story whether you got immunity or not? Weren't you?" Leibowitz asked.

"I was," said Schlitten.

Leibowitz asked if immunity didn't interest him and the witness said it did because it would save him from the electric chair. In Schlitten's mind, he didn't feel badly about the fact that Stein and Greenberg might face capital punishment because they had tried to pin the crime on him.

Schlitten finally said his conscience bothered him, a statement that led to more hard questioning by Leibowitz.

"That is why you made the confession?" asked Leibowitz.

"That's right," said Schlitten.

"It didn't bother you when you made the plan to go out to murder?"

"I didn't realize the horror of it."

"You went to murder for money, didn't you?"

"Yes."

"Was it your conscience that made you confess?"

"That is right."

"Or was it saving your own neck?"

"Partly," Schlitten answered.

Leibowitz's cross-examination succeeded in showing Schlitten to be an opportunist and sowing some confusion about why he decided to cooperate. Schlitten appeared not to be the most sympathetic witness. But it was when Leibowitz asked the witness about the "cackle" heard when Vivian died that Schlitten appeared to help the prosecution's case. Schlitten was reluctant to give such a demonstration but was pressed by Leibowitz. Finally, the witness made what seemed like a "rasping, gurgling sound" that the prosecution seemed very satisfied with.

The summations in the trial of Harry Stein and Samuel Greenberg took place the evening of June 29, 1931, and turned out to be as explosive as any seen in the Bronx in many years. Leibowitz had been a master of cross-examination in the case but it was prosecutor Adlerman who stunned the courtroom by alleging that the real person behind the killing of Vivian Gordon was her old attorney, confidant and lover, John A. Radeloff.

The basis for Adlerman's claim was in the testimony of Harry Schlitten, who said that when he pointed to a picture in the newspapers of Radeloff after Vivian's death, he was told by Stein, "That is the party we done it for—Radeloff." It was enough for Adlerman to turn and attack Leibowitz for not calling the attorney as a witness—presumably to refute Schlitten's testimony.

"If I were John A. Radeloff, I would tear down the doors of this courthouse in my eagerness to get here and take the witness stand to deny the testimony linking me to the case," Adlerman told the jury. "Why wasn't John A. Radeloff produced by the lawyer who has an office in the same building with him?"

With that Leibowitz jumped to his feet and objected to Adlerman's comment. But that didn't stop the prosecutor from continuing that attack over the missing witness in the case and to broadly tie Vivian's death to the wider scandal rocking the city.

"Was she about to make a complaint to someone about this lawyer?" Adlerman said. "Was she about to complain to the bar association or some other authoritative body? Vivian Gordon risked and lost her life because she was about to talk, and the gangster code was put into action. Stein took her life, and he took her life for the man who directed and inspired this horrible murder—John A. Radeloff, the lawyer."

"The death of Vivian Gordon is not the sole issue here," Adlerman continued. "There is a greater issue—that a witness about to give information was killed, and the killing of that witness is a challenge to our American institutions, to law and order. Marking a person for death, and taking that person for a ride, especially in New York, is a terrible situation for a civilized community."

Adlerman also attacked Leibowitz for a concocted defense and berated him for not producing investigator Noel Scaffa to back the defense claim that he had made up the whole story to dump on the lap of police commissioner Mulrooney.

Stein, said Adlerman, was as "guilty as a dog."

Although little noted in the news coverage, Greenberg's alibi was that he was at home the night Vivian was killed, sitting shiva for his mother. Greenberg's claim was labeled by the prosecution as "preposterous and ridiculous."

Leibowitz and his co-defense counsel had their say during summation and advanced the defense theory that it was Schlitten and Izzy Lewis, who hired the "death car," who were the sole killers. Schlitten testified because he was afraid of the cops and to frame Stein to save his own life, argued Leibowitz.

"There is something repugnant about the snitcher, even to honest men," Leibowitz said. "In the underworld the squealer is known as a rat—that little disgusting creature, the rat."

"Schlitten is a thief, a crook, a gorilla, a racketeer, a dope peddler, a lying coward," Leibowitz said in his excoriation of the prosecution's big witness. The entire case was "brewed" in the prosecutor's office.

At one point Leibowitz turned to his clients Stein and Greenberg and addressed them in front of the jury in stark terms, saying "Stein and Greenberg, they want to strap you in the chair and burn you, to satisfy public clamor, that is what they want to do."

Leibowitz again raised the specter that Schlitten was beaten by cops to get a confession out of him, wondering what had happened to him during the 12 or so hours he was in police custody when he made his statement. Although there wasn't any evidence in the case that Schlitten had been beaten by cops, Leibowitz made the most of the police brutality issue by raising suspicion that he had been. The deal Schlitten made was to give the cops Stein in exchange for his own life, argued Leibowitz.

The kind of name-calling seen in the closing arguments on both sides wouldn't be allowed in today's courtroom. But in 1931, the standards were different, and this was a hard-fought case. It was for the most part a circumstantial case and both sides posited different theories about what happened the night Vivian died.

As any good defense lawyer would have done, Leibowitz raised the specter of reasonable doubt for the jurors. If even only one juror bought into that, the case would result in a mistrial.

"The defendants," Leibowitz told the jury, "are presumed by law to be innocent. They don't have to prove anything. They don't have to take the stand. There is no confession here, although Stein and Greenberg were grilled for hours. The burden is on the district attorney to prove this case."

IT TOOK JUDGE Cohn less than two hours to charge the jury in the case. It took just about three and a half hours more for the jury to come back on June 30 with the stunning verdict of acquittal on the charges for both Stein and Greenberg. It didn't appear at all that the jury even seriously considered convicting the men. There were three ballots taken: the first was 10 to 2 for acquittal, the next 11 to 1 for acquittal and the last was unanimous for acquittal. The defense, with all its oration, theatrics, name-calling and raising the specter of reasonable doubt carried the day.

Stein broke into a broad grin with the acquittal. Greenberg was effusive, walking up to the jurors to thank them and kissing some of them outside the courtroom as he repeatedly said, "Thank you, thank you."

Leibowitz was beside himself with delight, saying the case had been from the beginning a "contemptible frame-up."

"I said it would fall flat as a pancake—and it has. A case tailor-made by the police department will never hold water before a jury of twelve sensible men," said Leibowitz.

Prosecutor Adlerman was seething with anger and left the courtroom immediately. He would later rail against the jury and for a short period considered if Radeloff could ever be brought to justice. The quick answer was no, Radeloff would escape any indictment. He would have had to confess and that Radeloff wasn't going to do.

"The jury which freed these two men, by its ridiculous and outrageous verdict frustrated any and all plans for his prosecution," Adlerman said of Radeloff. Had there been a conviction, the defendants could have offered to become government witnesses in any prosecution of Radeloff in exchange for taking the death penalty off the table. But with an acquittal nothing like that was going to happen.

Of Stein, Adlerman asked Judge Cohn to "let the jury know what kind of man this fellow Stein is... He's got a record as long as your arm." Cohn answered that the jury verdict was final, before he discharged the panel.

While the prosecution thought it had a strong case, clearly Schlitten wasn't a very convincing witness. Since the witness had been granted immunity, he could not be prosecuted. The case of Vivian Gordon's murder is officially carried to this day as unsolved.

Police Commissioner Mulrooney was also stunned and angered by the acquittal. His case, which he thought had been carefully constructed with interconnected circumstantial evidence, had simply failed to hold up under the concept of reasonable doubt.

But while Stein was cleared of the murder charge and spared the electric chair, his troubles did not end with the acquittal. As soon as the verdict was announced, Judge Cohn asked if either Stein or Greenberg had any additional charges. Yes, he was told, Stein was under indictment for a 1930 robbery and chloroforming of a woman in Manhattan. The charges alleged Stein took two rings from the woman, valued at about $1,200. With no lawyer to represent him in the robbery, Stein was immediately returned to jail, unable to make $50,000 bail. It would not be the end of his problems, not by a long shot.

CHAPTER FIFTEEN

"ПО! ПО! ПО!"

THE PROSECUTION'S STUNNING LOSS IN the Vivian Gordon murder case brought no end of criticism about the jury verdict. The case, as far as the police and prosecution was concerned, seemed to be strong. The testimony of Harry Schlitten seemed to be convincing. But as any seasoned attorney on either side of the coin will tell you, you can simply never tell with a jury. A case that seemed so solid from the law enforcement perspective hardly convinced any of the jurors. In fact, only two of the panel were initially convinced that there was enough evidence to convict beyond a reasonable doubt.

But Vivian Gordon was murdered and dumped like trash in Van Cortlandt Park. The question remains as to which person or persons were responsible and why. As this narrative has explained over the last 14 chapters, the theories about the motive stretched from robbery, to Vivian's plan to cooperate with the Seabury investigation, to her threats to disclose her old lover and attorney John Radeloff's criminal activity. In between were all of Vivian's incidents of bad blood with other women and men who crossed her in life, including former spouse John Bischoff and gangster Legs Diamond.

With the trial record in the case and available historical records the main theories about the motive for Vivian's killing can be examined.

With hindsight and some new historical materials from the National Archives, each of the theories can be looked at and for the most part eliminated—except for the theory that Radeloff was the prime mover.

The most talked-about theories included about motive for the murder: 1) Vivian's decision to cooperate with the Seabury investigation and implicate her former spouse Bischoff and vice cop Andrew McLaughlin in a plot to frame her on a prostitution charge; 2) Vivian's anger with old boyfriend Joseph Radlow over his attempt to have her arrested for extortion; 3) Vivian's awareness of criminal activity by Legs Diamond in stock swindles and extortion; 4) robbery of Vivian's jewelry and fur; 5) Vivian's threat to tell authorities about criminal activity by Radeloff, Stein and others involving a gem theft and their activity in the Oslo bank caper.

THE SEABURY INVESTIGATION: By late 1930 and early 1931, it was well known and widely publicized that Samuel Seabury was uncovering significant corruption within the NYPD vice squad. Vivian Gordon was well aware of the probe and saw the time as being ripe to give investigators information about the way she believed she was framed by police officer Andrew McLaughlin, who had already been revealed as a dirty cop. The added element for Vivian's case was that she believed McLaughlin and her former spouse, John Bischoff, had schemed together to get her arrested so that she would lose custody of her daughter, Benita.

The theory, one bandied about in the press, was that Vivian was killed before she could give significant evidence to Seabury. A closer look shows how implausible the idea was. Bischoff had filed a divorce action in Philadelphia in 1922, months before Vivian's arrest, and there was no evidence that he schemed with McLaughlin, much less even met him, to frame Vivian so that she would lose custody of Benita. McLaughlin was out of the country on a Caribbean cruise when Vivian was killed, and Bischoff provided police and prosecutors with enough evidence of his divorce action that he was dismissed as a person of interest.

The better view is that Vivian pushed the idea of the two men framing her as a convenient conspiracy theory stemming from the psychological trauma of losing custody of Benita. Vivian may have been right in the idea that she was framed but her allegations would have been icing on the cake in an investigation that had already focused on McLaughlin. Besides, there is no evidence that Seabury's staff leaked her name as a potential witness.

ANGER OF JOSEPH RADLOW: Vivian and Radlow had been lovers for a while, but their relationship had soured. Radlow had gone as far as to sue Vivian but the matter was dismissed in the courts. Could Radlow have been angry enough to want to harm Vivian? Possibly. But he was a man beleaguered by family troubles and a sick child. With distractions and concerns like that it is unlikely that Radlow could have pulled off a murder or had the nerve to plan such an act.

Radlow had numerous legal problems of a criminal nature involving stock swindles and Vivian was the least of his problems. To get out from under his stock swindling, Radlow began cooperating with the federal government. Additional records held by the National Archives show that Radlow and four others were indicted in 1929 on federal charges stemming from stock fraud involving shares of the Ford Motor Company's foreign subsidiaries and other entities. Records showed that Radlow gave "considerable assistance to the government" in the investigation of the case and had been given a promise by a federal prosecutor that he wouldn't be prosecuted, a promise that had to be kept. It is very doubtful then that Radlow, having escaped federal prison exposure, would put himself in more legal jeopardy by plotting to kill Vivian.

VIVIAN'S AWARENESS OF LEGS DIAMOND'S CRIMES: Vivian and Legs Diamond operated together for a time in the sex extortion racket until late 1930, when their relationship came to an end in a dispute over money. It is likely that Vivian knew of Diamond's other criminal interests but as a streetwise criminal she knew that any suggestion she was cooperating with cops could cause Diamond to strike first. By early 1931, Diamond was on law enforcement's radar and surveillance for a number of crimes in upstate New York and was the target of an assassination attempt which almost took his life in April 1931. Unless Diamond believed that Vivian posed some kind of threat to him, it is unlikely he would even think of bothering to kill her.

ROBBERY MOTIVE: Police and prosecutors initially advanced the theory that Vivian was a victim of a robbery, mainly because her valuable fur coat and jewelry were taken from her body. The theory received some credence after detectives determined from sources that some of the jewels were fenced. However, anyone who knew Vivian had jewelry also knew where she lived and could have robbed her at her Manhattan apartment, instead of taking her for a ride in a car and risking discovery if things went wrong for a few thousand dollars. Years earlier, two other Broadway Butterfly women who had amassed collections of jewels from their male friends—Dot King and Louise Lawson—were robbed and killed in their apartments. Like King and Lawson, Vivian made no secret of her jewelry holdings.

Attorney Radeloff raised the theory that Vivian could also have been killed by one of the taxicab drivers she used to bring her drunk rich men. Radeloff claimed in one news article that he heard Vivian argue with a driver who claimed to have been owed money, although she didn't seem worried. But if anyone was owed money by Vivian it made no sense to kill her because the money would never be collected.

THREAT TO DISCLOSE RADELOFF'S CRIMINAL ACTIVITIES: After all was said and done, this looks like the most likely motive for the killing. The idea that Vivian was killed because she was going to implicate her former lover and attorney John Radeloff in criminal activity came up in the Stein and Greenberg trial. Harry Schlitten testified that after he saw a picture of Radeloff in the newspapers, Stein told him Vivian was abducted and killed to keep the attorney from going to jail. The idea that the murder was done to protect Radeloff also came up in the prosecution summation in the case.

Vivian had caused problems for the married Radeloff when she disclosed to his wife that she had a relationship with her husband. Vivian would later apologize to Radeloff's wife, who suspected him, correctly as it turned out, of fooling around with other women. The big problem for Vivian and Radeloff was that they mixed business and pleasure. In Vivian's diary, additional details of which came out after the Stein trial, a number of entries detailed her business dealings with Radeloff as well as her awareness of some of his questionable and criminal activities with Sam "Chowderhead" Cohen.

The diary showed that, as Vivian's attorney, Radeloff picked up rents due on the Queens properties she owned but that he converted the money for his own use for a drinking binge. Vivian wrote in her diary that she suspected the money was misappropriated when the superintendent at the buildings told her Radeloff had already collected the rents. About a week after Vivian learned that Radeloff had used up the rent money she demanded payment and according to her diary got $50. "When I insisted on putting the screws to him he gave one of his usual threats—he and that Bill D. and his gang were out together they [were] plotting something phony," one diary entry stated. The "threat" wasn't explained.

If Radeloff had misused the rent money, as an attorney he would be subject to at the very least discipline, if Vivian wanted to press the matter as an ethical breach with the bar association. At the worst, she would have complained to prosecutors, although she seemed content to keep pressing him for repayment and according to her diary continued to lend him money. The rent theft, then, didn't seem to be a serious legal problem for Radeloff.

But one diary entry indicated that Vivian knew about something more serious. On February 4, 1931, just three weeks before she died, Vivian noted in the diary: "I believe that John A. Radeloff and Sam Cohen pulled that jewelry deal alone." The diary gave no further explanation of the jewelry deal but since it allegedly involved Cohen, a known felon, it was likely illegitimate.

More of Vivian's diary entries later disclosed asserted that it was Radeloff who negotiated a $1,500 loan to Stein to fund the mysterious trip to Oslo in July 1930. Stein would later claim that the trip was for bootlegging purposes, although Norway was not a major source country for booze during Prohibition—France and England were. New York police would later disclose that a police official from Norway did visit New York to confirm the presence of Stein in Norway for what was reported to be a million-dollar haul from the overseas bank. The financing for the trip, which police said was actually for a bank robbery, is mentioned at a number of points in Vivian's diary from 1929 to 1930 and implicates Radeloff in handling the loan to Stein (also known by the moniker H. Saunders). Vivian said in her diary that the loan was for Stein and two others for "passage to Oslo, Norway" to "clean up a bank there."

Vivian had hoped that the money would be cabled back from Oslo to her account. But according to her diary the money never came and Radeloff seemed particularly hard-pressed for cash, as were the trio in Oslo. The growing mistrust Vivian had for Radeloff was also apparent, and in a diary entry where she said she would have nothing to do with his efforts to revive their friendship—"No! No! No! I have had enough of him."

If Radeloff was involved in the financing of the Oslo trip, be it a bootlegging venture or a bank robbery or fraud, he would have been implicated in a crime, something Vivian was aware of and could tie him to since she was the source of the money. As it turned out, there was another crime involved in the Oslo trip and it involved a federal offense as well.

As uncovered by federal investigators, Stein, Morris Levine and Samuel Greenberg conspired beginning in May 1929 to submit false passport applications for the travel to Oslo. According to records in the files of the National Archives, Levine submitted an application for a passport using a fake name, Stein used a fake name when he filed a statement saying that he knew Levine for six years and Greenberg also used a fake name in applying for his passport. All three were indicted on federal charges in June 1932, and within a year pleaded guilty and received two-year prison sentences. Stein, as it turned out, was already serving a 25-year state prison term after being convicted following the Vivian Gordon murder trial in 1931 for the robbery of a different Manhattan woman.

Radeloff wasn't indicted in the passport case. But had he been connected by a witness—such as Vivian—to the Oslo caper he might have been implicated as someone who facilitated the passport offense as well. So Radeloff faced possible criminal exposure on a number of fronts and Vivian could have proved to be a witness against him. It seems clear that Stein was referring to Radeloff when he allegedly told witness Harry Schlitten that Vivian had to be killed to save the attorney from going to prison. Radeloff had criminal exposure on more than one front and Vivian could have been an important witness against him.

ABOUT TWO WEEKS after the acquittals, the Bronx grand jury that had heard the case and issued the original indictments formally ended its work. In doing so, the panel issued a document to Judge Cohn in which the grand jurors said the acquittal of Stein and Greenberg was a "great shock to the community and more so to us."

Bronx district attorney Charles McLaughlin, who had so much invested in the case, couldn't hold back his contempt for the jury. In a magazine article, McLaughlin said that "the verdict in this case is one of the rankest miscarriages of justice I have ever known. Verdicts like that—brought in by ignorant juries, juries that have been intimidated or juries that are easily fooled—are responsible for gang conditions in America today."

As far as NYPD commissioner Mulrooney was concerned, the acquittal in the Stein trial was a travesty of justice, something that would haunt him for the remainder of his days on the job. The Patrolmen's Benevolent Association had offered a $15,000 reward for the capture of Vivian's killer, and to salve the wounded pride of the department, Mulrooney had the money divided up among cops who worked the case.

PART THREE

CHAPTER SIXTEEN

"A WORLD GONE MAD"

T HE VIVIAN GORDON MURDER TRIAL was one of several big cases hitting the streets of New York in the spring and summer of 1931. Mob violence in particular was putting blood on the streets, including that of innocent child victims. Less than a month after the Stein-Greenberg verdict, five-year-old Michael Vengelli was gunned down and killed as he and some young friends frolicked on East 107th Street in Manhattan, victims of stray bullets fired by warring mobsters, including the notorious Vincent "Mad Dog" Coll. The death of little Michael and the wounding of his four friends so soon after Vivian's killing prompted the Patrolmen's Benevolent Association to post another reward, this time for $10,000, to find the child's killers. Coll and others were later arrested in upstate New York for the crimes, which were blamed as being part of a feud between Coll and Bronx beer baron Dutch Schultz. Coll and an associate would later be cleared of the killing after a key police witness was found to have been a liar.

Mobsters like Legs Diamond and Schultz were widely reported to be among the various gangsters living on borrowed time as the underworld became more unstable. The predictions about those two turned out to be remarkably prescient. In December 1931 Diamond was on trial in Albany, N.Y., on a kidnapping charge. Diamond was acquitted and that night after partying went to visit with his mistress Kiki Roberts, said to have the best legs in town. Diamond then went back to the rooming house where he was staying and was attacked by two gunmen who shot him in the head. Diamond's lucky streak ended on the night of December 18, 1931. Schultz was suspected of being behind the Diamond killing and was himself murdered in a Newark, New Jersey restaurant in 1935.

Numerous other gangsters were gunned down during 1931 on Manhattan streets. But the big incidents seemed to be related to the Italian gangs. While little known to the general public, the nascent Italian Mafia was going through a major bloodletting that began with the assassination of the old boss Joseph Masseria at a Coney Island fish restaurant on April 14, 1931, a murder that would lead in a matter of months to the rise of Lucky Luciano and his associates as the main, more powerful mob figures in town. Salvatore Maranzano, the Italian mob boss who tried to take over after Masseria's demise, was himself assassinated in his Park Avenue office in a preemptive strike arranged by Luciano, Costello and others in September of that year.

While she wasn't a Broadway Butterfly like Vivian Gordon, pretty socialite and Manhattan party girl Starr Faithfull was found dead on the sands of a beach in the Long Island city of Long Beach in June 1931. Her death, be it murder or suicide, filled the tabloids, which were no longer pursuing Vivian's case, for weeks that summer. Wherever the public turned, there was violent crime and it seemed more out of control. With an increase of 16 percent over the prior year, 1931 would end up with 489 homicides, more than half by gunfire. Some 16 cops were also killed in gunfights with criminals, and in one wild episode a cop killer named Francis "Two Gun" Crowley held 250 cops at bay in Manhattan until he finally surrendered for the killing of Long Island cop Frederick Hirsch.

Things were so bad, particularly for Walker, that the mayor initially decided to skip marching in the annual police parade but relented and did attend at the last minute, noted Thomas Reppetto in his *NYPD: A City and Its Police*, co-authored with James Lardner. He did the march in top hat and tails and, according to the gushing tabloid coverage, had a grand time.

Underscoring the sense of lawlessness that had characterized the city was the claim by the Wickersham Commission, the federal body studying the impact of Prohibition, that politicians and their underworld associates controlled the NYPD, causing a loss of public confidence in law and order. It seemed to be another smack at Tammany Hall and its coziness with the gangster element and came at a time when there was more justification to look at Mayor Walker, a creature of Tammany.

During the 1931 police parade, an annual event, Walker was initially met with a smattering of boos as he walked at the head of some 6,000 cops up Broadway and Fifth Avenue. But soon Walker heard cheers and instead of leaving the march as he had originally planned after a few short blocks, he was emboldened to continue for the entire route over five miles to a reviewing stand at Central Park At that point in time in his mayoral career, Walker needed to hear as many cheers as he could muster.

AGAINST SUCH A backdrop of violence in the city, Walker faced continuing challenges. Seabury's investigation of the magistrates' courts had succeeded in showing how deep the rot of corruption was in New York. The results not only impacted the police department, which saw a wholesale revamping of the vice squad, but also resulted in the removal of two magistrates: Jesse Silbermann and Jean Norris, the latter a woman. Norris in particular was cited for what the Seabury investigation found was her "severity, her unjudicial conduct and her callous disregard of the rights of defendants in the Women's Court." Silbermann was found to have been improperly influenced by political considerations in masking decisions on cases.

Shortly after Vivian's murder, in the face of the public clamor from the likes of Rabbi Stephen Wise and groups like the City Affairs Committee, Governor Roosevelt and the state legislature saw that they couldn't duck the responsibility any longer about paying attention to conditions in New York City. By late March 1931, with Vivian not even dead a month, the state assembly and senate passed a joint resolution providing for a joint legislative investigation of Mayor Walker and his administration. At this point Walker was having a vacation in Palm

Springs, joking around with fake cowboy holdup men and meeting with Native American chiefs, as well as fighting off a sunburn.

Samuel Seabury, who already had a full plate with the magistrates' courts investigation and the probe of Manhattan district attorney Crain, was to be the counsel who took charge of the legislative investigation. By approving the investigation, the legislature forced Roosevelt's hand. The governor had been seen as taking a more passive approach about Walker and his administration but now the train had left the station and Roosevelt had to go along with the program, no matter what his political calculation about the 1932 presidential race. Roosevelt had refused in April 1931 to take any action when Wise and others filed their charges against a vacationing Walker. But now they saw renewed hope with the legislative investigation.

"What Gov. Roosevelt has not found in our charges, Judge Samuel Seabury will," Wise and Rev. John Haynes Holmes said in a joint statement. "An indictment here so lightly dismissed will return to plague not merely the mayor, and his administration, but the governor and his decision."

Seabury didn't take long to get to work. His first move was to subpoena the records of a city agency known as the Office of the Commissioner of Accounts, the investigative arm of city government comparable to today's Department of Investigation. The aim was to give Seabury a sense of how serious Walker and the commissioner had been in probing charges of corruption and graft in city agencies. While investigations were done over the years, they weren't made public and sometimes were only made as verbal reports to Walker—all rather slipshod and secretive for such an important job.

Stories about the Office of the Commissioner of Accounts were not big headline grabbers for Seabury. But tales about broads and booze— or "dance hall" girls and sex—were sure to get attention. So it was in late July 1931 when a stuffy, puritanical group known as the Committee of Fourteen, which had been baying for years about sex and sin in New York City, came out with a report about dance hall vice and how police, because of the Seabury revelations about corruption in the vice squad, were afraid to make prostitution arrests. Arrests on vice charges had dropped to the lowest number in 24 years, at a time when the sex trade was one of the only ways men and women could find work in the Depression.

"The mushrooming growth of speakeasies and nightclubs, where gangdom congregates and prostitution is commercialized," was evidence of the increase in vice, the group said in its report. "The dance hall vice, which formally was limited to the old Tenderloin [in Manhattan] now flourishes in Broadway, Harlem and Brooklyn and is probably the greatest menace of all."

Dance hall sex trade was hardly a new scandal and the dives were known to attract a criminal element. It was a cut or two below the kind of trade Vivian Gordon had been plying with her more exclusive party girls and sex shakedowns. But the wrinkle now was that the Committee of Fourteen said a former city magistrate had an interest in the business. So Seabury had to dig into the claim to find out the extent of the scandal.

To make matters worse, the purveyor of women was a female "white-slaver" who operated a fake employment agency to provide dancers—a term used loosely—to the sex operations. Had Vivian lived she probably would have been cited by the committee as such an operator. But, according to Debby Applegate in *Madam*, the group had trailed Vivian's old cohort Polly Adler for years, making trouble for her and gaining her unwanted notoriety, but could never vanquish her. The committee said the sex businesses had the protection of city inspectors, undercover cops and even lady detectives. Prostitution was viewed as a victimless crime and New York was living up to its old reputation as place where any sexual appetite could be satisfied.

As a sign of the times, some newspaper editorial writers thought that the Committee of Fourteen had overplayed its hand. The organization was an offshoot of the old Anti-Saloon League and to some critics seemed to be trying to justify its existence by hyping the prevalence of commercial vice in New York.

"We think it's open to question whether the Committee of Fourteen can keep you from promiscuity if your family, friends, pastor and other ordinary restraints can't," said the *Daily News* in one editorial. As it turned out, the report on dance halls was the last hurrah for the committee, which wouldn't last another year.

Still, the cops and Seabury started looking at dance hall conditions—they almost had to after the report came out. Seabury assigned a couple of his assistants, notably Irving Ben Cooper, to see how many of the establishments were situated near schools. The investigation also focused on the allegation that the former magistrate was involved, and looked at a list of about 100 dance halls that had been on a special list of places with violations that had not been remedied by city officials.

As it turned out NYPD commissioner Mulrooney took the lead, setting up new regulations and registration requirements to keep gangsters out of the dance halls as hidden owners. Mulrooney also told an assemblage of dance hall owners that while it might have been popular to have gangsters in the clubs as part of the scenery, to attract clientele, that was no longer going to be allowed. Also barred were private booths where women could mingle with customers in privacy.

But sexual activity seemed to be of far lesser concern to the public than the continuing violence in the streets. The death of Vivian Gordon in February had galvanized outspoken public figures like Rabbi Wise and his associates to speak out against Walker and the atmosphere of lawlessness. While their initial efforts to oust the mayor failed, the issue had taken hold and City Hall, with Seabury breathing down its neck, was more and more on the defensive. In August, at a mass meeting at Madison Square Garden, 20,000 reform-minded citizens shouted their disapproval as they were told that public officials had put the city in the hands of racketeers who in recent days wounded or killed a dozen bystanders, including children, and shot dead two police officers.

Public officials of all stripes attended the rally, including Commissioner Mulrooney, although Walker didn't show up. Seabury sent a letter in which he said that gangsters flourished because of a "corrupt alliance with those who exercise political power." Meanwhile, Mulrooney, in a stunning admission of police impotence, said Prohibition had made "tyrants out of the police while the public makes heroes out of the bootleggers." The laws of Prohibition had allowed bootleggers and gangsters to accumulate enough cash to pay off the national debt, so it was time to change the laws, argued Mulrooney.

Sure, gangsters were into crime because it made them money by giving the public what it wanted, notably booze and drugs. But as the Seabury investigation continued through the summer of 1931, it became apparent that many of those making money through crime were in city government. A sheriff in New York City, a patronage plum if there ever was one, was supposed to carry out certain laws, execute eviction orders and enforce judgments. Actually, the job was shown to be a form of banditry. If a sheriff couldn't be a bootlegger, just having the office was enough to give him a nest egg far beyond his legal remuneration. Such was the case of Sheriff Thomas M. Farley.

A Tammany leader in Manhattan, Farley was a big Irishman with a full head of black hair and a fleshy face indicating he went a bit too heavy on butter and mayonnaise. He was questioned at a public hearing by Seabury about a large amount of cash he had in some boxes. It seems that Farley had accumulated over $360,000 in just over six years, a period in which his public salary ranged from $6,500 to $15,000 a year, which even at the highest level would only have totaled about $100,000. The money, Farley said, was kept in two boxes, one a large tin box in a safe in his home and another a bank safe-deposit box. Farley said the money represented all that he had saved from his years as a union business agent and his salary as an alderman, a city official. Whenever he had to pay bills, Farley said he dipped into one of the two boxes, took out the cash and used the money to write checks.

Clearly, Farley was lying about the source of his money. He was making what were large deposits over the years, including over $93,000 in 1929. Farley's obstinacy over his refusal to sign a waiver of immunity actually was reported to have forced Seabury to raise the issue of his unexplained cash deposits and storage boxes. Seabury originally just wanted to question Farley about a gambling raid at his political club, during which the sheriff tried to interfere with the police.

What was particularly memorable about the exchange between Seabury and Farley was the way the sheriff characterized the boxes where he kept his cash.

"Sheriff, where did you keep these monies that you had saved?" Seabury asked.

"In a big box, in a big safe," answered Farley.

"Sheriff, and was this big box that was safely kept in the big safe, a tin box or a wooden box?" queried Seabury.

"A tin box," said Farley.

"Kind of a magic box, wasn't it, Sheriff," replied Seabury.

Said Farley: "It was a wonderful box."

The exchange, which was gobbled up by the newspapers, earned Farley the moniker "Tin-Box Farley."

But in Albany, Roosevelt was not amused about what he had learned. Farley may have been known in his neighborhood for having an annual May party in Central Park for his constituents and children where he gave out 15,000 baseball bats, 15,000 balls and 5,000 jump ropes. But clearly he was crooked. After months of consideration, Roosevelt, on Seabury's recommendation, removed Farley in February 1932 from his job as sheriff. In doing so, Roosevelt said that whenever it appeared that a public official was living beyond his means or had unexplained bank deposits he had to give an explanation or else face removal. This was a new standard and an ominous sign for any other public official, including Walker.

Farley and his tin box were the big news but not the only cases of city officials being caught in possession of large amounts of cash. Working in public service seemed to be a way on the road to riches if you had the right political connections. Vivian Gordon may have died nearly penniless but a government job could make you wealthy during the Depression when so many were scratching around for something to eat.

James J. McCormick, as first deputy city clerk, somebody whose duty was to perform civil marriage ceremonies, pulled in over $385,000 in six years of work. The marriage fees were $2 at the time but it turned out that Seabury learned that McCormick had a habit of keeping a desk drawer open in his office. Bridegrooms, spotting money in the drawer, would add a bit to the pile of cash as a tip, with encouragement from McCormick.

Over in Brooklyn, James A. McQuade was a county register for Kings County and bragged about the library he had in his political club. But as Seabury discovered, the club didn't have a library at all but served as a gambling den. Tammany politicians were using clubs for gambling, obviously reaping some of the profits from what the local gangsters pulled in. Cops may have had gambling clubs like those of McQuade and big political bosses like Jimmy Hines in Manhattan under surveillance, but it seemed that City Hill kept the police in check. Out of some 514 people arrested in political clubs from 1926 to 1927, only two were convicted and even they got suspended sentences.

Such paltry enforcement of gambling laws in the Tammany club-houses appears to have been by design at the highest levels of the NYPD. Former commissioner Whalen may have talked a good fight about going after speakeasies and Prohibition, but that was low-hanging fruit. Seabury's investigation determined that over the years when he led the NYPD, Whalen abolished the special "confidential unit" which, under the command of Inspector Valentine, had done a creditable job of going after gambling at the political clubs. Whalen transferred everybody to outlying commands, sort of the modern-day equivalent of sending a cop who has angered top brass to Staten Island or some other post remote from their homes. Valentine was demoted to the rank of captain and, with one of his assistants, assigned to a job that essentially restricted him to patrolling a cemetery.

Whalen's message to his commanders was clear: stay away from the political clubs. This created what Seabury said was a "vicious relationship" between gamblers and political district leaders. With the right political connections, the gangsters could act with impunity.

Gambling could amass a good deal of money for the political leaders. McQuade accumulated a pile of $520,000 in his bank accounts in six years when his salary amounted to only a total of $50,000. Asked how he got such a fortune, McQuade said he had a big family for which he was the only breadwinner and had to borrow to support so many hungry mouths, some 34 in all. When asked by Seabury who loaned him the cash, McQuade said he couldn't remember and gave some long-winded explanation about how he borrowed from Peter to pay Paul, so to speak. It was confusing and nonsensical. Newspaper reporters tracked down some of McQuade's 34 relatives and found most of them had city jobs and were prospering.

It seemed that some city officials had access to a printing press, given the amount of cash Seabury discovered passing through their bank accounts. While Farley and McQuade banked hundreds of thousands of dollars, they were outdone by Under-Sheriff Peter J. Curran, a Farley deputy, whose bank account saw deposits of over $662,000 in some six and half years. Curran told Seabury that he got some of the money from his various businesses, including a funeral home and livery stable, but couldn't be specific. Curran also said that he had been in the habit of cashing checks for people he knew and that his practice of taking money out to cash the check and then replacing it accounted for the large sum going through his account.

"So we have got that account straight, haven't we?" Seabury said with a touch of sarcasm.

IN THE MONTHS after Vivian Gordon was strangled and dumped in the park, her death and the resulting public outcry set off a political brush-fire, which by the end of 1931 had burned Tammany Hall and many of its allies and had grown to a full conflagration threatening to engulf City Hall and its main occupant—Mayor James Walker. By December, Samuel Seabury's big investigation of New York City government had gone on for six solid months and had taken testimony from over 2,000 persons in private and 125 more in public sessions that often proved embarrassing to those on the stand. Millions of words had been transcribed and by the time the end of the year rolled around the evidence amassed showed that George Washington Plunkitt's idea of "honest graft" being an on-the-job benefit for those in government was still business as usual. For that reason, investigators had subpoenaed over 3,500 bank books and other records.

By the summer of 1931 there had been intimations that Walker himself had secret accounts. So Seabury indicated that he wanted to take a look at the mayor's finances. Knowing that Seabury wanted to look at his affairs, Walker did what he often did when things got uncomfortable—he took a vacation, this time to Europe.

In early August, Walker hopped on the liner *Bremen* and sailed to Southampton on the way to a final destination at the city of Bremen in Germany. But as usual, Walker couldn't resist talking to reporters, who had gone out in a rowboat to shout out questions to him as he stood on the vessel's promenade deck.

"I am not afraid of any investigation into my private affairs," Walker said in response to news that Seabury had asked for his financial records. "I have nothing to be ashamed of and nothing to hide.

"Tell them I have wired my attorneys to show the Seabury committee my bank books or anything else," Walker added. He again said he had nothing to worry about.

Walker was committed to having a good time on the trip, Seabury be damned. When he landed in Germany the reporters said he had a special railway saloon car set aside for his trip to Berlin, courtesy of the railway authority. He also had to keep up his sartorial splendor on the trip, as one British journalist noted.

"Jimmy was dressing in his suite aboard the *Bremen*. A valet handed him a double-breasted sky-blue waistcoat and pleated jacket of the same hue," the correspondent wrote. "Mr. Walker adjusted the belt on his gray check trousers, fastened the laces on his black-and-white kid shoes, donned the waistcoat and jacket and hunched his shoulders as a final touch."

"I have had enough of City Hall," said Walker. "When my term is up so am I."

CHAPTER SEVENTEEN

"I LOVE BEER"

For MAYOR JIMMY WALKER THE trip to Europe was turning into a wonderful distraction from all of the growing problems looming back home in New York City. The Seabury investigation might have made it seem like he was some sort of gangster but the Germans, the French, they loved him. In Berlin the newspaper headlines featured his picture and the words "Hello Jimmy." In the French city of Cannes, Walker's vivid blue suit ensemble caused a pleasant stir and when he went to visit a soldier's memorial and deposited a wreath, the French greeted him with "Hip, Hip, Hurrah Jimmy."

With his reputation for being an opponent of Prohibition, a deputy mayor in Cannes proposed a champagne toast for Walker, saying, "With French champagne, I toast the greatest wet in America." To which Walker agreed and put the glass to his lips.

In Hungary, Walker took another shot at Prohibition when he was asked what his greatest experience was in Europe. That was easy for Walker: "I love beer and hate Prohibition, which exists only on paper. Its evil result is only that we get bad, unhealthy alcohol in America."

Everywhere he went in Europe, Walker was greeted with pomp, adulation and good cheer. If he was tardy in Vienna, the Viennese loved him. In Carlsbad, Czechoslovakia, he got a greeting that was bigger than that given British royalty. Things were going so well that he decided to extend his trip and didn't plan to be back in New York until the fall.

Back in New York, Seabury was in no hurry to have Walker come back from his trip for any questioning. Instead, the investigator was in a frustrating search for one Russell T. Sherwood, who had once worked with Walker at their old law firm. Sherwood had been the bookkeeper and accountant at the firm and had acted as Walker's agent in financial matters. But Sherwood had been trying to make a concerted effort not to be seen. He was absent from New York and was followed to Mexico City in October, where he was on his honeymoon, where he refused to accept service of a subpoena from Seabury's staffers, even in the face of a $100,000 fine.

Sherwood was a potentially critical witness for Seabury because other witnesses said that he and Walker shared a "tin box" in the vault of a safe-deposit company on Broadway, an allusion to the tin box Farley had testified about. The box was a relatively small one and was rented not quite a year before Walker was first elected mayor in 1925, with both Sherwood and Walker listed as holding the title. But Sherwood was proving to be stubborn and Seabury finally got a court order to hit him with a $50,000 fine, of which bits and pieces were collected through court proceedings. In the end, Sherwood never cooperated with Seabury.

By January 1932, Seabury issued yet another report dealing with the wider investigation he had conducted on city corruption and waste. Walker wasn't targeted in the report but Tammany Hall was painted as the entity that controlled widespread graft and corruption in the city and in the process had tried to thwart Seabury's investigation. Critics had also tried to pin the city's dismal financial condition on Seabury's investigation but he said the sole blame lay with the waste, graft and corruption which infested the city. It seemed that everyone, from a lowly police commander to connected lawyers, had their hands out.

What about Mayor Walker? The safe-deposit box Sherwood shared with the mayor was raising questions, as was a secret brokerage account Sherwood had opened for Walker which by August 1931 had seen deposits of $1 million, with over $750,000 in cash. With Sherwood essentially a fugitive and refusing to testify or cooperate, the next best witness would have to be Walker himself. By early March 1932, just a year after the death of Vivian Gordon, it was announced that Walker would be called to testify in public around May about his financial dealings, despite the fact that Sherwood proved to be missing in action and not cooperating.

With the hearings closing in on him, Walker had time for a diversion close to his heart. He accepted the chairmanship of the Beer for Taxation parade, which took place on May 14. It aimed to be a serious demonstration for the legalization of beer during Prohibition, something that Walker believed could bring $500 million in tax revenues into the U.S. Treasury. After all, Walker had said during his recent trip to Europe that he loved beer. In fact, he liked his drink so much that it was reported that he had what was called a "hangover room" in the depths of City Hall, reachable by a private circular staircase and where there was a bed. Walker promoted the event but some churches adopted a resolution condemning it and applauding the exposure of graft and corruption made by Seabury. Clearly, Walker's diversions weren't playing with the public like they used to. He could always drown his sorrows in some speakeasy.

As the spring of 1932 came, Walker showed that he was aggravated by the Seabury inquiries, which he knew were edging closer to him and his friends. In particular he took aim at the magistrates' courts' finding about vice squad graft and turned it into an argument that the investigation had made the city streets unsafe for New Yorkers, particularly school-age girls and boys. Speaking at one event, Walker said that the investigation had so shattered the morale of cops that they didn't want to make vice arrests because they feared being accused of framing innocent victims.

"The morale of the department was broken," said Walker. "Those who were promoting vice in the city have the slogan 'The cop has not got the nerve to arrest you, and if he does we shall charge that he has framed another innocent woman.'" As Walker spoke, police commissioner Mulrooney nodded in agreement.

But leaks from the Seabury probe showed that the ties between Walker and questionable financial transactions were greater than initially thought. There were reports of $1 million in stock deals done by the missing business agent Russell T. Sherwood. Seabury also had evidence that a taxicab financier named J. A. Sisto had given Walker a gift of over $26,000 in bonds a short time before the mayor backed a measure for closer supervision of the taxicab industry. Even Walker's various trips to Europe and California, going back five years, were being examined by Seabury, and reports in the press suggested the financial dealings might result in charges of malfeasance against the mayor.

Could Walker have been such a fool to have been tainted by the flow of money? It seems that he could have been. In his lengthy history of modern New York, Donald L. Miller said that Walker liked money but was terrible at managing it, leaving big bills and uncashed checks in clothing sent to the cleaners. He was cavalier about finances and it seemed to be reflected in a devil-may-care attitude about money and where it came from. "Money to him is entirely unimportant, a commodity made to be spent and utterly useless in the bank," one commentator wrote. Walker seemed constantly broke but always had friends who were eager to "lend him more money than he could possibly use."

Like previous mayors, Walker had to provide his own housing and got no reimbursement from the city for living expenses or accommodations. At one point Walker mentioned to a friend that he needed over $25,000 to renovate his apartment, an amount equal to his yearly salary. The rich friend, Jules Mastbaum, told Walker to have the work done and send him the bills. It wouldn't be the last time Walker got the benefit of a friend's largesse. It may have seemed all right to Walker to live that way, off the benefit of friends, but he would soon find out that it raised the perception that he could be bought and was an easy mark for corruption.

CHAPTER EIGHTEEN

"I AM STILL THE MAYOR OF NEW YORK"

I N OLD NEW YORK, DUELS both personal and political could be settled in an open field with firearms. On May 25, 1932, the biggest duel in decades was about to unfold in the courtroom of the New York State Supreme Court at 60 Centre Street. The combatants would be Mayor James Walker and the man who had emerged as his greatest nemesis, Samuel Seabury, special counsel to the Hofstadter Committee, the joint legislative body empowered to look into city corruption. The battle was a long time coming, two years exactly since the first investigations started into the magistrates' courts. The death of Vivian Gordon impelled more demands that something be done about the corrupt and lawless state of the city and on this day the big showdown was to take place.

Anyone who picked up the *New York Times* this particular day and read the editorial entitled "Not Even Standing Room" would easily sense what was at stake. It was going to be more than just a personality clash between Walker and his "flashy and brilliant personality," as the *Times* said. The nation was watching to see what "Governor Roosevelt will do when a transcript of the evidence is laid before him by Judge Seabury," the newspaper said. It seemed clear that Seabury wanted to force Walker out of government. But it would be Roosevelt who would ultimately have to make that decision. Walker was expected to use his wits and sharp tongue in sparring with Seabury's questioning. But what everyone, including the limited number allowed in the courtroom and the wider public devouring the news coverage, wanted to know was if Walker had satisfactory answers to the questions that went to the core of his competence and character.

It was the committee chairman Senator Samuel Hofstadter who a day earlier had notified Walker by subpoena that he was required to attend the hearing and to bring certain documents and other evidence regarding his business dealings, including those handled by the mysterious Russell T. Sherwood, a man whose business affairs, as one reporter said, "were so entangled with the mayor that it sometimes was hard to tell where the interests of one left off and the other's began." Just as serious were details about a city bus contract, including questions why one of the men seeking to get the bus contract got Walker a $10,000 letter of credit for use on his trip to Europe in 1927. Walker was also going to be questioned about other gifts, including over $26,000 in bonds given by stockbroker J. A. Sisto.

Days earlier, Walker had once again blasted the Seabury inquiry as a political hit job. But the time for that kind of posturing and political rhetoric was over. As he rode a limousine over to the courthouse, Walker was decked out in a double-breasted suit, with blue accessories color-coordinated down to his tie and socks. When dressed, Walker is reported to have turned to his valet and said, "Little Boy Blue is about to blow his horn—or his top."

The courtroom on Centre Street only had room for about 300 people. But more crammed in, about 700, for the spectacle and sometimes stood five deep. Those allowed to enter had special invitations and a special cadre of cops made sure only the anointed could enter. The room was hot—this was late May and the courthouse had no air-conditioning—and those inside included friends of the mayor, their spouses, labor leaders, civic group heads and many more.

"The scene all about the courthouse at the hour the hearing started resembled a mass shot from the movies," was how the *Times* captured the scene. "The little room was so crowded that the participants stood two deep in one foot of space back of the jury box. They were up on the window ledges and sitting on the floor. They stood everywhere, even on each other. The doorway was so jammed that no one could move in and no one wanted to move out." The scene was like a sporting event and the news coverage promised to be that way as well. Newsboys barked out headlines of special additions like MAYOR WALKER WINS FIRST ROUND. Ice cream vendors and sellers of pineapple drink and peanuts were having a field day, giving the scene the feel of a country fair.

When Walker arrived at about 10:45 A.M., the crowd of about 5,000 outside the courthouse pushed forward to greet him, taking the phalanx of cops on the stairs with them in the surge of humanity. Walker was greeted with "Atta boy," "Good luck, Jimmy" and "You tell 'im, Jimmy." Walker was the overwhelming favorite of the crowd. Going through the revolving doors, Walker put out his left arm in a boxing gesture and grinned. Inside the courthouse, another crowd of about 1,200 who couldn't get a seat in the hearing room gave Walker more cheers. Inside the courtroom, when Walker entered he was greeted with more cheers that went on for so long that it was hard to hear Hofstadter's gavel as he tried to call for order. Seabury had actually entered the courthouse before Walker and was greeted by a smattering of boos. But in the main, Seabury got cheers which drowned out the catcalls. Seabury was, one writer said, "dignity personified."

But the press coverage approached the hearing as if it were a battle of gladiators, and not a search for evidence of the truth. The *Daily News* said the hearing resembled a battle between an airplane (Walker) and a tank (Seabury) staged in the "glamorous excitement of [a] gladiatorial arena." Walker was portrayed as firing back at Seabury from the air with "repartee and wit" and soaring away before Seabury could come back at him. Approaching such serious hearings as a sporting event runs the risk of trivializing the substance, which is something that had to be expected given Walker's popularity on the street. But it was clear that Seabury was making a case. The question was how badly damaged Walker would be in the end.

On the first day of the hearing, under questioning by Seabury, Walker had to address a number of financial transactions and gifts. One thorny subject was the so-called Equitable Bus Company deal to provide a bus franchise for the city. The problem was that Equitable actually had no buses, although a rival bidder known as Service Bus Company had vehicles. Equitable also didn't offer the city any security payment while Service Bus handed over a check for $100,000. However, Walker testified that he approved and signed the Equitable franchise. Seabury then pointed out that the day the bus deal was approved a promoter of the Equitable franchise presented Walker with a $10,000 letter of credit just before he left for a European trip, with another $3,000 made good by the company.

The timing of the letter of credit so close to the Equitable deal sounded fishy to Seabury. Walker could sense that and pointedly wagged his finger and asked Seabury if he was accusing him of taking a bribe. After the crowd erupted in applause and hisses, Seabury finally said, "The facts, in my judgment, are extremely suspicious."

Walker and Seabury had a number of tense exchanges over the Equitable deal. At one point Walker shouted out, "Remember, I am still the mayor of New York City."

"I recognize that. You are also a witness here," responded Seabury.

"That's correct. Thanks to you!" was Walker's retort.

As the day progressed, Walker showed more and more irritation. His sniping got very personal, making it a point that unlike city residents Seabury lived in an affluent area of East Hampton on Long Island. When Seabury admonished him about making speeches, Walker had a reply about his own speeches that got approval from the crowd in the courtroom.

"Well, they're not so bad," said Walker. "Did you ever listen to any of them? I heard your Cincinnati speech, and it wasn't so good."

"I don't doubt your speeches, Excellency," said Seabury. "I only doubt the pertinency to my questions."

The letter of credit related to the Equitable deal was the smallest financial deal of interest to the committee. Walker acknowledged that wealthy newspaper publisher Paul Block gave him over $246,000 between 1927 and 1929, the shares of profits from a brokerage account which at one point had Walker's name on it, only to have it later removed to conceal the paper trail.

Block would later reveal that the reason why he was so generous with Walker was that Block's ten-year-old son, Billy, was curious as to how the mayor could live on a salary of $25,000 a year. Block said he told his son that the mayor somehow managed but that it was difficult. It was then, Block told Seabury, that he resolved to make a little money for Walker and set up the account.

The profits for a five-month period alone in 1927 amounted to $102,500 for Walker and Seabury asked him to account for what he did with the money. Walker essentially said such a question was really none of Seabury's business, unless there was evidence he tried to use the cash to pay off public officials. It was a reply from the mayor that brought laughter and boisterous approval from the crowd.

"That's telling them, Jimmy," said one in the crowd.

Pressed by Seabury, Walker said that the money from the stock account was kept in cash in a safe in his apartment—not a "tin box," said the mayor to laughter, in reference to the Sheriff Farley testimony about the "wonderful" box. The cash was spent by both Walker and his wife, he said.

At times Walker took a sip from a glass of water by the witness chair and, alluding to his fondness for beer and booze, winked at the audience and said, "I better not drink too much of this, it might become as habit."

The hearings picked up the next day, August 26, and dealt with the momentous issue of the joint account set up by Russell T. Sherwood, the missing witness and former employee of the law firm where Walker once worked. The Sherwood brokerage accounts had accumulated a total of nearly $1 million over a five-year period, a sum that would amount to about $17.5 million under today's dollar value. Walker said he had no idea where Sherwood was but admitted sharing a safe-deposit box with him as a way of safeguarding some legal papers when he had to leave the old law firm in 1926 after being elected mayor.

"I know nothing about his personal affairs, his personal accounts or his personal operations," Walker said of Sherwood. When it was pointed out that Sherwood withdrew nearly half a million dollars in cash from the account, Walker quipped, "I hope they can prove it is mine and I will try and collect it."

It didn't seem through the mayor's testimony that Seabury had connected Walker definitively to the Sherwood account. This prompted

Walker to voice his strong suspicion that the entire hearing was just an attempt to torpedo his political career.

"It looks as somebody is seeking my political life," Walker said at one point, adding, "Is this an inquiry or a political inquest?"

Indeed, there were some observers of the political spectacle who didn't think the stock transactions for his benefit were anything terrible. No, said writer E. B. White in a *New Yorker* piece, the real issue was a problem with Walker's style of dress and the impact on his brain.

"We have always believed the one completely incriminating thing about Jimmy Walker was his necktie: the knot is too tight. No blood can get up to his head; or, if it gets there it can't get down again," wrote White.

The second day of the hearings ended as a mixed bag for Seabury. Walker stood his ground on a number of issues and when he left the witness stand had sustained applause and shouts of support for about three minutes. As Walker left the courthouse, more of the crowd pressed in on him and a dozen women showered him with roses. As he descended the courthouse steps, Walker greeted each of the women. It was a clear sign that Walker still had public support for what was turning into the political battle of a lifetime.

But while the tabloid headlines showed that Walker appeared to have won the day with his Tammany supporters and the public, the *New York Times* had a more critical view. In an editorial titled "His Own Worst Enemy," the *Times* said Walker was playing the victim but in so doing was tacitly admitting that the same thing that got Sheriff Farley thrown out of office might work against him as well. The sober public saw that the mayor of the nation's biggest city had been "so extremely careless about taking money from people having business with the city, and so strangely irregular about keeping large sums of cash in his safe at home.

"There may have been no technical crime in this. It may not be sufficient to warrant Mayor Walker's removal from office," the *Times* concluded. "But it was morally and politically a high crime and misdemeanor for a public servant in whom the city had so strikingly reposed its confidence thus to abuse the proprieties and disregard the decencies of official life."

If the position of the *Times* bothered Walker he didn't show it. The day his testimony ended, the mayor appeared before a new class of police department recruits who were graduating from the Police College—the forerunner of the modern Police Academy—and found an audience that loved him. Some 18,000 people filled the old Madison Square Garden and shook the place with applause, particularly after he repeated the line he had used with Seabury: "I am still the mayor of New York."

Walker also made a not so veiled reference to the political jealousy he believed was behind everything that was happening to him. The event was a love fest between Walker and the cops, at a time when both were feeling under siege. Mulrooney had been shown up by the stunning loss and failure to win a conviction in the murder of Vivian Gordon. As if a reminder of the vice fiasco was needed, at the time Walker was appearing before Seabury two vice cops, including Officer McLaughlin—the officer Vivian Gordon accused of arresting her under false pretenses, allegations that exploded into scandal with her murder—went on trial for perjury. Walker repeated his complaint that the entire vice squad scandal, another case engineered by Seabury, had broken down police morale. In a sense, the police and Walker needed each other in the face of great uncertainty about what lay ahead.

After the hearings finished and Walker returned to City Hall to go about whatever business he felt he needed to carry out, it was up to Seabury to decide what he would do next with the mass of transcripts and evidence he had compiled. Overhanging everything was the fact that Roosevelt was vying for the Democratic Party nomination for the presidency. Roosevelt had already compiled a big number of delegates but didn't have enough yet to beat his only real competition, Alfred Smith, also from New York.

In terms of what to do about Walker, a waiting game ensued. "For reasons of his own, Seabury sat back and let the case against Walker simmer for several days after the hearing ended," observed historian Herbert Mitgang. "He thought Governor Roosevelt should make the first move, Roosevelt thought Seabury as counsel to the legislative committee should do it."

By June 15, the transcripts of the Seabury hearings were sent to Roosevelt through two lawyers he appointed as his agents to receive the materials. Seabury was again playing things close to the vest. He wouldn't even say publicly if he recommended that Walker be removed at this point. But Seabury's feelings became known when earlier in the month he sent a letter to Roosevelt saying he thought Walker was unfit to remain in office.

Seabury described the familiar financial dealings such as those surrounding the Equitable Bus franchise and the gift to Walker from Mr. Sisto, who was doing business with the city and had a financial interest in the outcomes. Seabury also said Walker took improper gratuities from people and companies doing business with the city. Walker also did nothing to uncover the whereabouts of the mysterious financial agent Russell T. Sherwood, thus preventing a disclosure of important facts about the way the mayor conducted his business, Seabury charged. In one act that strongly smacked of corruption, Walker allowed the city attorney to pick the doctors in city compensation cases, who then split their fees with the mayor's brother.

Walker was playing fast and loose in the way he ran the city, even refusing to bring financial records to the hearings when subpoenaed to do so. The bottom line for Seabury was that Walker acted as mayor with such "malfeasance and nonfeasance" that it amounted to conduct unbecoming a person who was in charge of the city. He had to be removed from the office, Seabury concluded.

Roosevelt got the letter from Seabury, as well as the evidence, and promptly decided to do nothing; he needed time. He had good reason not to act to quickly. Vying for the presidential nomination, Roosevelt was walking a fine political line. The more conservative elements of the party would have loved to see Walker, the symbol of big-city corruption and crime, canned and dumped on the scrap heap. But Tammany still had some clout in New York and started lobbying against Roosevelt, putting forward Smith as an alternative.

But as it turned out, some of the new Mafia in New York, which had influence with Tammany, broke away and supported Roosevelt. It was a story that became part of Mafia lore as a testament to Frank Costello's power. At the Democratic National Convention, Costello was among a group of New Yorkers who in late June 1932 prowled the halls of the Drake Hotel to work for Roosevelt's nomination. It was a way of hedging a political bet, no matter who won the nomination.

"Here in Chicago what did it turn out to be?" wrote Costello's attorney George Wolf years later. "Guys running up and down hotel corridors day and night trading votes and offering jobs and threatening political revenge just like old Tammany Hall."

In the end, on the fourth ballot at the convention, Roosevelt won the nomination to run for president. Smith placed a distant second. John Nance Garner, Speaker of the House of Representatives, was picked as Roosevelt's running mate.

Throughout the 1932 presidential campaign, Roosevelt's arrival was often signaled at campaign stops by the song "Happy Days Are Here Again." But it wouldn't turn out to be good times for Mayor James Walker.

CHAPTER NINETEEN

"JIM, YOU ARE THROUGH"

T HE ONE THING THAT WAS perfectly clear about Mayor James Walker during the entire controversy over his personal finances and questionable dealings with friends who did business with the city was that—no matter what editorial writers and his critics might say—he could still have a crowd in his corner.

On August 11, 1932, Governor Franklin D. Roosevelt commenced his own hearing into the allegations of misconduct and summoned Walker to Albany. Roosevelt called the hearing to determine if he should fire Walker for the various financial transgressions—some 15 in all—that Seabury had found. The mayor's arrival in the state capital was reminiscent of the way he had arrived at the Manhattan courthouse nearly three months earlier. Wherever he went, Walker created a spectacle.

Arriving a day early by a special train from Grand Central Terminal with his wife, Janet, and a small entourage of lawyers and officials, Walker was greeted by a brass band and the boom of fireworks. When he arrived at his hotel, a throng of 500 jammed the street and cheered him.

"He stepped from his car, mounted the steps where all could see him, and indicated by the gesture of a clenched fist, shaken at an imaginary adversary, that he expected to make the proceedings a fight to the finish," was how the *New York Times* reported on Walker's arrival. "Then he clasped both hands together, in the manner of a prizefighter shaking hands with himself in acknowledgment of the plaudits."

Walker appeared before Roosevelt in the governor's office, where both men were seated across from each other at a flat-topped desk. At this stage in his life Roosevelt was feeling the full crippling impact of polio, and when he entered the room for the hearing, "[a]s he moved through the dead silence, the creak of his leg braces could be distinctly heard," Herbert Mitgang observed years later.

Roosevelt, arguably the most important Democrat in the country, was about to decide the fate of the one man who had him beat as a popular celebrity. Roosevelt would handle some of the questioning but a great deal of the interrogation would be led by the governor's special counsel Martin Conboy, who had what was described as a "rapid and none too gentle" form of questioning. But unlike the raucous atmosphere that had been part of the Seabury hearings in Manhattan, things in the executive chamber offices were sedate. State police officers were stationed in the room and the only cheering occurred outside.

Roosevelt appeared to have a calm, patient demeanor as he questioned Walker. At times the mayor fidgeted in his chair as Roosevelt and Conboy queried him about two very contentious deals: the Equitable Bus contract and the large gift of a $246,000 account set up by Paul Block. Walker insisted that while he didn't put up any money for the Block account, he had potential tax liability all the same, although when pressed he admitted that it was Block who paid the income tax on the profits.

Yes, while Block had an interest in a company with tiles to sell for the city subways, he got nothing for his generosity, Walker insisted, adding that as far as the account was concerned "there wasn't a dollar of taxpayers' money in it."

Roosevelt hit on something that seemed to him odd. Walker had taken $104,000 from the Block account before any profits had been realized. Walker said he had taken the money unwittingly. Roosevelt finally observed that Walker got something before he really was entitled to get it under the arrangements of the joint account.

The Equitable deal remained problematic as well for Roosevelt. It seemed that one of Walker's close political friends, Senator John A. Hastings, had a secret interest in the company, something Walker claimed he didn't know about until later. But when Roosevelt pointed out that Hastings said he had kept his relationship with the company secret at the request of the mayor, Walker said he couldn't recall having that conversation, which under the circumstances sounded like a suspicious evasion.

The first hearings before Roosevelt took two days and on Friday, Walker and his entourage headed back to New York City by train. Roosevelt had gone through about half of the issues that formed the basis of Seabury's charges but had some important ones, namely the account set up by the still-missing Russell T. Sherwood, to deal with the following week.

When Walker's train made its way back to Manhattan from Albany, he was greeted once again as if he were a conquering hero. A crowd of 5,000 packed Grand Central and a band struck up stanzas of "Hail, Hail, the Gang's All Here." Two young women sprinkled rose petals and one elderly woman eluded a cordon of cops, rushed up to Walker and grabbed him as she planted three kisses on him.

How did Walker think he did? In a short statement he said, "I feel so far, that I have met every challenge and I propose to meet every challenge on my official conduct."

It had been a grueling week in Albany and Walker, whose health despite all his bravado was not very good, had one thing on his mind for the weekend—sleep.

"I am going right to bed. I'm going into a sleeping contest with the world, I want to relax," he said before getting into a limousine for a trip to Larchmont in Westchester County. There, Walker would stay at the estate of his friend, real estate executive and wealthy theatrical businessman A. C. Blumenthal.

By the time the weekend was over, Walker would have needed the rest. When he returned to Albany on August 16 for more questioning by Roosevelt, things seemed to be going the wrong way for the mayor. The top item on the agenda was the infamous Russell T. Sherwood account, the one started by Walker's old law-firm colleague. Seabury had found through a check of bank and other records that at one time the account had about $1 million.

Walker stuck to the story he had told Seabury: that Sherwood simply handled routine matters for him at the law firm and was never his confidential agent. Sherwood was little more than an errand boy, said Walker.

Roosevelt cautioned Walker that if any money in the Sherwood account belonged to the mayor, he had to explain the source of it. If not, then Walker might suffer the same fate as old Sheriff Farley, who Roosevelt removed from office when he couldn't identify the source of all the money that went into his "wonderful tin box." As far as Roosevelt was concerned, any official who had no explanation for cash holdings could be removed from office. While that might not have been the law, the governor said it was his policy. Walker was now on notice that Roosevelt could fire him if there was money that was untraceable.

As the week progressed, Walker's attorney asked Roosevelt to dismiss the charges, which he declined to do. Walker returned to Manhattan yet again for the weekend, this time to another band playing for him in Grand Central and a smaller crowd of about 2,500 waiting for him. But there were no young ladies strewing roses this time.

Perhaps it was a sign of how things were progressing. When Walker took the train back to Albany for another round of hearings, he was accompanied by only one aide. No big entourage. His wife was ill so she didn't appear. The hearing atmosphere deteriorated so that at one point Walker was overheard saying he wanted to "sock" his nemesis Seabury.

To stop the proceeding, Walker's lawyers filed a lawsuit in Albany seeking to have the entire hearing declared unconstitutional. If Walker were removed, the city would fall into financial and political chaos, argued the lawyers. Bankers wouldn't lend money to the city and for all practical purposes the municipality would grind to a halt, so went the argument. But like many of Walker's legal moves, the lawsuit went nowhere and didn't stop what Roosevelt was doing.

Walker was not without his political supporters. But the possibility that he might be booted from office had grown. As the hearings wound down, Roosevelt picked the brains of Felix Frankfurter, a law professor who would go on to be a U.S. Supreme Court justice. As far as Frankfurter was concerned, Roosevelt was right to be worried about the unexplained income or cash deposits of any public official, including Walker. So if Roosevelt was troubled about that, it certainly would be a strike against the mayor.

Walker's friends were moving toward the inevitability of his removal, and he got it straight from Al Smith, the man he had pushed in a futile effort for the presidential nomination a few weeks earlier.

"He asked Al Smith, who still carried weight with the power brokers in New York and Catholic voters around the country, for advice," said Mitgang. "'Jim, you are through,' Smith told him. 'You must resign for the good of the party.'"

Oddly enough, despite the growing political issues facing Walker, his lawsuit to stop Roosevelt had some legal traction. A state judge in Albany criticized the way Roosevelt was conducting the hearings but said he was powerless to stop him. The decision turned on a quirky, arcane aspect of the law. Under the concept of home rule, New York City is allowed to preempt state government on certain issues and had the right to change the existing provisions for removing the mayor through a bill passed by the city government and ratified in the general election. The city could have yanked the removal process from the governor but had not done so. As a result, the court said, Roosevelt was "immune from interference" in the removal process and free to do what he wanted.

Although the judge said that Roosevelt had acted unfairly in not allowing Walker the opportunity to cross-examine witnesses against him, the governor still had the right to hold the hearings as he wished. Walker could always appeal but he was now deflated in his fight with Roosevelt. Then, on top of everything, Walker's ailing brother, George F. Walker, died from tuberculosis at the age of 48. It was another personal setback for Walker and hit him hard. His victory in the courts was really moot and now he entered a period of deep depression as he stared at the prospect of losing his job as mayor. His doctor ordered him to bed for rest to avoid any further physical and mental breakdown.

On September 1, 1932, Walker gathered his strength and trooped out to St. Patrick's Cathedral for the funeral of his brother George.

Walker, dressed in funereal black, was ashen in appearance, his face long and drawn. "His appearance shocked those who saw him," said one journalist. Walker seemed to grit his teeth and fought to stay erect as he entered the cathedral. With the 45-minute mass completed, Walker endured the walk arm in arm with his brother's widow to a wait-ing limousine, for the drive to Calvary Cemetery. There, the interment ceremony was brief and Walker dabbed his face with a handkerchief.

The entire funeral was symbolic of what was happening in real time for Walker. Stories that day in the newspapers said that he was expected to resign rather than continue to fight with Roosevelt over the removal process. His publisher friend William Randolph Hearst wrote that morning in the *New York American* that Walker should resign and then run for reelection in the fall. The once jubilant, happy-go-lucky Walker, the man who personified the Jazz Age life of New York, was in his own political death spiral as he watched his brother's casket disappear into the ground, under a mass of floral displays.

"I DO NOT know."

That was the most Walker's lawyer John J. Curtin could say when asked after the burial at Calvary if the mayor was going to resign. It gave the impression he was totally out of the loop. But if Curtin truly didn't know, the rest of New York City was burning up with word that the tenure of "Beau James" Walker was coming to an end. Law-yers sometimes are the last to know what their clients really intend to do, so Curtin conceded that his client may not have told him his true intentions.

The first hint that something was happening came when some vig-ilant reporters noticed that the city clerk's office on September 1 was staying open beyond the normal 5:00 P.M. closing time. Reporters had gathered at Mayfair House where Walker lived and watched as he ap-proached in the evening after his brother's funeral and answered "Great-Great" when asked how he felt.

To the more important question of whether he was resigning, Walked told the scribes to "get down to City Hall, I'm telling you." There the whole "shebang" was waiting for them.

Walker's resignation letter filed with City Clerk Michael J. Cruise was terse: "I hereby resign as mayor of the City of New York, said resignation to take effect immediately."

It was a dramatic end to a story in which Walker had only days earlier sounded defiant with the stance that "I am no quitter."

The instant Walker resigned, Joseph V. McKee, the aldermanic president, which today would be the equivalent of city council president, took over as acting mayor. So ended the tenure of one of New York City's most colorful mayors. As the *Daily News* said, "The Walker administration will go down in the annals as a good-time Charlie, whoop-de-do, never-to-be-forgotten three-ring circus that may or may not have maltreated the taxpayers as Samuel Seabury contends." In any case, Wallker clearly had become an institution, the best promoter for the city at a time when the booze and good times were flowing in abundance.

But to other critics, Walker might have been able to muddle through in his first term. But as the Depression took hold in later years and the city budget became stressed, Walker, as the *Times* said, never adjusted from the easygoing style he had acquired to becoming the leader who was needed to run a city in financial straits.

The resignation ended the Roosevelt inquiry and spared the governor the angst of having to remove Walker, something that held political risks for the presidential candidate. But Walker didn't go quietly. At about the same time he resigned, Walker issued a 30,000-word scathing rebuttal of the Seabury charges and the way Roosevelt conducted the Albany hearings, which Walker said were a mock trial and a travesty. Roosevelt was "studiously unfair," charged Walker.

But Walker was firing blanks with such a vitriolic screed. He couldn't reverse his decision and he had to figure out now how to repair his health. Run for reelection? He would wait and see if there was a public groundswell for him to do so.

"The Democratic Party and the people of New York have my case," Walker said in an interview a couple of days after he resigned. "I am not going to urge them one way or another."

Walker admitted the decision to resign was sudden, but he wouldn't go into details about any meetings he had with political allies, such as Al Smith, that led up to his quitting. What did it matter if he wrote out his resignation in a taxi or a subway, he said with some testiness. When two photographers outside the Mayfair tried to take his photo, he berated them and walked into a waiting limousine. It was a radical change in behavior for a man who always courted the press and would always pose for a picture.

Finally, on September 10, Walker got on the S.S. *Conte Grande* for what was to be a three-week trip to Europe to get away from things—including the press. But as fate would have it, six journalists had already booked passage on the vessel to get to Italy to cover the maiden voyage of the Italian liner *Rex*. Some guys just can't catch a break, and with the journalists sharing the voyage Walker's trip would again be in the newspapers. Walker wasn't actually traveling alone, as he had a party of six, including his old wealthy friend from Westchester, A. C. Blumenthal. Also in tow was Walker's Japanese spaniel, Admiral Togo, who was named after a Japanese admiral.

The voyage and sea air seemed to benefit Walker's health. He would walk the vessel's promenade and take lunch and dinner without the fuss of formal dress. He still seemed irritated by the journalists on board. But he had some issues with his spaniel as well. The dog would run away from his valet, and tried to fight with other canines on board and steal their food. Walker said that he was thinking of changing Admiral Togo's name to "Al Capone."

"He is just a gangster, unworthy of the name of a famous Japanese admiral," quipped Walker.

When asked about why Mrs. Walker didn't make the trip, Walker said that she was still not feeling well. While it wasn't widely known at the time, it seemed that Walker's girlfriend, Betty Compton, had already sailed ahead of him to Europe for the summer months. How convenient. After meeting together, Walker and Compton toured the ruins of Pompeii and made plans to return to the city aboard the new Italian liner *Rex*. Walker might no longer be king of New York City but he could travel aboard a ship with a royal name.

But Walker and Compton didn't return immediately to New York. Instead, they decamped to the Riviera, taking golf and dance lessons. He even stopped shaving for a few days. Walker also mused about taking a villa where he could write his memoirs. Back in Miami where she was living, Mrs. Walker finally decided she had had enough and filed for divorce, saying Walker had deserted her four years earlier. "He just left," Mrs. Walker sobbed at a court hearing on the divorce. Although Walker kept supporting his wife throughout the period of separation, he rebuffed her when she asked him if he was ever coming back to her. On hearing that, Mrs. Walker's anguished response was "Oh, my God!" A final decree of divorce ending Walker's marriage was signed in Miami on March 27, 1933.

WAS THERE ANY good that came from the time James Walker spent as mayor? The Municipal Archives of the City of New York contains the papers of Walker's tenure. Author Kenneth B. Cobb posted an article to the archive's website, along with city photographs, which describes some of Walker's accomplishments that have been overshadowed by the financial and political scandal that led to his resignation. Of late, Cobb notes, historians have suggested that Walker's time might be worth some reconsideration.

Walker was an aviation buff and was enthralled with the feats of the early pioneers like Amelia Earhart and Charles Lindbergh. It was Walker who presided over the construction and dedication in 1931 of Floyd Bennett Field in south Brooklyn, one of the city's first significant airports. It was a sign, noted Cobb, "that Walker and his administration understood their greater purpose in promoting the possibility of commercial aviation," something that would become part of the economic life of the city.

On the ground, Walker pushed for the construction of the West Side Highway in Manhattan, an elevated roadway that for its time was a marvel of mobility. Walker also made efforts to expand the subway system and in 1927 approved a plan for what was then the Independent (IND) subway system, later commonly known as the Eighth Avenue line. Cleaning city streets had been done by the Street Cleaning Department, which in 1929 Walker renamed the Department of Sanitation, the agency that handles solid waste and garbage collection. Walker's sanitation effort is also credited with improving sewage treatment, a vital aspect of such a large city's infrastructure.

So there are certain things that Walker should get credit for during his scandal-scarred tenure. But, unlike the legacy of his tumultuous days in office, not everything Walker did endured. Floyd Bennett Field is still around but relegated to the role of a training facility, eclipsed by LaGuardia and JFK Airports. The West Side Highway, while innovative, couldn't stand the test of time. It became decrepit from poor maintenance and was torn down in the 1970s, along with the plaques which listed Walker as being the mayor, all resigned to the scrap heap.

CHAPTER TWENTY

KARMA CAN BE A BITCH

IT WAS EIGHTEEN MONTHS BETWEEN the time Vivian Gordon was found strangled in Van Cortlandt Park and New York City was upended with the resignation under fire of Mayor James Walker. In that time, the metropolis found itself sliding deeper into the financial pit of the Depression and unemployment, despite Walker's efforts. The old way of doing things with Tammany Hall and the politics of favoritism and corruption, as well as the "honest graft" espoused by George Washington Plunkitt, was coming to an end. Tammany wouldn't disappear as a power immediately and would persist through the leadership of Carmine DeSapio, the last of the old-time political bosses. But clearly the reform movement was gaining strength and would propel Fiorello LaGuardia to the mayoralty in 1932.

Walker had much of himself to blame for his demise. His cavalier, inattentive attitude toward running the city created the perception that he wasn't engaged in the job. He fostered that by his embrace of the speakeasy and nightlife, which was so important to the growing gangster culture. For anyone who cared about the rule of law, public safety and good government, Walker's approach to his private affairs, his taking of financial benefits and loose governance at a time of economic stress were as dangerous as spreading gasoline over the ground floor of a building. It took the match of Vivian's death to ignite the fire that would consume him.

Unless they met in a speakeasy or nightclub, it seems unlikely that Walker and Vivian ever crossed paths. When he wasn't enjoying himself, Walker lived in the world of politics. Vivian trolled the underground activities of Broadway, Wall Street and the legal profession. Walker certainly knew who the big mobsters were, but it was Vivian who worked and consorted with some of them.

As it turned out, a number of people who Vivian who crossed paths with or worked with suffered personal misfortunes and unwanted continued notoriety. To some pundits, these events became known as the "jinx of Vivian," a special display of karma for those who had dealt with her in a bad way. The first person who comes to mind is John A. Radeloff, her former lover and attorney who worked with Vivian on attempted shakedowns and bogus legal claims to squeeze various victims for money through extortion. Radeloff was also a two-timer. He was married but chased women with abandon. In one example, Vivian learned that Helen Dorf, whom she introduced to the aging, rich businessman Henry Joralmon, had caught Radeloff's eye. It wasn't enough that Dorf had received over $30,000 in gifts and had "invested" it through the attorney. He also pursued her, even though, as Vivian said in a fit of jealousy, she wasn't that attractive.

It was August 1932, just as the Roosevelt hearings on Walker were heating up, that Radeloff was caught red-handed—so to speak—in a hotel with a woman who wasn't his wife. As Radeloff's wife related the incident in court testimony, she and her brother went to the Hotel Montel in Manhattan about 9:00 P.M. one evening and found Radeloff and another woman in a room, both wearing pajamas.

"There was mighty hot argument, I can tell you," Byrdie Radeloff told the judge. The other woman wasn't identified and although Mrs. Radeloff didn't want any alimony, the judge awarded her $10 a week. But Radeloff didn't get off that lightly. The couple had apparently worked out a financial settlement before the case got to court. All the judge had to do was grant Radeloff's wife an expensive divorce so she could care for their two children, who remained in her custody. Although he was never formally charged with the crime, for the rest of his life Radeloff, no matter what he did, would be unescapably associated with the Vivian Gordon murder.

When Dr. Max Eagle was going through marital problems, his Tammany Hall–connected law firm suggested he hire Vivian as a private investigator to get some dirt on his wife, Mrs. Rae Eagle. However, whatever Vivian did failed to find anything incriminating against the woman so a divorce was granted and the good doctor was hit with an alimony award, used in part to help his ex-spouse raise their child. But after Eagle was linked to Vivian, he said his professional practice was hit hard by the notoriety and his income slid. The court eventually cut the alimony payments to $30 a week, down from the original $125.

While Eagle protested that he couldn't afford to pay any more, his ex-wife said that was a fake excuse and claimed he had married a former showgirl and put her and her mother in an expensive apartment at 239 Central Park West. The court was not impressed by the former Mrs. Eagle, calling her an "uncompromising woman embittered by hate." But, nevertheless, the alimony was raised to $50 a week, with Eagle also required to pay $10 a week to cover some arrears. At least he wasn't sent to alimony jail.

More serious and deadly things haunted the affairs of Joseph Radlow, the crooked stockbroker and onetime lover of Vivian who somehow managed to avoid serious prison time by becoming a government witness on Wall Street. Well, it seems as though Radlow couldn't stay away from stock rackets and by 1934 had opened up another business in Manhattan, employing one David Bacharach as a salesman. Although arrested 11 times, Bacharach had only one conviction, which netted him a two-year federal prison term.

It was on January 8, 1934, that Bacharach, while walking in Midtown with an ex-con named Frank Shaeffer, was fired upon by assailants shooting from a slowly moving car. Shaeffer was killed instantly, and Bacharach wounded and taken to hospital. One bullet passed through the window of a nearby café filled with about 50 patrons although none were hurt. Schaeffer had been a hardcore criminal, with a record for forgery and a short-lived escape from an Atlanta prison.

Bacharach and Radlow had a falling-out stemming from the short time they shared a suite at a Midtown hotel. Radlow left the hotel and

Bacharach said he would stay an extra day and pay the $165 due on the bill. But instead Bacharach stayed on at the hotel and ran up the bill, which Radlow had to pay. Since Bacharach sold no stocks and had stuck him with the hotel bill, Radlow fired him. Was it Radlow who set up the shooting? Knowing his record, cops pulled in Radlow for questioning, getting him more unwanted attention but in the end finding no evidence to charge him.

Harry Stein and Sam Greenberg escaped a possible death sentence with their acquittals in the Vivian Gordon murder trial. But Stein was almost immediately stalked by the bad karma of his bad personal choices. While Greenberg walked free, Stein was immediately taken into custody on charges he tried to strangle a Manhattan woman as he robbed her of some jewelry. Stein wasn't so lucky in that case as he got convicted and was given a hefty sentence of up to 25 years. It is a fair bet that the sentencing judge gave him such a stiff sentence because of all that was known about Vivian's murder, although that could never be proved. Despite the lengthy sentence, Stein got out of prison in 1950, at the age of 52, after serving about 18 years. One would think that Stein would relish the chance to stay straight and not go back to a life of crime. But he was a very troubled man, a career criminal who tried to play for big stakes but never got that far.

What happened in April 1950 on a rural road in Westchester showed just how unlucky Stein was with karma. Stein and two other hardcore thugs, 43-year-old Calman Cooper and Nathan Wissner, 38, got wind of what they thought was an easy armored-car target in the town of Pleasantville, the headquarters of *Reader's Digest* magazine. It seemed that on certain days the armored car would leave the magazine plant and take money and checks to the local bank. Driving the cash-laden vehicle was a 23-year-old driver named William Waterbury, while seated in the passenger seat was a local man from Mount Kisco, Andrew Petrini, who was 30 years old.

The armored car stopped at a traffic sign on Route 117 when suddenly a dilapidated truck pulled up alongside. Petrini was shot through the neck and would die later in a hospital. The driver, Waterbury, appeared to be unhurt. Stein and his two accomplices took about $5,000 in cash and some $30,000 in checks from the armored car and fled. Stein's share of the cash take was about $1,200 since there was a fourth man involved in the heist.

The killing of Petrini, who had merely been a helper on the truck, was a particularly callous act since he didn't even have time to submit to the robbers. However, Waterbury was able to give police a description of Wissner and together with help from the NYPD and New York State Police were able to arrest him, Stein and Cooper in early June on first-degree murder charges. The crucial lead was the discovery that the dilapidated truck used in the holdup was rented by a man who used a fictitious driver's license sometimes used by Cooper. Unlike the dragged-out legal fight in the Vivian Gordon trial, Stein and his accomplices saw the evidence against them was strong and quickly confessed to the fatal robbery.

But the trio went through the motions of a trial and in December 1950 were convicted of first-degree murder—a capital offense. The jury didn't come down with any recommendation of mercy so that meant that Stein and the others were going to have a date with the electric chair. In February 1951, about a week after the verdict, all three were sentenced to die in the electric chair, although automatic appeals would delay that date. It took until the end of 1951 for the appeals to finally go up to New York State's highest court, which rejected Stein's and the others' claims that their confessions had been coerced. Execution was set for April 21 at Sing Sing.

However, as often happens in capital punishment cases, the defendants asked U.S. Supreme Court Justice Robert H. Jackson for a stay so they could have time to file an appeal to the full high court. That bought them more time and as it turned out the court granted Stein and his co-defendants the right to a full review of their convictions. But in the end the Supreme Court ruled in a six to three vote to uphold the convictions. The execution clock began to run yet again.

But in New York State there was always the appeal to the governor for clemency, and Stein and the other two condemned men took that route but also to no avail. Even last-ditch appeals to the federal courts didn't help. The three men alleged that a Yiddish-speaking detective was planted in the courtroom during the trial to eavesdrop on conversations by the defense in violation of attorney-client privilege. But the appeals court noted the cop was in court as part of increased security because there was information indicating the defendants might try to escape during a lunch hour. By July 10, 1955, nearly five years after their conviction, Stein, Cooper and Wissner were ready to spend their final day on death row in Sing Sing prison. Stein doodled on a writing pad in his cell, did crossword puzzles and derided the notion that he knew anything about the disappearance of Judge Crater decades earlier. Stein did say that he met the jurist casually at Vivian Gordon's apartment but that he had no idea what happened to him.

"If I knew anything about him, I'd let it out," Stein said. He also had nothing to say or admit about Vivian's murder.

(In a strange postscript, C. Weston Leyra, who had been an inmate on death row with Stein, would claim in 1956 that Stein did confide that he knew the details of Judge Crater's murder. Leyra was freed from the death penalty after his conviction was overturned and gave an interview for compensation that appeared in the *American Weekly* in which he said Stein described how Crater was killed in an abandoned New Jersey paper mill after he failed to fix a criminal case after taking a $5,000 payoff. The story created a brief stir but nothing much more. Leyra died in August 1963 in Las Vegas.)

For executions, the newspapers embraced a macabre tradition of relaying what the last days of a condemned person's life were like, down to what the last meal contained. In Stein's case he ordered Southern fried chicken, ice cream, coffee and cigarettes. He had two visitors, his brother Louis and his wife. Then, Stein and the other condemned had a final bath and shave and were outfitted in what was called a "death uniform" of black pants and a white shirt.

Before he was transferred to the pre-execution cell, Stein talked with another inmate on death row and said, "Sorry to have to meet under these circumstances."

Stein was the first to enter the death room. A witness described him as shuffling uncertainly in slippers to the electric chair. Stein gave no sign of emotion as electrodes were secured to his right leg and like Cooper and Wissner would later do, seemed to ignore the prayers of a rabbi. Then, the current was turned on.

"A deep-chested, hairy man, he was hurled against the straps as the current was turned on with the clash of the switch," was how the *Daily News* described the moment of execution. "Then, as the current rose and fell in four waves, wisps of smoke curled four times from his right knee."

Wissner and Cooper seemed subdued and resigned to their fates. In his last moment, Cooper seemed to recognize someone among the witnesses who waved to him. Wissner stared far off into the distance as he was strapped into the chair. Each took five jolts of electricity before they were pronounced dead.

It took two minutes for Stein to die. He was 56 years old. It was nearly a quarter century after Vivian's death, but karma finally played out for the man police to this day still believe killed her. His body was taken to a funeral home on Grand Street in Manhattan. Only his brother Louis and his wife attended the brief service.

EPILOGUE

CEMETERIES ARE SOMETIMES THE BEST places to begin and end stories about a life. A place of burial can be evocative and a symbolic element in a biography. For that reason, I thought it important to try and find the final resting place of Vivian Gordon. It wouldn't be any easy task. She had been buried in Mount Hope Cemetery in Hastings-on-Hudson, that was clear. The old news photos showed her grief-stricken brother Pierre Franklin near collapse at the grave. However, the images provided no clear reference point with which to locate where Vivian was finally laid to rest. There was also another issue: Vivian was known by different names, something that created some very basic problems in cemetery searching.

It was a spring day in 2022 when I first started to research this book that I drove up to Mount Hope, armed with the name Vivian Gordon and the expectation that with the aid of the experienced cemetery researcher who accompanied me, I could easily find the grave. We had already visited nearby Westchester Hills Cemetery, which is just down the road from Mount Hope. Since we knew the date of death, I expected that the cemetery staff would have no trouble putting us in the right direction on the grassy grounds. But for "Vivian Gordon" there was no listing, not for 1931 nor any other year, even under her maiden name Franklin. She just didn't seem to be there. There was a third cemetery next door but there was no record of a person by those names being buried there, either.

After weeks it became clear that Vivian's stage name wasn't going to be helpful. The tip I needed finally came after I got to review her death certificate and saw that her name on the record was "Benita Bischoff," her married name. With that new information, the cemetery was able to confirm that indeed Vivian (Benita) had been buried there in March 1931 and was in a particular location. We trooped back to Mount Hope, expecting to find the grave. But again, there was nothing, no stone nor a metal marker. Since it was a Sunday the cemetery office was closed, and I had to wait for the next business day to call, at which point I learned that Vivian was in an unmarked grave. You could walk around the grounds all day and wouldn't find anything. Of course, all interments are noted on cemetery records and the business office sent me a copy of a very detailed map showing Vivian's final resting place, next to one John Hirvela, a Finnish seaman who died just days after Vivian as a possible homicide victim from a fractured skull.

Finally, with enough new information and the plot map, we went back up to Mount Hope and walked over to Hirvela's grave, which was clearly marked with an upright metal marker. To the left of his grave was Vivian's, nothing more than an expanse of green grass with no indication there was someone buried beneath. But we knew that was the place and for a moment we stood in silence at the spot, content with our discovery. I walked around the spot and recalled the old news photos, noting the particular gentle slope and seeing that some of the old trees from nearly a century ago were no longer there.

But what happened next was unexpected. As we got ready to leave the grave, I suddenly noticed that a ladybug with its tiny but distinctive red and black shell had alighted on the map of Vivian's plot. I am not one to easily find symbolic or mystical messages in things that happen unexpectedly. But for those of a more spiritual bent, the ladybug can mean, as Chinese mystics tell us, that there will be good things: good luck, prosperity and good fortune. It can also mean that persistence will pay off, something that I knew was needed in my attempt to uncover the life of Vivian Gordon.

This book took many months of painstaking work and is a welcome addition to my collection of true crime stories. Yet I kept thinking back to the unmarked plot of earth where Vivian Gordon lies, unbeknownst to anyone passing through the cemetery. Gangsters are buried all around the New York City metropolitan area, including crime bosses Joseph Profaci, Frank Costello and Lucky Luciano, who are in impressive mausoleums in Queens, locations that become places of pilgrimage for Mafia buffs. Vivian was her own kind of gangster but she also played a unique role in New York history since her murder contributed to events that led to Mayor Jimmy Walker's resignation and the long decline of Tammany Hall. Coincidentally, Rabbi Stephen Wise, the clergyman who used Vivian's death to decry the lawlessness of New York City and Mayor Walker's ineptitude as a way of encouraging various investigations, was entombed in a mausoleum just down the road at Westchester Hills Cemetery. For those reasons alone it seemed that there should be something to mark her existence. She was also a celebrated crime victim who deserved more than anonymity in death.

Vivian has no family that can be traced. Her sisters and brothers have been dead for decades. If there are any distant relatives, even Ancestry.com doesn't indicate who they might be. So I thought that there had to be something I could do for a woman whose life story absorbed me for so long and resulted in this book. I decided to pay for a modest metal plaque. Hopefully, by the time this book is published, if the cemetery concurs there will be a marker at Vivian's place of eternal sleep. Anyone looking for the resting place of the Broadway Butterfly can now find her more easily than I first did. Just go to Section 88, Lot 50, Grave 87. The cemetery staff should be happy to help with a map. On a warm, sunny day you might even spot a ladybug.

NOTES

INTRODUCTION   Details of the discovery of Vivian Gordon's body and the crime scene are described in a number of newspaper accounts: *New York Times,* Feb. 27, 1931; *New York Daily News,* Feb. 27, 1931; *Yonkers Herald,* Feb. 27, 1931. A great deal of the information in this chapter is reprised at greater length and detail in the subsequent chapters so the source material will be stated further along in this notes section. But in the case of George Washington Plunkitt, made famous for his discussion as a politician about "honest graft," his story is found on Wikipedia, as well as in William L. Riordan's *Plunkitt of Tammany Hall.* Descriptions of the NYPD process in 1931 for processing fingerprints relied upon the author's personal familiarity with the practices of the department, gained through many decades of reporting. The author visited a number of cemeteries and it was on that basis that observations were made about the interments and graves of President Roosevelt, Mayor James Walker and Vivian Gordon.

CHAPTER ONE   Descriptions of the early days of the city of Guelph, Ontario, and the development of the Catholic institutions can be found in materials of the Guelph Museums, as well as the recollections of some of its staff. Also used were documents provided by the Loretto Sisters, notably the dissertation on *Academic Excellence, Devotion to the Church and the Virtues of Womanhood: Loretto Hamilton, 1865–1970,* by Christine Lei. The school records of the Loretto Academy detailed to some extent the attendance and activities of Vivian (known at the time as Benita) and her two sisters, Arnolda and Lillian. The academy records also show the travels of the Franklin family to Detroit. The

New York Times of Feb. 27, 1931, also contains details of the Franklin family travels and Vivian's meeting of John Bischoff in South Carolina. Vivian's association with the Shubert shows can be found in programs held by the Shubert Archive in New York City. A description of the Lorton Reformatory was provided by David Turk of the U.S. Marshals Service, as well as various postings found on Wikipedia. The history of Polly Adler is found in Debby Applegate's book *Madam* as well as Wikipedia. The particular association between Adler and Vivian in the sex trade is found in *Madam*. The deterioration of Vivian's marriage, her association with Al Marks and her arrest by police are detailed in *the Daily News*, March 2, 1931.

CHAPTER TWO   The substance of the letters of Vivian's daughter Benita to her as well as the substance of the letters written by Vivian to her sister Arnolda are contained in stories of the *Daily News* on Feb. 21, 1932. Descriptions of the conditions at the Jefferson Market Court and the influence of Tammany Hall on the criminal justice system are found in the official report *In the Matter of the Investigation of the Magistrates' Courts, First Judicial Department, Supreme Court, Appellate Division, final report, 1932.*

CHAPTER THREE   Information about the economic and social conditions in New York City after World War One and during Prohibition can be found in a variety of sources, notably on Wikipedia and in *Supreme City: How Jazz Age Manhattan Gave Birth to Modern America* by Donald L. Miller. Arnold Rothstein's rise in the underworld is described in *Rothstein: The Life, Times, and Murder of the Criminal Genius Who Fixed the 1919 World Series* by David Pietrusza. A relationship between Rothstein and Vivian Gordon is mentioned in *Madam* and indicated in the *Daily News* of March 18, 1931. Rothstein's relationship with Nellie Black is described in the *Daily News* of June 14, 1922. The murders of Dot King and Louise Lawson are described in Wikipedia entries. Lawson's murder is also described in detail in the *Daily News* of June 15, 1924. Rothstein's involvement in the futile Juniper Swamp development is described in *Gangland New York: The Places and Faces of Mob History* by Anthony M. DeStefano. The narcotics case brought by federal officials after the death of Rothstein is described in *Rothstein* and in the *Daily News* of December 11, 1928, and the *Evening Herald* of December 8, 1928.

CHAPTER FOUR   Details on the career of NYPD commissioner Grover Whalen can be found on Wikipedia. Reports on the corruption of Officer Mullarkey during Prohibition are summarized in the official report *In the Matter of the Investigation of the Departments of the Government of New York City, pursuant to joint resolutions adopted by the New York State Legislature, final report, 1932.* The criminal career of Legs Diamond is summarized in a number of places, including Wikipedia and the *Miami News* on October 5, 1930. Diamond's activity with Vivian Gordon is reported in the *Daily News* on March 5, 1931. Vivian's activities in compromising competitors on Long Island were described in the *Daily News* on March 10, 1931, while reports of the impact on the competition and the resulting criminal cases were described in the *Daily News* on November 11 and December 21, 1929.

CHAPTER FIVE   The life and career of Oscar Hammerstein is contained in a biography on Wikipedia. Stories about his wife Emma Swift Hammerstein and her arrest and conviction on charges of "immoral conduct" are found in the *New York Times* on May 13, 1930, and June 7, 1930. The robbery of Judge Albert Vitale at the Bronx restaurant Roman Gardens was covered by the *New York Times* on December 9, 1929. The Vitale episode is also described in *The Tiger: The Rise and Fall of Tammany Hall* by Oliver E. Allen, and *Once Upon a Time in New York* by Herbert Mitgang. Vitale's suspension and removal from the bench was reported in the *New York Times* on February 18, 1930 and March 14, 1930. Judge Ewald's legal troubles were reported in the *Daily News* on June 6, 1932, and in the *New York Times* in his obituary on July 7, 1964.

CHAPTER SIX   Jean Stoneham's story about Vivian Gordon and her viciousness was carried in the *Daily News* on March 4, 1931. Marion Davies and her long relationship with William Randolph Hearst are described in her Wikipedia profile. Judge Crater's life and disappearance are described in *Vanishing Point: The Disappearance of Judge Crater, and the New York He Left Behind* by Richard J. Tofel. Vivian Gordon's relationship with Judge Crater was described in the *Daily News* on May 12, 1931. Samuel Seabury's legal career was described on the New York State court system website detailing the history of state judges. Seabury's appointment to referee the investigation in the magistrates' courts was reported in the *New York Times* on August 26, 1930, and the *Brooklyn Daily Eagle* on August 31, 1930.

CHAPTER SEVEN   The testimony of Chile Mapocha Acuna, the main informant for the Seabury investigation into the magistrates' courts and vice squad corruption, was compelling and covered extensively in the newspapers. A key story appeared in the *New York Times* on December 4, 1930. The entire investigation was summarized in the report *In the Matter of the Investigation of the Magistrates' Courts, First Judicial Department, Supreme Court, Appellate Division, final report, 1932*.

CHAPTER EIGHT   The barrage of newspaper stories about Vivian Gordon's murder and immediate aftermath appeared around the country and abroad. In New York, the *New York Times* had a story on February 27, 1931, as did the *Daily News*. The coverage was extensive in the days following that date. Revelations about Vivian Gordon's diary contents were described in part in the *New York Times* on March 3, 1931. The career of Commissioner Edward Mulrooney was the subject of a lengthy story in the *Times* on May 21, 1930, when he was appointed to the post. Pierre Franklin's discovery that his sister Vivian Gordon had been murdered was detailed in the *Halifax Mail* (Halifax, Canada) on March 10, 1931, and the *Montreal Daily Star* (Canada) on March 14, 1931.

CHAPTER NINE   The circumstances surrounding the suicide of Benita Fredericka Bischoff were widely reported. In particular, the *New York Times* described the incident in a story on March 4, 1931. Related stories appeared in the *Republic* (Columbus, Indiana) on March 4, 1931, the *Courier Post* (Camden, N.J.) on March 5, 1931 and the *Daily News* of March 8, 1931. The funerals of both Benita and her mother, Vivian Gordon, were extensively covered by the newspapers, including the *New York Times* and the *Daily News* on March 7, 1931. The emotional and physical breakdown of Pierre Franklin was covered in the *New York Times* on March 9, 1931.

CHAPTER TEN   Andrew McLaughlin's return to New York, his interrogation and the problems he faced with the NYPD were described in the *New York Times* on March 2, 1931. Dr. Ann Gibson's recollections of Vivian and her daughter were described in the *Daily News* on March 2 and March 4, 1931. The statements of Rabbi Wise and other religious officials about the crime problem and the death of Vivian appeared in the *New York Times*, notably on February 28, 1931.

CHAPTER ELEVEN   The Manhattan Surrogate's Court administration file on Vivian Gordon is *In the Matter of the Application for Letters of Administration upon the goods, chattels and credits of Vivian Gordon, also known as Benita M. Bischoff (deceased). The Surrogate's Court, the County of New York, A-1331 1931*. Comments by Pierre Franklin about his sister Vivian appeared in the *Montreal Daily Star* on March 14, 1931. Vernon Repez's statements about Vivian's activities appeared in the *Daily News* on March 6, 1931. Helen Dorf was interviewed and her comments about Vivian appeared in the *Daily News* on March 5, March 8 and March 30, 1931. John Radeloff's interview and recollections of Vivian Gordon's relationship with him and her activities appeared in the *Daily News* on March 27, 1931. Noel Scaffa's history as a private investigator in the recovery of jewels is described in *Top Hoodlum* by DeStefano. Scaffa's involvement in the Vivian Gordon investigation was described in the *Daily News* on April 28, 1935 and September 7, 1941. News of the arrests in the Gordon murder was extensively reported in both the *New York Times* and the *Daily News* from April 10 through April 14, 1931.

CHAPTER TWELVE   The biography of Thomas Crain can be found on Wikipedia. Criticism of Crain's record as Manhattan district attorney was described in the *New York Times* on May 1, 1931. The full text of the Seabury report on Crain's tenure as district attorney was carried in the *Times* on September 1, 1931. The efforts by the Society for the Prevention of Crime to call attention to lawlessness in New York City was detailed in the *New York Times* on March 11 and March 12, 1931. Vivian Gordon's relationship with a number of wealthy and prominent men, such as William Thornburgh and Samuel Herriman, was detailed in the *Daily News* on March 31, 1931.

CHAPTER THIRTEEN   Legs Diamond's travails and assassination attempts in 1931 were chronicled in the *Daily News* on January 1, April 24 and December 29, 1931. In addition, the *Daily News* ran a nearly full-page interview with Diamond on August 9, 1931 in a story by Grace Robinson. The murder of dance hall girl Virginia Brannen was covered in the *Daily News* on April 28, 1931 and April 30, 1931. The arrest of Rudolph Duringer for the murder of Brannen was covered in the *Daily News* on May 8 and May 9 of 1931. The *News* also covered the trial of Duringer from May 29 to June 4, 1931, as well as his execution on December 11, 1931.

CHAPTER FOURTEEN   The court records and records of the Bronx district attorney's office related to the trial of Harry Stein could not be found after requests were made. To reconstruct the trial, newspaper accounts were consulted, along with excerpts of the trial record contained in *The Defender* by Robert Leibowitz and *Not Guilty! The Story of Samuel S. Leibowitz* by Fred Pasley. The Stein trial was covered extensively by the *New York Times* and the *Daily News* in the month of June 1931 through the verdict and final coverage on July 1, 1931.

CHAPTER FIFTEEN   The facts included in the discussion of the various motives for the killing of Vivian Gordon have been described largely in previous
chapters. A good summary of what was found in Vivian's diaries, along with excerpts, was described in the *Daily News* on July 9, 1931.

CHAPTER SIXTEEN   The Mafia bloodshed in 1931 is described in a number
of books, including *Top Hoodlum* and *Gangland New York* by DeStefano, as well
as *Five Families* by Selwyn Raab. The killing of Michael Vengelli was described
in the *Daily News* from August 10 through August 13, 1931. The subsequent arrest of Vincent "Mad Dog" Coll for the Vengelli killing and his subsequent
beating of the case was described in the *Daily News* on October 11, 1931 and December 27, 1931, as well as the *New York Times* on December 29, 1931. The
capture of cop killer Francis "Two Gun" Crowley was covered by the *Daily News*
on August, 8, 1931. See *NYPD: A City and Its Police* by Thomas Reppetto and
James Lardner for a description of Mayor Walker's activity in the 1931 NYPD
parade. For a summary of the results of the Seabury investigation into the magistrates' courts, see *In the Matter of the Investigation of the Magistrates' Courts, First
Judicial Department, Supreme Court, Appellate Division, final report*, 1932. The
death of Starr Faithfull was described in the *Daily News* of August 4, 1931. The
public pronouncements of Rabbi Stephen Wise on the state of affairs in New
York City and Mayor Walker's inaction was reported in the *New York Times* on
March 18, 1931. The scandal about dance halls was described in the *New York
Times* on July 19, 1931. The joint legislative resolution calling for an investiga-
tion of New York City government was first reported in the *New York Times* on
March 24, 1931. The resolution and its aftermath are further described in *Once
Upon a Time in New York* by Mitgang. Magistrate Farley's troubles and his later
firing by Governor Roosevelt are described in *Once Upon a Time in New York* and
The Tiger by Allen. A recap of the investigation into various city officials, including Farley, can be found in *In the Matter of the Investigation of the Departments of
the Government of New York City, pursuant to joint resolutions adopted by the New
York State Legislature, final report*, 1932. Mayor Walker's statements about not
being afraid of the investigation and his readiness to leave politics at the end
of his term were reported by the *New York Times* on August 10, 1931.

CHAPTER SEVENTEEN   Mayor Walker's European trip to various capitals
and the warm reception he received in places like Cannes, Vienna and Carlsbad
were covered by the *New York Times* from August 10 through August 24, 1931.
The coverage of the preliminary public hearings on the Seabury investigation,

not including testimony of Mayor Walker, was covered in the *New York Times* on various dates from September to December 1931. Crucial stories included a summary of the evidence described in a *Times* story on December 20, 1931. See also *The Tiger* by Allen and *Once Upon a Time in New York* by Mitgang.

CHAPTER EIGHTEEN   The Seabury hearings were described in all New York City newspapers, notably, the *New York Times* on May 25 through May 27, 1932 and the *Daily News* from May 25 through May 28, 1932. The *Times* reports included daily transcripts of the testimony. Useful book accounts of the hearing in New York County State Supreme Court are found in *The Tiger* by Allen and *Once Upon a Time in New York* by Mitgang. E. B. White's observations about Mayor Walker's sartorial issues were published in the *New Yorker* magazine in 1932 and can be found on the website newyorkerstateofmind.com. The report of Mayor Walker's address to the graduating police academy class can be found in the *Daily News* on May 26, 1932. A summary of Frank Costello's activity at the 1932 Democratic National Convention was reported by Costello's lawyer in the book *Frank Costello: Prime Minister of the Underworld* by George Wolf and Joseph DiMona.

CHAPTER NINETEEN   The *New York Times* provided extensive coverage of the hearing on Mayor Walker before Governor Franklin Roosevelt in August 1932. Specifically, the *Times* ran stories August 13–August 14, 1932; August 16–August 17, 1932; August 20 and August 30, 1932. The death of Mayor Walker's brother was covered by the *Times* and other New York City newspapers on August 29, 1932. Mayor Walker's resignation was reported in the *Times* and the *Daily News* on September 2, 1932. Walker's trip abroad after his resignation was reported in the *Times* on September 13, 1932. The *Daily News* also described the trip on September 11–September 12, 1932. The divorce of Walker and his first wife, Janet, was covered extensively in the *Daily News* on March 22, 1933. The reassessment of Walker's tenure as mayor, including some of his public works contributions, can be found in the blog post of Kenneth B. Cobb titled "Mayor James J. Walker" at www.archives.gov/blog, published February 2021.

CHAPTER TWENTY   The term "jinx" related to Vivian Gordon first appeared in the *Sault Daily Star* in Canada on February 4, 1934. John Radeloff's seamy divorce was covered by the *Daily News* from November 14 through November 17, 1932 and on December 1, 1932. The killing of Joseph Radlow's business partner was described in the *Daily News* on January 6, 1934. The robbery of the

Reader's Digest truck in 1950 and the subsequent trial and execution of Harry Stein and two accomplices was extensively written about in New York newspapers from 1950 to 1955. Their executions were detailed in the *Daily News* on July 9, 1955.

WHATEVER
HAPPENED TO THEM?

PEOPLE CONNECTED TO THE VIVIAN GORDON CASE

POLLY ADLER Perhaps the most famous madam in the history of New York City prostitution and an associate of Vivian Gordon's, Adler eventually quit the life around 1945 and moved to California, where she attended high school and eventually earned an associate's degree. With writer Virginia Faulkner, she penned a best-selling autobiography, *A House Is Not a Home,* which sold about two million copies. The book was later made into a movie with Shelley Winters playing Adler. Adler died in 1962 and is buried at Mt. Sinai Memorial Park in Los Angeles.

ISRAEL J. P. ADLERMAN After working eight years in the Bronx district attorney's office, including as lead prosecutor in the Vivian Gordon murder case, Adlerman was named a justice of the City Court in April 1933. He died in September 1941 at the age of 62. Adlerman was buried at Riverside Cemetery in Rochelle Park, N.J.

BENITA FREDERICKA BISCHOFF The daughter of John Bischoff and Vivian Gordon, Benita committed suicide at the age of 16 on March 3, 1931, just days after her mother's murder. Benita was shattered by her mother's death and what she had been doing with her life. Benita's death, combined with the killing of her mother, fueled the outrage that erupted in New York City over crime, lawlessness and official corruption. She was interred in Upper Darby, Pennsylvania.

JOHN BISCHOFF   The ex-spouse of Vivian Gordon, Bischoff was never considered a suspect by police in her murder, despite claims she made to investigators that he helped frame her on her 1923 prostitution arrest. Bischoff died in June 1936 at the age of 48 and is interred at Arlington Cemetery in Drexel Hill, Pennsylvania.

SAM "CHOWDERHEAD" COHEN   Also known as Samuel Harris, and once Vivian Gordon's bodyguard, Cohen was arrested in 1932 as a material witness in the passport fraud case against Harry Stein and Morris Levine. He went on to become a proponent of what the newspapers called "muscular mediation" in labor disputes, getting arrested a number of times in 1936 and 1937 for alleged strike-breaking tactics. Cohen pleaded guilty in 1937 to charges he defrauded a government relief fund and was sentenced to an indeterminate prison sentence, at which time he complained that he was not a strikebreaker and was being hounded by "every newspaper in the country." His best praise for a fellow criminal was "He is a great guy, I stolen with him." After 1956, Cohen, who had complained that he was constantly broke, was never heard from again.

JUDGE ALBERT COHN   After presiding over the trial of the suspected killers of Vivian Gordon, Cohn was elevated to become a justice on the appellate division, the intermediate court of appeals in New York State. He was reappointed to the higher court a number of times until he retired in 1955. Upon leaving the bench, Cohn joined the law firm of his son Roy Cohn, who earlier had been special counsel to the U.S. Senate committee chaired by the infamous senator Joseph McCarthy. Cohn died in January 1959 of a stroke. At his funeral, over 70 judges and a number of politicians, including Mayor Robert Wagner, served as honorary pallbearers. Cohn was interred at Cypress Hill Cemetery in Queens.

VINCENT "MAD DOG" COLL   It was in September 1931 that Coll was hired by aspiring mob boss Salvatore Maranzano to kill Charles "Lucky" Luciano, Frank Costello and Vito Genovese. Alerted by Thomas Lucchese about the planned hit, Luciano got some hired Jewish gunmen to ambush Maranzano in his office, the place where he planned to kill Luciano and the others. When Coll arrived at Maranzano's office to kill the trio, he learned that Maranzano had already been assassinated. With a reported $50,000 bounty on his head, Coll dodged one assassination attempt in the Bronx in February 1932. But a week later, while at a telephone booth outside a drugstore on Eighth Avenue in Manhattan, Coll was shot dead by an assailant wielding a tommy gun. Coll is buried in St. Raymond's Cemetery in the Bronx. His killers were never arrested.

IRVING BEN COOPER   After working with the Seabury investigation, where he interviewed Vivian Gordon about her allegations of a police frame-up, Cooper served as special counsel to the New York City Department of Investigation from 1934 to 1937. Then, in a bit of irony, he was appointed to the magistrates' court, the very entity he investigated with Seabury, for two years. Cooper then went on to become a judge of the New York Court of Special Sessions. In 1961, Cooper was appointed a federal judge by President John F. Kennedy for a new vacancy in New York City and was confirmed by the Senate in 1962. Cooper served in the Southern District of New York and took senior status in 1972 but still worked on an active docket of cases. He died in September 1996 at the age of 94.

JUDGE JOSEPH FORCE CRATER   He is still missing. The jurist whose disappearance in 1930 mystified New York City for decades was officially declared dead in 1939. In 2005, officials disclosed that following the death of a Queens woman a note was found, apparently written by her, which stated that her husband, an NYPD officer, had learned that Crater was killed by another cop working for Murder, Inc. The note went on to say that Crater was buried in Coney Island at the site of the current aquarium. However, police said there were no records of any bones being found when the facility was being built.

JACK "LEGS" DIAMOND   After dodging assassination attempts for years, Diamond was finally shot and killed on December 18, 1931, as he rested in a hotel room in Albany, N.Y., following his acquittal on a kidnapping charge. Diamond was buried at Mount Olivet Cemetery in Maspeth, Queens, in an unmarked grave. Even to this day cemetery staffers won't reveal its location. His wife, Alice Kenny Diamond, made some appearances as an attraction in Coney Island after his death. She was shot dead in her Brooklyn apartment by unknown assailants in July 1933. She is also buried in an unmarked grave in Mount Olivet Cemetery.

THOMAS M. FARLEY   After his removal from the office of sheriff by Governor Roosevelt, Farley was tried on and acquitted of charges he kept the interest on money entrusted to him as sheriff. Farley was attempting a political comeback in a run for the state assembly when he died in April 1934 of complications from an appendicitis operation. Tammany Hall leaders served as honorary pall-bearers at his funeral. An overflow crowd packed the Church of St. Vincent Ferrer in Manhattan for his funeral and later the street was lined with spectators. He was buried at Calvary Cemetery.

ARNOLDA FRANKLIN   After the publicity about Vivian's murder, Arnolda disappeared from public view.

PIERRE MOREHEAD FRANKLIN   Reportedly, Franklin returned to Canada where he had a business address. But like his sister Arnolda he disappeared from public view.

SAM GREENBERG   In February 1932 Greenberg was arrested on a vague charge under the "Public Enemy" law of consorting with another suspect for an illegal purpose, a case a group of appeals judges reversed. He was sentenced in 1933 to two years in federal prison after being charged in a passport fraud related to a trip to Oslo, Norway, which officials believed was part of a scheme to rob a Norwegian bank.

CHARLES "VANNIE" HIGGINS   Like his confederate in crime Legs Diamond, Higgins escaped numerous shootings and assassination attempts. During Prohibition he moved into the Manhattan liquor market and along with Diamond and others competed violently with Dutch Schultz. Higgins became the biggest Irish gangster in Prohibition, expanded his operations into Long Island and was accused of snuffing out some bootleggers in the Long Beach area. Often accused of homicide, Higgins was never convicted and dodged a couple of major bootlegging indictments. In June 1932 Higgins had attended a tap dance recital with his daughter at the Knights of Columbus building in Prospect Park, Brooklyn, when he was shot at as he exited the premises. Wounded, Higgins was taken to a local hospital but refused to tell cops who did the shooting. Higgins died the day after being shot. He was 35 years old. A Navy veteran, Higgins is buried under a plain military-style grave marker at St. John's Cemetery in Middle Village, Queens, opposite the grave of slain gangster Carmine Galante.

REV. JOHN HOLMES   A minister of the Unitarian faith, Holmes was known for his pacifism and antiwar activism. He teamed up with Rabbi Stephen Wise on a number of initiatives, as well as their both going after Mayor Walker in the furor over the death of Vivian Gordon and lawlessness in the city. Holmes helped found the National Association for the Advancement of Colored People and the American Civil Liberties Union. He died in April 1964 at the age of 84. After the funeral, Holmes was cremated.

HENRY JORALMON After dying at age 68 from a long illness at the Hotel Pennsylvania on the same day Vivian's body was discovered, the wealthy and lonely Joralmon was buried at Mount Pleasant Cemetery, near Newark, N.J. His wife, Katherine, was also buried there.

DR. LOUIS LEFKOWITZ Appointed assistant medical examiner for the Bronx in 1929, Lefkowitz was just two years in the job when he performed the autopsy on Vivian Gordon. Lefkowitz died suddenly at the age of 44 at his Bronx home of a heart attack. He was buried at Mount Hebron Cemetery in Flushing, Queens.

SAMUEL LEIBOWITZ After he defended the accused killers of Vivian Gordon, life did not slow down for Leibowitz. A year after the conclusion of the trial of Harry Stein and Sam Greenberg, Leibowitz was indicted by the Brooklyn district attorney's office on charges he coached a witness to lie in a trial of police officers. Leibowitz was likely targeted for prosecution because he had been a thorn in the side of cops and prosecutors, claiming that their cases against his various clients were frame-ups. A judge dismissed the indictment of Leibowitz, noting there was no evidence to support the charges. That same year, 1932, Leibowitz got Vincent Coll acquitted for the innocent bystander shooting of a boy in East Harlem.

Leibowitz became well known for his defense, for free, of the Scottsboro Boys, a group of nine Black men accused of raping a white woman in Alabama. Leibowitz took on the case at great personal risk as Southerners didn't like his aggressive tactics. Leibowitz's client Haywood Patterson was found guilty in 1933 but a new trial was ordered which resulted in another guilty verdict and a death sentence. Eventually, Leibowitz took part in an appeal of Patterson's conviction to the U.S. Supreme Court on the grounds that Blacks were systematically excluded from Alabama juries. The Supreme Court agreed after Leibowitz showed the justices doctored Alabama jury rolls and reversed the conviction. All of the Scottsboro convictions were ultimately reversed.

Back in New York, Leibowitz, after winning 139 of 140 murder cases as a defense attorney, became a criminal court judge. He earned a reputation for toughness against defendants, remarking that "I was tough with hardened criminals, toughness is all they understand." He acquired the label "hanging judge" because of the way he handled criminals. He supervised a special grand jury from 1949 to 1951 which probed police corruption and led to indictments of a giant gambling ring. In 1953 he sought the Democratic nomination for mayor but was turned down. Leibowitz went to the New York State Supreme Court where he served as a justice until retiring in 1969. He died of a stroke in January 1978 at the age of 84.

ANDREW J. MCLAUGHLIN   After being fired from the NYPD over the vice squad scandal, McLaughlin made small efforts to stay in touch with his old friends in the department. McLaughlin remained silent about the arrest of Vivian Gordon and allegations about corruption in the squad. Eventually, he became ill and suffered from depression. In June 1950, he went into the basement of his home in Forest Hills, Queens, and shot himself to death. To kill himself, McLaughlin used the service revolver of his son, also named Andrew, who was an NYPD patrolman. McLaughlin left no note.

CHARLES B. MCLAUGHLIN   He served as Bronx district attorney from 1930 to 1933, handling not only the Vivian Gordon case but also organized crime investigations. He was appointed a New York State Supreme Court judge in March 1933 and then won a regular 14-year term in November of that year. McLaughlin died on December 8, 1948, at the age of 63, shortly after winning a second term in 1947. He is buried at Gate of Heaven Cemetery in Valhalla, N.Y.

ABRAHAM "AL" MARKS   After leaving New York City, Marks married and set up a cosmetics shop in Long Branch, N.J. He told police he was visiting friends in Manhattan with his spouse the day before Vivian Gordon was murdered.

EDWARD P. MULROONEY   He was NYPD commissioner from 1930 to 1933, at which point he resigned to take appointment as the chair of the State Alcoholic Beverage Control Board, a new entity formed with the end of Prohibition. In 1936 Mulrooney was appointed State Commissioner of Correction, a post he held until 1939. In 1951 he was named to a special board by Governor Thomas Dewey to investigate crime. Mulrooney died in May 1960 at the age of 85 in his Manhattan home. Mayor Robert Wagner ordered all flags in the city to be flown at half-mast the day of his funeral. Mulrooney is buried at Gate of Heaven Cemetery in Valhalla, N.Y.

JOHN RADELOFF After the Vivian Gordon case, Radeloff struggled in his law practice and had to settle with his wife in an expensive divorce case. He later disappeared from public view. He was never charged in connection with Vivian's murder.

JOSEPH RADLOW After the flurry of news about the murder of his associate in the stockbroker business, Radlow disappeared from public view.

ARNOLD ROTHSTEIN His natural head for business in the underworld earned Rothstein the moniker "The Brain." He loved to gamble and will always be remembered for fixing the 1919 World Series, something he denied doing. Over the years of Prohibition, Rothstein helped Charles Luciano and Frank Costello get into the bootlegging rackets and stressed to them the need to be organized. Because of his skill as a mediator, he was called upon by businesses and organized crime to settle disputes, becoming one of the most influential and powerful mob figures of the day. Rothstein was shot on November 4, 1928, during a meeting at the Park Central Hotel in Manhattan. Rothstein had balked at paying a debt of over $300,000 he accrued after a high-stakes poker game, claiming it was rigged. Rothstein refused to tell police who shot him and was reputed to have told investigators "my mudder did it." He died on November 6, 1928, at the age of 46 and is buried at Union Field Cemetery in Queens. His estate was said at one point to be valued at $25 million but finally was whittled down to about $2.5 million.

NOEL C. SCAFFA During the 1920s and 1930s Scaffa was considered one of the best private investigators of his time. He specialized in stolen gem cases and by one estimate recovered over $10 million in jewelry in his career. Scaffa never disclosed his modus operandi, but police believed he was able to develop contacts in the underworld and negotiate the return of stolen merchandise. One of his more celebrated achievements was the recovery of nearly $700,000 in jewels stolen from Mrs. James P. Donahue, the daughter of retailer F. W. Woolworth, in 1925. His ability was of important use in the Vivian Gordon case because he was able to put the NYPD in contact with a fence who was believed to have handled some of the dead woman's stolen jewels. Scaffa was in and out of trouble a few times, once arrested with mob boss Frank Costello, and was found guilty of perjury in 1935. While a success in his business, Scaffa once said he only was able to secure recoveries in 10 percent of his cases. In September 1941 Scaffa died in Pennsylvania of a heart attack and stroke at the age of 53. At his death, Scaffa's estate totaled $30,000.

HARRY SCHLITTEN The major witness in the trial of the two men accused of murdering Vivian Gordon, Schlitten was arrested by federal agents in July 1934 on charges he and others ran a drug ring. Investigators said the group brought drugs to New York City and sold them to high-end clientele, including actresses. Schlitten used the alias "Peter Benson." The customers were known only by code. In September 1934 Schlitten and the gang's alleged ringleader, Max Webber, pleaded guilty and were sentenced to two years in federal prison on McNeil Island. A key witness was a Chinese character actor named Raymond Fong, who also pleaded guilty.

DUTCH SCHULTZ If there was any trouble going on among the gangster elements in New York City during Prohibition, Schultz (whose real name was Arthur Flegenheimer) was invariably in the middle of it. He fought with Jack Diamond and is believed to have been involved in setting up his murder. He fought with Diamond's allies over beer routes and gambling concessions in the Bronx and elsewhere. Hotheaded, Schultz even wanted to kill special prosecutor Thomas Dewey because of the legal troubles he was causing the mob. The ruling commission of the Mafia rejected the idea and eventually authorized the killing of Schultz in October 1935 in a New Jersey restaurant. Schultz was seriously wounded in the shooting and died later of peritonitis at the age of 34. While born a Jew, Schultz received the last rites from a Catholic priest and was buried at the Catholic cemetery Gate of Heaven in Hawthorn, N.Y. His mother was allowed to bury him in his Jewish prayer shawl.

SAMUEL SEABURY Following the wrapping up of his investigation into Mayor Walker, Seabury from 1934 to 1937 was special counsel on transit matters for the New York City Board of Estimate, a body that went out of existence in 1990. His effort to bring about transit unification was not successful. He was president of the Association of the Bar of the City of New York from 1939 to 1941. After Seabury's wife, Josephine, died in 1950, he moved permanently to his estate in East Hampton. Seabury injured himself in a fall in 1955, and then lived in a nursing home on Long Island. He died on May 7, 1958, at the age of 85. He is buried in the graveyard of Trinity Church in Manhattan. Since Seabury and his wife had no children, the bulk of his estate including his house in East Hampton and 361 acres of land went a total of ten nieces and nephews. Samuel Seabury Playground in Manhattan was dedicated in his honor.

RUSSELL T. SHERWOOD   After Mayor Walker resigned, federal officials in New York started a grand jury investigation into his income. Sherwood, who was absent from the city for 21 months during the Seabury investigation, returned in June 1933 and gave documents and testimony to the federal investigators. The documents related to Walker's financial accounts, as well as those of his wife Betty Compton and a woman named Yvonne Arango. But after a three-month investigation, the grand jury voted no indictment and the panel's service was ended. No charges were lodged against Walker. But in 1953, a state court ordered that some $37,000 of Sherwood's money be used to pay an old contempt fine against him for dodging subpoenas in the Seabury investigation.

HARRY STEIN   As described in this book, after his acquittal in the Vivian Gordon murder case, Stein was jailed for a 25-year term for the forceful robbing of a Manhattan woman. After his release, Stein carried out a life of crime and met his final comeuppance in the robbery of the *Reader's Digest* armored car which took the life of a truck worker. After his conviction for first-degree murder in 1950, Stein was sentenced to death but delayed his execution by legal appeals until July 1955, when he went to the electric chair in Sing Sing prison. His place of burial is unknown.

JEAN STONEHAM   A pretty brunette of French-English ancestry originally from Canada, Stoneham had an affection for the gangster life. A friend for a time of Vivian Gordon's, she was close to both Diamond and Higgins, who was said to have physically abused her. Stoneham had been living next door to Kiki Roberts, Diamond's girlfriend. In 1930 Stoneham was questioned about the shooting and wounding of Diamond in Manhattan and the disappearance and death of Long Island bootlegger Leo Steinberg, who was suspected of having been killed by Higgins. By 1931 Stoneham decided she had had enough of the Broadway gangster scene and moved to Detroit where she got married. After Higgins was slain in 1932, police in Brooklyn questioned Stoneham about his activities but got no useful leads.

MAYOR JAMES F. WALKER   After he resigned in September 1932, Walker traveled through Europe with Betty Compton, whom he married in Cannes, France, in 1933 after he divorced his first wife. The Walkers bounced around Europe and eventually settled in Dorking, England, with frequent trips to London and the continent. Walker for a while wrote a column for a London newspaper and earned $102 a week. Still, money was tight and after he was taken to court by creditors in London, Walker admitted he was broke and living off his wife's money. After the threat of prosecution for tax evasion ended in 1935, Walker and his wife returned to New York City. In 1937, he was given a job of assistant council to the State Transit Commission for $12,500 a year, which helped qualify him for a pension.

In 1936, Walker and his second wife adopted a girl and a year later a boy. In 1940 Mayor Fiorello LaGuardia appointed Walker impartial chairman for a segment of the garment industry, a job that required him to settle labor disputes. Walker and his second wife lived in relative quiet and eventually moved to a home in Northport, Long Island, to breed Irish terriers and chickens. But the couple's marriage foundered and in March 1941, Mrs. Walker won a divorce on grounds of mental cruelty. She died in July 1944.

Around 1945, Walker served as president of Majestic Record Company. Walker died in a hospital on November 18, 1946, after he was stricken at his home with a blood clot on the brain. He was 65. As he lay dying, Walker, as one reporter wrote, "still looked, even on his deathbed, while asleep, the ruddy-cheeked, black-haired young Irishman who walked into City Hall twenty years ago as mayor." Walker's funeral at St. Patrick's Cathedral drew a crowd of about 14,500 inside and outside the cathedral. Some 300 cops provided security. Walker was buried at Gate of Heaven Cemetery in Valhalla, N.Y.

RABBI STEPHEN WISE   Following the resignation of Walker, Wise remained a political activist, ardent Zionist and opponent of Nazism. In 1942 Wise held a press conference announcing news about the extermination of Jews by the Nazis, an event that garnered little publicity. He received criticism for asking that the public not send food packages to Jews in occupied countries because such action might be considered under U.S. policy to be aid to the enemy. Wise died on April 18, 1949, in New York at the age of 75. He is interred in an unmarked mausoleum in Westchester Hills Cemetery in Hastings-on-Hudson, barely a mile from where Vivian Gordon, the woman whose death sparked his outrage against Walker, reposed in an unmarked grave.

SOURCE: Wikipedia, news reports and Findagrave.com

BIBLIOGRAPHY

BOOKS

Allen, Oliver E. *The Tiger: The Rise and Fall of Tammany Hall.* New York: Addison-Wesley Publishing Company, 1993.

Applegate, Debby. *Madam: The Biography of Polly Adler, Icon of the Jazz Age.* New York: Doubleday, 2021.

Aylesworth, Thomas and Aylesworth, Virginia. *New York: The Glamour Years (1919–1945).* New York: Gallery Books, 1987.

Breslin, Jimmy. *Damon Runyon: A Life.* New York: Ticknor & Fields, 1991.

Bugliosi, Vincent and Stadiem, William: *Lullaby and Goodnight: A Novel Inspired by the True Story of Vivian Gordon.* New York: New American Library, 1987.

Charyn, Jerome. *Gangsters and Gold Diggers.* New York: Four Walls, Eight Windows, 2003.

DeStefano, Anthony M. *Top Hoodlum: Frank Costello, Prime Minister of the Mafia.* New York: Citadel Press Books, 2018.

———. *Gangland New York: The Places and Faces of Mob History.* Connecticut: Rowman & Littlefield, 2015.

Downey, Patrick. *Gangster City: The History of the New York Underworld 1900–1935.* Fort Lee: Barricade Books, Inc., 2004.

Fellows, Gordon. *They Took Me for a Ride.* Toronto: Thomas Nelson and Sons, Ltd., 1934.

Gilfoyle, Timothy J. *City of Eros: New York City, Prostitution, and the Commercialization of Sex, 1790–1920.* New York: W. W. Norton & Company, Inc., 1992.

Gosch, Martin A., and Hammer, Richard. *The Last Testament of Lucky Luciano.* New York: Little Brown & Company, 1975.

Hortis, C. Alexander. *The Mob and the City: The Hidden History of How the Mafia Captured New York.* Amherst, New York: Prometheus Books, 2014.

Lardner, James, and Reppetto, Thomas. *NYPD: A City and Its Police.* New York: Henry Holt and Company, LLC., 2000.

Leibowitz, Robert. *The Defender: The Life and Career of Samuel S. Leibowitz.* New York: Prentice-Hall, 1981.

Miller, Donald L. *Supreme City: How Jazz Age Manhattan Gave Birth to Modern America.* New York: Simon & Schuster, 2014.

Mitgang, Herbert. *Once Upon a Time in New York: Jimmy Walker, Franklin Roosevelt, and the Last Great Battle of the Jazz Age.* New York: Free Press, 2000.

——. *The Man Who Rode the Tiger: The Life and Times of Judge Samuel Seabury.* New York: Fordham University Press, 1996.

Pasley, Fred D. *Not Guilty! The Story of Samuel S. Leibowitz.* New York: G. P. Putnam Sons, 1933.

Pietrusza, David. *Rothstein: The Life, Times, and Murder of the Criminal Genius Who Fixed the 1919 World Series.* New York: Carroll & Graf Publishers, 2003.

Raab, Selwyn. *Five Families: The Rise, Decline, and Resurgence of America's Most Powerful Mafia Families.* New York: Thomas Dunne Books, 2005.

Rudin, James A. *Pillar of Fire: A Biography of Stephen S. Wise.* Lubbock, Texas: Texas Tech University Press, 2015.

Tofel, Richard J. *Vanishing Point: The Disappearance of Judge Crater and the New York He Left Behind.* Chicago: Ivan R. Dee, 2003.

Tosches, Nick. *King of the Jews.* New York: Ecco/Harper Collins Publishers, Inc., 2005.

Whalen, Bernard and Messing, Philip and Mladinich, Robert. *Case Files of the NYPD: More than 175 Years of Solved and Unsolved Cases.* New York: Black Dog & Leventhal, 2018.

NEWSPAPERS

Boston Globe

Bradford Evening Star and Bradford Daily Record (Bradford, Pennsylvania)

Brooklyn Times Union

Cincinnati Enquirer (Cincinnati, Ohio)

Courier News (Bridgewater, New Jersey)

Courier-Post (Camden, New Jersey)

Daily News (New York, New York)

Daily Notes (Canonsburg, Pennsylvania)

Daily Record (Long Branch, NJ)

Evansville Journal (Evansville, Indiana)

Evansville Press (Evansville, Indiana)

Evening Herald (Shenandoah, Pennsylvania)

Evening Standard (London)

Evening Star (Washington, D.C.)

Evening World (New York, New York)

Fairbanks Daily News-Miner (Fairbanks, Alaska)

Gazette (Montreal, Canada)

Guardian (London, England)

Halifax Mail (Halifax, Canada)

Indianapolis Times (Indianapolis, Indiana)

Kokomo Tribune (Kokomo, Indiana)

Miami News (Miami, Florida)

Montreal Daily Star (Montreal, Canada)

Morning Call (Paterson, New Jersey)

New York Age (New York, New York)

New York Times

Orlando Sentinel (Orlando, Florida)

Passaic Daily Herald (Passaic, New Jersey)

Philadelphia Inquirer

Province (Vancouver, Canada)

Record (Hackensack, New Jersey)

Republic (Columbus, Indiana)

Richmond Item (Richmond, Indiana)

Sault Daily Star (Sault Ste. Marie, Canada)

Seminole Producer (Seminole, Oklahoma)

Standard Union (Brooklyn, New York)

Sun (New York, New York)

Virginia Pilot and the Norfolk Landmark (Norfolk, Virginia)

Windsor Star (Windsor, Canada)

Yonkers Herald (Yonkers, New York)

Yonkers Statesman (Yonkers, New York)

PERIODICALS

Anonymous prominent police official. "The Woman Who Paid with Her Life: The First Inside Woman Police Revelations of Why Vivian Gordon Was Murdered." *Illustrated Detective Magazine*, September 1931.

Mosca, Alexandra. "Low Key Cemetery, High Profile Permanent Residents." *Cemetery & Cremation*, October 2022.

Shteir, Rachel. "The Dead Woman Who Brought Down the Mayor." *Smithsonian Magazine*, February 2013.

WEBSITES

www.archive.nyc
www.FBI.gov
www.Findagrave.com
www.guelphmuseums.ca
www.history.nycourts.gov
www.loc.gov
www.nara.gov
www.nexis.com
www.newspapers.com
www.newyorkerstateofmind.com
www.nyc.gov
www.shubertachive.org
www.usinflationcalculator.com
www.wikipedia.org
https://guideyourpet.com/ladybug-meaning
www.youtube.com

BLOG ARTICLES

Cobb, Kenneth R. "Mayor James J. Walker" at www.archives.gov/blog, published February 2021.

Miller, Tim. "The Lost Hotel Marguery—No. 270 Park Avenue" at DaytonInManhattan.Blogspot.com/2015/11/the-lost-hotel-marguery-no-270-park.html, published November 9, 2015.

ACADEMIC THESIS

Lei, Christine. *Academic Excellence, Devotion to the Church and the Virtues of Womanhood—Loretto Hamilton, 1865–1970.* A thesis submitted with the requirements for the degree of Doctor of Philosophy, Department of Theory and Policy Studies in Education, Ontario Institute for Studies in Education of the University of Toronto, 2003.

GOVERNMENT REPORTS

In the Matter of the Investigation of the Magistrates' Courts, First Judicial Department, Supreme Court, Appellate Division, final report, 1932.

In the Matter of the Investigation of the Departments of the Government of New York City, pursuant to joint resolutions adopted by the New York State Legislature, final report, 1932.

COURT CASES

In the Matter of the Application for Letters of Administration upon the goods, chattels and credits of Vivian Gordon, also known as Benita M. Bischoff (deceased). Surrogate's Court, County of New York, A-1331, 1931.

John E. C. Bischoff and Benita Bischoff. Court of Common Pleas of Philadelphia County, divorce proceeding Number 2261.

ACKNOWLEDGMENTS

In researching and writing *Broadway Butterfly*, I had the assistance of some people of varied backgrounds whose expertise was very helpful in pulling a story together about events from so long ago. No one who lived through events described in the book is alive today so I was able to rely on people who proved to be helpful guides through the maze of historical evidence.

For a start, at Mount Hope Cemetery, Pietra Carrea, family assistance associate, provided needed assistance in finding out where Vivian Gordon was buried in an unmarked grave. Some cemeteries aren't as cooperative, but Mount Hope was different.

Alexandra Mosca, author and funeral director, knows her way around New York's burial grounds. She was able to provide extremely useful help.

In piecing together Vivian and her sisters' early convent education in Canada, I had the patience and assistance of the staff affiliated with the Loretto Sisters of Canada. In particular, I would like to thank Julie Denovan, administrative assistant. At the Loretto Archives, Michelle Pariag and Robert Little were instrumental in providing materials about the history of the schooling of Vivian at the convent.

Vivian Gordon's stage career was largely undocumented, that is until Sylvia Wang of the Shubert Archive was able to find material about Vivian's role in a couple of Shubert shows in the World War One era. The information proved valuable in documenting Vivian's stage career.

Over at John Jay College of Criminal Justice, Kathleen Collins, of the special collections section for the Lloyd Sealy Library, facilitated my visit and gathered appropriate materials from the collection. A particularly useful find was an old NYPD poster displaying Vivian's pictures which had been distributed to taxi and limousine drivers in the hopes of generating clues.

At the National Archives and Records Administration in Kansas City, archivist Bob Beebe was able to secure the recovery of certain criminal case files dating back to the 1930s. In New York, Eirini Melena Karoutsos at the Municipal Archives patiently helped me through the process of accessing old records related to Vivian Gordon's case and various court records related to the Jefferson Market Court.

Old surrogate's court records are sometimes difficult to find, but Kim Silik at the court in Manhattan quickly was able to uncover the administration file related to Vivian's meager estate, which nonetheless contained some critical biographical information.

At the NYPD, Lieutenant John Russo made an effort to uncover the criminal files on the Vivian Gordon murder. David Turk, resident historian for the United States Marshals Service, highlighted details of the Lorton jail facility where Vivian's husband worked. Writer, producer, journalist and friend Nicholas Pileggi offered his special enthusiasm for the book.

My agent Jill Maral once again helped me navigate the editorial process. Lastly, Gary Goldstein, my longtime editor at Kensington Publishing, decided not to retire and remained in the saddle as the editorial director for *Broadway Butterfly*, and other projects, something for which I am especially grateful.

INDEX